Freud's Foes

Polemics

Stephen Eric Bronner, Series Editor

The books in the Polemics series confront readers with provocative ideas by major figures in the social sciences and humanities on a host of controversial issues and developments. The authors combine a sophisticated argument with a lively and engaging style, making the books interesting to even the most accomplished scholar and appealing to the general reader and student.

Media Wars
News at a Time of Terror
By Danny Schechter

The Collapse of Liberalism
Why America Needs a New Left
By Charles Noble

Imperial Delusions
American Militarism and Endless War
By Carl Boggs

Murdering Myths
The Real Story Behind the Death Penalty
By Judith Kay

Primetime Politics
The Truth about Conservative Lies, Corporate Control, and Television Culture
By Philip Green

Gay Marriage and Democracy
Equality for All
By R. Claire Snyder

Servants of Wealth
The Right's Assault on Economic Justice
By John Ehrenberg

Freud's Foes
Psychoanalysis, Science, and Resistance
By Kurt Jacobsen

Freud's Foes

Psychoanalysis, Science, and Resistance

Kurt Jacobsen

ROWMAN & LITTLEFIELD PUBLISHERS, INC.
Lanham • Boulder • New York • Toronto • Plymouth, UK

ROWMAN & LITTLEFIELD PUBLISHERS, INC.

Published in the United States of America
by Rowman & Littlefield Publishers, Inc.
A wholly owned subsidiary of The Rowman & Littlefield Publishing Group, Inc.
4501 Forbes Boulevard, Suite 200, Lanham, Maryland 20706
www.rowmanlittlefield.com

Estover Road
Plymouth PL6 7PY
United Kingdom

British Library Cataloguing in Publication Information Available

Library of Congress Cataloging-in-Publication Data:

Jacobsen, Kurt, 1949–
Freud's foes : psychoanalysis, science, and resistance / Kurt Jacobsen.
p. cm. — (Polemics)
Includes bibliographical references and index.
ISBN 978-0-7425-2263-3 (cloth : alk. paper) — ISBN 978-0-7425-6634-7 (electronic)
1. Psychoanalysis—History. 2. Freud, Sigmund, 1856–1939. I. Title.
BF175.J27 2009
150.19'52—dc22 2009010031

Printed in the United States of America

™ The paper used in this publication meets the minimum requirements of American National Standard for Information Sciences—Permanence of Paper for Printed Library Materials, ANSI/NISO Z39.48-1992.

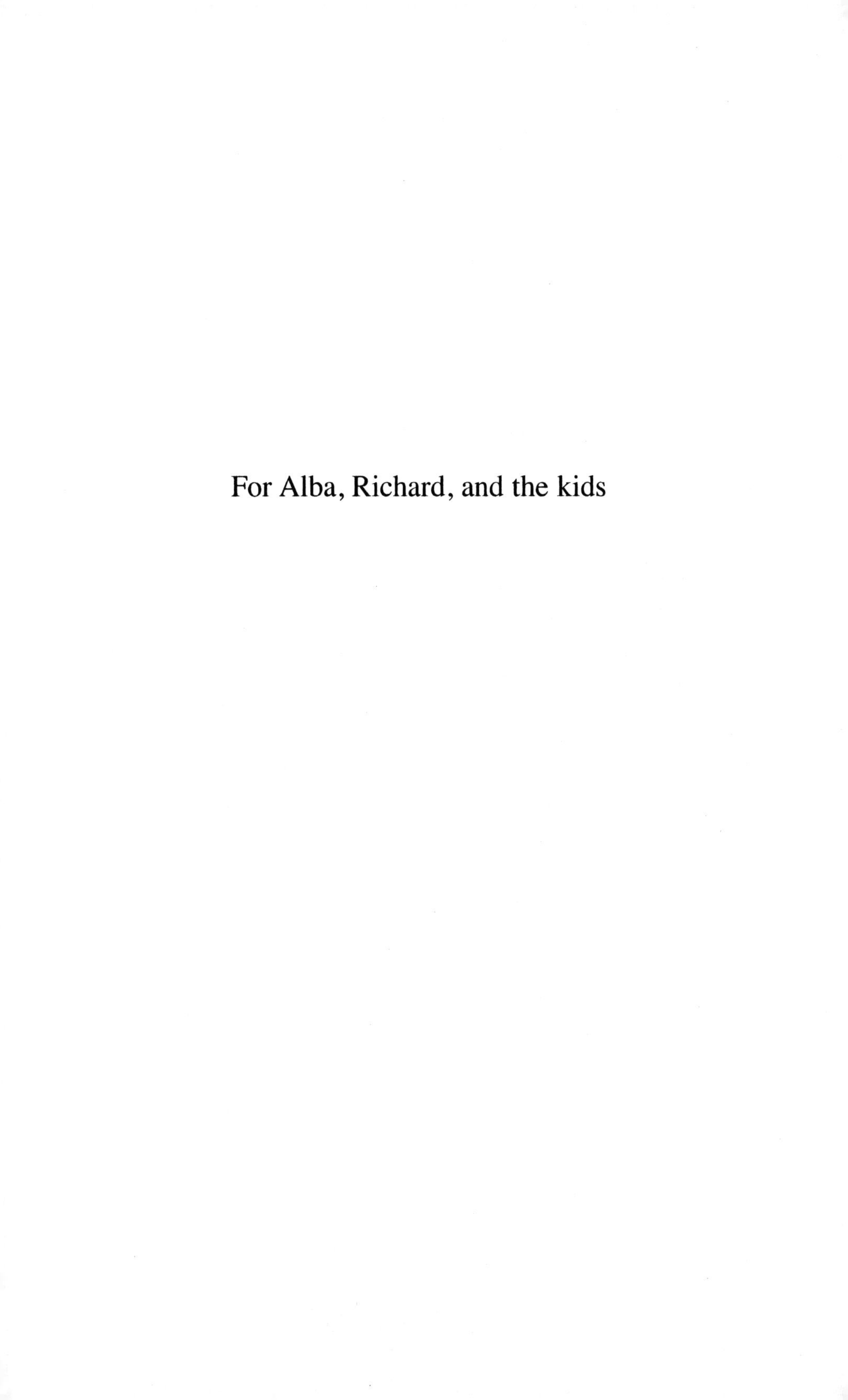

For Alba, Richard, and the kids

Contents

Introduction

Most well-educated people know that Sigmund Freud was a charlatan who abetted child molesters, snorted cocaine, started a messianic cult, denigrated women, bullied patients, and lusted for his sister-in-law. According to the relentless scourging words of Frederick Crews (*The Memory Wars* and *Unauthorized Freud*), Richard Webster (*Why Freud Was Wrong*), and Jeffrey Masson (*The Assault on Truth* and *Against Analysis*), Freud would be the twentieth century's supreme con artist if only he had not been dumb enough to believe in his own pseudoscience. Historian Frank Sulloway, who compiles twenty-six myths Freud allegedly concocted, asserts that the history of psychoanalysis is one of "myth formation and propaganda production," a record he is happy to set straight.[1] Debunking Freudian psychoanalysis has been all the rage for ages.

With unabashed panache English professors, social scientists, philosophy professors, and journalists led the latest wave of the anti-Freud crusades on the presumption that their skills are superior to the clinical experience of mere psychoanalysts. They argue that Freud—who, by the way, was not himself a "strict Freudian"[2]—and his besotted followers exhibited a "waywardness of reasoning, a refusal to countenance crucial but inconvenient factors, and rhetorical sleight of hand" as well as failing to notice that "self-contradiction is a sign of trouble" in an argument.[3] Yet, on examination, no one exhibits all these faults more acutely than the latest crop of Freud's foes.

Knowledge ideally is refined though a process of rigorous criticism, reconsideration, refutation, and/or refinement.[4] Innumerable critics, in and outside the analytic fold, approached Freud's work with reasonable wariness. Indeed, it seems impossible for the most admiring reader to sift through Freud's rich and wide-ranging output without raising an eyebrow now and then or heartily contesting elements of it. Morton Schatzman, for example, has it right that the late and prolific Paul Roazen was a sharp critic whose "wish was to add perspective to our understanding of Freud and his followers, not to undermine them."[5] Critical scourings attend all scientific endeavors, as Freud fully expected. This volume is entitled *Freud's Foes*, rather than *Freud's Critics* or *Freud's Rivals*, because it addresses a fiercely disdainful group who are intent on annihilating—not updating, modifying, correcting, or refuting—Freud, on denouncing him and all his diabolical works in which they affect to detect not the slightest redeeming value.

Consider Jeffrey Masson's accusation that cowardly Freud, buckling under professional pressure, ditched his "seduction theory," which held that neuroses usually originate from sexual molestation. Then compare this febrile accusation with Crews's assertion that Freud is to blame for all the tragic excesses of the 1990s repressed memory movement.[6] Yet Masson nonetheless dangles a license for anyone who wants to commit exactly those excesses when he scolds us that "free and honest retrieval of painful memories cannot occur in the face of skepticism and fear of the truth."[7] So, apparently, accused parents are guilty as charged by their offspring, whose stories need not be checked by skeptical authorities.

Psychoanalysis, for better or worse, is inherently suspicious of surfaces. Freud stated that psychoanalysts accept "that there are unconscious mental processes, the recognition of the theory of resistance and repression, the appreciation of the importance of sexuality and the Oedipus complex—these constitute the principal subject matter of psychoanalysis and the foundations of its theory."[8] Crews denounces psychoanalysis anyway for its "distrust of any patient's conscious 'screen memory' of molestation"—and yet, several pages later, ridicules the "memory of illusory events that the therapist is duty-bound to credit." Crews does so as if these contrary charges needn't be reconciled, or even acknowledged, by the people making them.[9] So Freud is held responsible for the "sinister revival of veridical memory retrieval" in the same breath as he is condemned for denying that possibility.

Yet, in this notorious instance, Freud very early questioned "whether we have any memories at all *from* childhood; memories *relating to* childhood may be all that we possess."[10] What patients recall was not always, or often, gospel truth. Psychoanalysis, Masson himself admits, began only when Freud abandoned the notion of retrieving trustworthy memories.[11] A contributor in one of Crews's caustic anti-Freud collections admits as much, too.[12] So analysts, while hardly foolproof, have been least liable among all mental health professionals to treat memories as facts. Many of Freud's foes have yet to get the word, or bother to notice the contradictions lacing their condemnations of psychoanalysis. These are the sort of reckless, ill-thought-out charges that partisans toss around when they are sure that the social climate is on their side, and therefore believe their accusations won't be inquired into too closely because everybody knows—and has been conditioned to know—that they are correct. Why is this? How do they get away with it?

Freud's recent batch of foes enjoyed an exceptionally easy ride, escaping the kind of scrutiny that they say they courageously train on shifty analysts. I emphasize the word *recent* because, although attackers pose as daring savants, they are only the latest round in repetitious critiques that psychoanalysis faced ever since its controversial birth—a birth which prominent opponents even try to deny was controversial. What we encounter here are enemies who rely for their rhetorical ammunition mainly upon half-digested neurological research and pharmaceutical advertising copy. What is at stake is preservation of a view of psychotherapy, and of medicine, as treating troubled people in their full humanity, rather than as little more than defective appliances. Disparaging Freud is one key tactic in the resurrection of a primitive and often misguided medical model for treating or, rather, suppressing human anguish. Fortunately, this seductive model is not synonymous with the best knowledge and practices in modern medical science. But the best, by definition, tends not to be what most people are in any field.

Scattershot critiques of Freud grow unchecked and unhindered. Every analyst who contributed to the psychoanalytical enterprise has been a critic of Freud insofar as every research enterprise is by definition incomplete and open to critical elaboration. Psychoanalysis, like any dynamic mode of inquiry, contains flaws, exaggerations, and blind spots that require criticism and correction. But the remorseless outpouring of conflicting charges suggests that the current cohort of enemies long ago left the realm of reasoned criticism.

Still, one need only scan Crews's *The Memory Wars*—containing eminent analysts' lazy parries alongside Crews's deft ripostes—to see psychoanalysts have done a lackluster job defending themselves in a public sphere where they are unaccustomed to maneuver.[13] The public intellectuals who once communicated psychoanalytic ideas to a broader public—Erik Erikson, Erich Fromm, Bruno Bettelheim—are long gone and go mostly unreplaced.[14] With too few exceptions, Freud's card-carrying defenders come across as stuffy, arrogant, inward-looking, overprivileged, and out of touch. So analysts become easy prey for ambitious ideologues who wield a good line of patter, a narrow grasp of science, and personal or partisan hatchets to grind. Still, this vulnerability—partly self-inflicted—points to genuine problems within contemporary psychoanalysis, which I also address. It says a great deal, though, about diversity within the field today that some psychoanalysts are bound to regard this book as too favorable toward Freud.

This volume is a brisk intervention in the debate whether "Freud is dead" or, more to the point, whether psychoanalysis in all its guises should be snuffed out.[15] Given the pat answers that the finest nineteenth-century minds of our era expect science to wring from reality, Freud lamented that in psychology what people really wanted "is not progress in knowledge but satisfaction of some other sort; every unsolved problem, every admitted uncertainty is made into a reproach against it."[16] The inclination to seize upon "magic bullets," ballyhooed medical boasts, and pop psychology bromides as answers to human problems is widespread as ever. Perhaps the supreme misguided assumption in psychoanalytic critiques is that a magical medical science, with which all critics piously side, set impeccable standards from which analysts such as Freud irresponsibly deviated, and at a great human cost.

This comic-book idealization of science has little to do with the messy historical realities of research, even in the loftiest realms of microbiology or physics.[17] The trouble with ardent debunkers is that they are always gullible about some other, favored creed: in this case, a positivist version of science that is thought utterly objective, precisely measurable, and perfectly predictive. What we have witnessed in the last few decades is a resurgence, especially in newsrooms and English departments, of physician Ernst Brucke's conviction—shared for a while by Freud—that "no other forces than common physico-chemical ones are active within the organism."[18] A revived article of faith in popular lore is that the environment cannot contribute to serious mental disturbances—or perhaps does so in a grudgingly conceded and minor way. Medicine, unlike Freud, gets remarkably worshipful press these days. Many historians have good cause to scratch their heads over this stark contrast in treatment.

Consider the claim that Freud blamed "neurasthenia on excessive masturbation and nocturnal emission," and punished patients with his "obsessions with masturbation, adultery and homosexuality."[19] To the fleeting extent that the charges were true, Freud reflected the standard medical opinion of his day. The tactic employed by Freud's foes is to bowdlerize history or, at least, to rely on their audience's ignorance of it, although one can never entirely rule out their own convenient and considerable ignorance.

The doctrine that mental illness must have a somatic origin gained wide acceptance in mid-nineteenth-century Europe, despite a shocking absence of evidence for it. Freud's foes need to appreciate the sway of medical orthodoxies. In an epoch justly labeled one of "medical terrorism," many texts, authored by the most celebrated practitioners, solemnly related masturbation and nocturnal emissions to incipient insanity. Freud, like any good intern, went along with prevailing medical opinions but, unlike most, eventually discarded them, sometimes with fanfare, sometimes quietly. Yet Freud alone is pilloried for purveying cranky ideas and is deemed as nothing but an impediment to the majestic march of medicine.

Dubious medical practices never vanished. The 1930s featured many dangerous treatments for mental illness: electroshock, amphetamine shock, cardiazol shock, and insulin shock among them. A tradition of what Valenstein rightly calls "great and desperate cures" continues into the twenty-first century. In the 1940s and 1950s, psychiatrists—pillars of their communities—were performing deranged psychosurgeries, electroshocking three-year-old children, and, as new pharmaceuticals appeared, drugging everyone in sight. This is the pristine establishment in which our critics place such touching faith. One may cite a long list of medical breakthroughs and a roll call of humane figures, but unsavory events are part and parcel of medical history too. Physicians (and medically trained psychoanalysts) do not care to be reminded of a seamy past because of the doubts it might cast on the present.

So it is praiseworthy to promote a belief that all illness is physical illness and thus exculpate people, especially people with power and status, from affecting others adversely and with impunity. In the 1990s the American Psychiatric Association acquired generous drug company support earmarked to prove "psychological suffering is a biologically based medical problem." Disease or dysfunction is genetic or biochemical even when evidence is absent or, at very least, thin or mixed. A *New York Times* book reviewer and author of a popular biography of a famous schizophrenic mathematician plays up to such facile popular misunderstanding when she casually says that schizophrenia is a proven brain dysfunction.[20] It is not.

Does the "dopamine theory of schizophrenia" withstand scrutiny? Does Ritalin correct a neurochemical imbalance in hyperactive kids, as the public has been led to assume? Can 10 percent of all children suddenly suffer a genetically based outbreak of misbehavior? After many years of accumulated and powerful evidence, the manifold problems attending antidepressant drug treatment are finally receiving some front-page attention.[21] The cultural gullibility needed to enable these groundless beliefs required the resurrection of much the same mechanistic-minded climate in which Freud commenced his work.

The breakneck commercial societies we reside in prize quick fixes and symptom relief over the lengthy in-depth therapy that Freud and a squabbling cohort of analysts practiced. Unlike contemporary biopsychiatry and nineteenth-century psychiatry (which are eerily similar), Freud viewed mental disturbances as occurring along a continuum of human behavior that we are all capable, under certain circumstances and pressures, of manifesting. The notion that "we are all a little bit schizophrenic or a little bit manic-depressive is total anathema to biopsychiatry because it would rule out a genetic basis for these illnesses."[22]

The answers science seeks more likely "lie in a cross-fertilization of the disciplines of medical science and of psychology without privileging either, at least until more conclusive evidence is in."[23] For Freud, "it was the host himself—or rather his moral character—that must be treated . . . [psychoanalysis] addressing itself not to diagnostic categories but moral agents," Rieff writes.[24] Biopsychiatry, in the hands of the lesser lights in its ranks, succeeds only in erecting barriers to empathy and useful insight. This book aims to provide an appreciative and well-grounded examination of Freud's enduring contributions to therapy and knowledge.

Chapters 1, 2, and 3 explore the debate and compare it to earlier rounds of critiques of psychoanalysis during two fin de siècles, the tail ends of the nineteenth and the twentieth centuries. I examine the rhetorical strategy of the foes. Freud may have established, as W. H. Auden wrote, a "whole climate of opinion," but a parallel climate tenaciously persisted—a climate comprised of an indiscriminately applied medical model and of positivist science. In the United States especially, psychoanalysis, contrary to Freud's wishes, became incorporated into medicine and rendered housebroken. These chapters winnow out vacuous and ill-judged criticisms as well as attending to those that are quite valid.

Chapter 4 sets the critique of psychoanalysis in the context of the state of medicine and its animating philosophy. Uncertainty caught up with the "hard" sciences and the savviest scientists in those fields appreciate and cope remarkably well with it. Freud, in a sense, incorporated uncertainty so as to understand and treat human anguish. Certainly, by limiting gullibility regarding the influence of heredity, psychoanalysis expanded the hopeful influence of therapy. Chapter 5 traces the "second biological psychiatry" as it regained dominance and meshed with powerful economic institutions to push psychotherapies of all kinds aside.

Chapter 6 takes us beyond idealizing or demonizing Freud. Despite a long list of shortcomings, alleged or real, Freud attracts us as scholars, as healers, and as human beings. Despite a conservative emphasis, in some hands, on "adjusting the individual to his environment," psychoanalysis remains a rebellious phenomenon at its core. This chapter emphasizes the importance of recovering the humanism of Freud for the new high-tech age of pill cures and one-dimensional diagnoses. For their helpful comments on parts or the entirety of the manuscript I am grateful to series editor Steve Bronner, David Edgerton, Mattihias von der Tann, Nick Temple, and Sylvia Zwettler-Otte.

By no means is it my intention to defend psychoanalysis as the catechism that some—hardly all—followers have made of it.[25] Every form of knowledge is liable to suffer this fate. I certainly do not deny that some caricatures that foes have made of analysis actually exist. Self-caricaturing practitioners exist in every field where people overidentify with their roles.[26] Had Freud been such a young zealot as this he would have played out his career as a very good but unremarkable neurologist.

Freud's foes are advocates, not dispassionate critics, and what they advocate are idealized medical practices they do not understand. They operate in effect as advertising agents for the least admirable facets of the medical profession. No matter how many horrors medicine inflicted in the past, the practitioners meant well and will never revert to the bad old days, even though those "bad old days" remain implicit in their basic belief system. Stoked on Philosophy of Science 101 fancies, the foes divide "good" medicine from "bad" science. Partly this follows the zeitgeist fashion, partly it is opportunism, and partly it is dogmatism unnoticed as such because it is so widely shared. In contrast with this carnival of conformity, psychoanalysis, as Philip Rieff long ago argued, "even that part of it which claims to be most orthodox, is a very successful heresy."[27] That heresy is the orthodoxy that I defend.

NOTES

1. Frank J. Sulloway, *Freud: Biologist of the Mind* (New York: Basic Books, 1979), p. 485. For the list, see pp. 489–95.
2. See Paul Roazen, *How Freud Worked* (Northvale, NJ: Jason Aronson Inc., 1995).
3. Frederick C. Crews, ed., *Unauthorized Freud: Doubters Confront a Legend* (New York: Penguin Putnam, 1998), p. 144.
4. See Robert Musgrave and Imre Lakatos, eds., *Criticism and the Growth of Knowledge* (Cambridge: Cambridge University Press, 1975).
5. Morton Schatzman, "Paul Roazen: Obituary," *Independent* (UK), 16 November 2005. Roazen broke the news that Anna Freud's analyst was her father.
6. See Lawrence Wright, *Remembering Satan* (New York: Knopf, 1994). Also, more recently, Jon Henley, "Victims of False Paedophilia Charges Tell French MPs of Ruined Lives," *Guardian*, 19 January 2006.
7. Jeffrey Masson, *The Assault on Truth: Freud's Suppression of the Seduction Theory* (New York: Farrar, Strauss and Giroux, 1983), p. 192.
8. Sigmund Freud, in *Standard Edition of the Complete Psychological Works of Sigmund Freud*, ed. James Strachey et al. (London: Hogarth Press, 1957), 18:247 (Hereafter *SE*). Rycroft defines psychoanalysis as "theories and therapies—whether Freudian, Jungian, or existentialist—which assume the existence of unconscious mental processes, which concern themselves with elucidation of motives and which make use of transference—and which can be differentiated from the organic school of psychiatry and from behaviorism (learning-theory) by the fact that they regard subjective experience as a central object of study and not an awkward contaminant

which has to be ignored or eliminated." Charles Rycroft, "Introduction: Causes and Meaning," in *Psychoanalysis Observed* (London: Constable & Co, 1966), pp. 9–10.

9. Crews, *Unauthorized Freud*, pp. 22, 25.

10. Freud, "Screen Memories," *SE*, 3:322.

11. Masson, *Assault on Truth*, p. 188.

12. Mikkel Borch-Jacobsen, "Self-Seduced," in Crews, *Unauthorized Freud*, pp. 49–50. "It is no accident, then, that during this whole period, Freud speaks of '*reproductions*' of the infantile sexual scene, and not 'memories,' or 'reminiscences'" (p. 49).

13. Frederick Crews, *The Memory Wars: Freud's Legacy in Dispute* (New York: New York Review of Books, 1995).

14. See Russell Jacoby, *The Last Intellectuals* (New York: Basic Books, 1987).

15. See Todd Dufresne, *Killing Freud: Twentieth Century Culture and the Death of Psychoanalysis* (London: Continuum Books, 2003), and Joel Paris, *The Fall of an Icon: Psychoanalysis and Academic Psychiatry* (Toronto: University of Toronto Press, 2005).

16. Freud, "Preface," *SE*, 22:6.

17. See Bruno Latour and Stephen Woolgar, *Laboratory Life: The Construction of Scientific Facts*, 2nd ed. (Beverly Hills, CA: Russell Sage, 1986).

18. Paul Robinson, *Freud and His Critics* (Berkeley: University of California, 1995), p. 25.

19. Elaine Showalter, *Hystories: Hysterical Epidemics and Modern Culture* (London: Picador, 1997), pp. 85, 116.

20. Sylvia Nasar, "Loved Humanity. Hated People," *New York Times*, 29 April 2001, p. 12.

21. Sarah Boseley, "Prozac, Used by 40m People, Does Not Work, Say Scientists," *Guardian*, 26 February 2008. Published in the *Public Library of Science Medicine* journal, the study, using data the manufacturers chose not to reveal, revealed that placebos were just as effective as the drugs themselves.

22. Edward Shorter, *A History of Psychiatry* (New York: John Wiley & Sons, 1997), p. 178.

23. Mark Solms, "What Is Consciousness?" *Journal of the American Psychiatric Association* 45, no. 3 (1997): 688.

24. Philip Rieff, *Freud: The Mind of a Moralist* (London: Victor Gollancz, 1960), p. 29.

25. On internal bickering among the various psychoanalytic tribes see, for example, Douglas Kirsner, *Unfree Associations* (London: Process Press, 2000).

26. Paul Roazen recalls a Viennese analyst who "was so pious as to have a fresh bouquet of flowers before an etching of Freud in his waiting room" and stonewalled his questions. His point is that this man was the exception among the scores of analysts he interviewed. Roazen, *Freud and His Followers* (London: Allen Lane, 1976), p. 28. Also see his criticisms of the Ernest Jones official biography of Freud, pp. 36–37.

27. Rieff, *Freud: Mind of a Moralist*, p. ix.

Chapter One

Science and the Psyche

> Science cannot solve the ultimate mysteries of nature and that is because, in the last analysis, we ourselves are part of the mystery we are trying to solve.
>
> —Max Planck

"Sometimes a cigar is just a cigar," is as shrewd a remark as Sigmund Freud ever uttered, if he uttered it. A splendid candidate for second shrewdest remark is Freud's comment that when analyzing any subject it often is "hard to know where to draw the line."[1] What he meant was that it is difficult for even the most sharp-witted investigators to say precisely where one subject stops and another begins, or how far to proceed in pursuit of worthwhile answers. No single scientific method, as he knew, can encompass all influences that affect its object of study.[2] Most scientists appreciate this humbling fact even if they don't always act like it. So when we study ourselves, what is relevant and what is not will be a matter of fine judgment.

Scientists tend not to broadcast the news that judgment calls are involved in much of what they do.[3] In our slick pragmatic culture we want to pin things down with schoolboy logic or do laboratory tests before anything is regarded as real. If the unconscious or the Oedipus complex or defense mechanisms cannot be chloroformed and exhibited on test slides, then these ghostly notions cannot exist. The cavalier consignment of these concepts to oblivion is regarded as the fault of the subject, not of research methods. So, from the start, psychoanalysis was at a deep disadvantage in a superficially scientific popular culture because it acknowledged that human discretion cannot be expelled from the study of humanity without distorting what we find and what we say about it.[4]

For all Freud's toil in developing psychoanalysis, he cautioned any frisky followers that symbolic meaning does not always trump the everyday use of a given item. (An airplane may be a penis symbol, early analysts joked, but "all the same it got you from Vienna to Berlin.") This temptation to overdo symbolism is among many reasons why psychoanalysis would always be, as Freud put it, his "problem child."[5] Indeed, in typically contradictory charges, foes rebuked Freud for making too much of symbolism and in the next breath scorned him for disregarding symbolism's power.[6] So it goes in the Freud wars.

This chapter aims to clear some ground by demonstrating that Freud's foes propagate a naive and misleading notion of scientific inquiry, that public images of Freud are invidiously skewed, that Freud's views on hot-button issues such as women, deviance, and social influences are mischaracterized, that "resistance" has legitimate uses as a concept, and that Freud, for all his real shortcomings, was a scientist of great acuity whose conscientious work is entitled to balanced reappraisals, not jihads. Some key foes I address below include former analyst Jeffrey Masson, literary critic Frederick Crews, historian Peter Swales, philosophy professor Adolf Grunbaum, scholar Ernest Gellner, and a hostile branch of feminism.

IMAGES OF FREUD

Freud was reluctant to incorporate new findings or hypotheses until he thought them through within his own investigative system to see if or how they worked out. (Roazen suggests this was a way for Freud to protect himself from his own hostility, which is possible, but how can one know?)[7] Unless the core principles of psychoanalysis were contested, Freud rarely rejected new propositions or lines of inquiry outright but instead held them in abeyance, saying he "didn't understand" them, at least as yet. Reluctance eventually gave way to evidence where it did favor the unfamiliar element, as can be seen by the revisions Freud made in his own lifetime and the evolution of psychoanalysis ever afterward.

Freud, a staid Viennese gentleman in manner if not temperament, confessed that he couldn't understand the "oceanic feeling" or paranormal phenomena, but he never denied that they might exist.[8] You might count on fingers of one hand the scientists (*pace* Richard Dawkins) today who are as open-minded.[9] As for his "obsession" with sexuality,[10] Rieff long ago noted that Freud "used the term 'sexuality' very widely, in the same comprehensive sense as ordinary language uses the word 'love.'"[11] For Freud love, in the sappy Hollywood sense, was just a "normal prototype of the psychoses."[12]

Biographers attest that Freud had personal experience.[13] As young Freud blurted to future wife Martha, "One is very crazy when one is in love."[14] One suspects at times when perusing his writings that Freud had all the makings of a droll stand-up comedian.[15]

The sour old zealot gracing the covers of most foes' books is a shriveled shadow of Freud. The twenty-three agonizing jaw operations over Freud's last sixteen years would likely make a Robin Williams or a Jim Carrey look a trifle grim, too. Another niggling problem with this portrait is that virtually every scientific advance stems from an initial burst of zeal, which is adjusted and refined later.[16] As Erikson, doyen of ego psychology, remarked about Freud's fix on sexuality, "it may be that in a particular repressive era it is better to call too many things sexual than not, in order to integrate them and eventually understand where they fit in the changing cultural scheme of things."[17] Freud even referred knowingly to his own "one-sidedness" (*einseitgkeit*) as necessary for delving into hidden or otherwise mystifying aspects of life.[18] Sometimes a tower is only a tower, a cigar a cigar, and a penis a penis. Then again, these protrusive items may mean far more to a particular individual or a culture than is apparent to unwitting outsiders.

In this self-reflexive vein Freud said that there was an excellent reason why he entitled his book not *The Dream* but *The Interpretation of Dreams*.[19] Rather than foist prefabricated definitions on us, an analyst works out the meaning with the dreamer. Judgment—savvy, sober, seasoned—is called for when tiptoeing around this strange protean realm. Textbook formulas were as likely to hinder as to help one to navigate the tricky shoals of the psyche. Good judgment, alas, is not easily come by. No umpire, no scientist, no scholar, no community of saints gets every call right. The psyche is not a chalkboard where one of this and two of that always, or ever, add up to three. Human beings are not constructed so conveniently as to fit mere mathematical equations or thumbnail bromides. Unlike human beings, chemicals, rocks, and planets never get angry at or, for that matter, fawn over their investigators.[20] Scientists, for their part, do not always resist temptations to adjust data to fit investigative frameworks, as Freud himself is routinely accused of doing.[21]

Scientific appraisals should test hypotheses, weigh alternative views, revise conclusions in light of evidence, explore the outer (and innermost) reaches of human experience, and use methods appropriate to the nature of the subject. Although performing all these tasks admirably, Freud, who started out as a neurologist (and is praised by enemies for being a talented one), rarely is given his due as a genuine scientist.[22] "The medulla oblongata is a very serious and lovely object," Freud recollected of his early career activities. "I remember how much time and trouble I devoted to its study many years ago. To-day, however, I must remark that I know nothing that could be of less interest to me for the psychological understanding of anxiety than a knowledge of the path of the nerves along which its excitations pass."[23] Freud's foes now simply cannot understand—as Freud on occasion could "not understand" new propositions—why Freud regarded this stance as a major scientific advance.

Scientists, according to ardent anti-Freudians, operate according to a secondary-school textbook picture of the remorseless forward march of knowledge. In their glassy-eyed view, as in that of generations of militant positivists, probing human consciousness requires methods not one whit different than those applied to chemistry or astronomy.[24] A worrisomely widespread attitude in many disciplines today is that just one method—rational choice or econometrics or pharmacology—fits all, encompasses all, and illuminates all, or all that matters anyway. The spoilsports who differ are regarded as trying to pull a fast one. Few notice that it is the prim one-size-fits-all proponents who are doing so. In any case, every action or scientific innovation breeds a reaction. Psychoanalysis ignites recurrent reactions. From its controversial inception audiences were primed to be leery toward psychoanalysis, ranging from its repugnant idea of infantile sexuality to the unnerving discovery that we are not necessarily "masters in our own house."

No system of thought is, or ought to be, immune to criticism. Psychoanalysis has been no exception to the rule, contrary to overwrought or undereducated critics.[25] Perhaps, for example, Freud tended to "identify the social structure of his social class and its problems with the problems inherent in human existence"—although one is hard-pressed to find a rival that likewise fails to reflect the prejudices and preoccupations of his or her own time.[26] Freud was not quite so trapped within bourgeois Viennese convention as foes imply.[27] He was wise enough to his indelibly hypocritical milieu to advise a new foreign patient "that analysis demands a degree of honesty which is unusual, and even impossible in *der burgerlichen gesellschaft* [bourgeois society]."[28]

Freud relentlessly is derided for male chauvinism, stuffy bourgeois attitudes, overdoing sexuality, and valuing subjective states over conscious ones. Yet, as feminist Juliet Mitchell retorted, that Herr Doktor Freud "partook of the socials mores and ideology of his time whilst he developed a science that could overthrow them is neither a contradiction nor a limitation of his work."[29] Just what background is it that would endow Freud with the acumen that fussy foes demand? Might it be the shiny resume of a twenty-first-century liberal arts professor or a Manhattan journalist or an Ivy League literary critic or a psychiatrist whose therapeutic talents begin and end with the jotting of prescriptions? With few exceptions, the latest wave of bitter assaults on psychoanalysis are based on lazy vulgarizations, tendentious readings, a selective heightening of minor aspects of his work into the status of key elements, and sheer misunderstandings.[30]

The ultimate insult that the latest adversaries inflict is the accusation that Freud's earlier opponents were imaginary.[31] It was all in Freud's head. Yet a few foes, like Sulloway and Masson, shored up their prosecutorial strategies by confirming that Freud encountered hard going. The plain contradictions arising from the foes' flurries of charges tend to go unnoticed outside the fray. Scoffing at Freud is a safe intellectual sport, which is why so many rush in to play at it.[32] So the screenwriter of the 2006 film *The Departed* wriggled out of his invented Freud quote about the Irish ("impervious to psychoanalysis") by remarking it was to be regretted only "because it is the only statement of truth to which his name has ever been connected."[33] In a climate badly tilted against Freud, anyone can take refuge in a plainly lame remark and not get called out on it.[34] Irish commentators to this day, of course, treasure the fabricated quote.[35]

In 1981 *Newsweek*'s special issue on Freud asked only whether the Viennese geezer was a fraud or a fantasist.[36] Even during better days, the 1956 *Time* magazine cover story described Freud with stinting praise and reprised the mocking ditty that from psychoanalysis we "know that when we think a thing the thing we think was not the thing we think but only the thing we thing makes us think this thing we think we think."[37] These weary jibes recycle cobwebbed diatribes stretching back to satirist Karl Krauss. The twenty-first-century media revel in portraying psychoanalysis as "a degraded profession, a pseudo-science whose existence is now in doubt."[38] Terry Johnson's play *Hysteria* pictured refugee Freud in London as a slow-witted danger to feisty young women and, to boot, made him the butt of Salvador Dali's jokes.[39] Hence, Dali, fey Franco sympathizer, was treated more sympathetically than Freud, who in 1938 just fled the Gestapo and would lose four sisters in the death camps. Never mind that Stefan Zweig, who introduced Dali to Freud, failed to share anything like the playwright's denigratory view of Freud and of the meeting.[40] The playwright depended for laughs on the reliable assumption of his audience's knowledge being two book pages or three web pages deep.

The iconic image, too, of Freud scribbling or snoring beside the couch is another stereotype.[41] Yet these images, even at their most contemptuous, contain strong traces of underlying apprehension. The cartoonists force a laugh at the healer who might flush out one's dark secrets. No less so, the cartoons ignite fears of charlatans acquiring power over our souls and our bank accounts. Freud unabashedly talked of a soul, but in the deepest human and secular sense.[42] Freud's foes remorselessly hunt down any iota of evidence against him. They mean well so how could they go wrong? Whatever else students of Freudian analysis know, they know that meaning well does not always mean that you really mean well.

ONLY THE LATEST EDITION: MASSON AND COMPANY

Jeffrey Masson became chief reinvigorator of the assault on Freud when he exited a brief tenure as keeper of the Freud Archives in the early 1980s to accuse Freud of a stunning scientific crime. Freud, Masson said, ditched his seduction theory of neurosis "not for theoretical or clinical reasons but because of a personal failure of courage."[43] Psychoanalysis was born of a fainthearted lie.[44] Freud could not endure the opprobrium his hypothesis generated and so caved in to the abusive establishment of Vienna.[45] Freud, in short, could not bear the isolation that other foes say he never suffered.[46] It's clear that the many foes don't compare notes—so much for conspiracy theories.[47]

Masson contends that the average psychoanalyst "is trained to believe that her memories are fantasies."[48] Nowhere in the subsequent annals of psychoanalysis is there a shred of evidence to that effect. Freud, even after recanting seduction theory, never denied that real sexual abuse occurs, and more often than most people credit.[49] Still, the publicized upshot was Masson's jape that, if his charge were true, one "would have to recall every patient since 1901. It would be like the Pinto."[50] Yet even fellow foe Adolf Grunbaum repudiates Masson's rash attack on Freud as "etiologically unfounded."[51]

Masson underwent psychoanalytic training (with incompatible analysts, which, as bumper stickers say, happens) and smartly wangled his way into the prestigious post of projects director of the Freud Archives under boss Kurt Eissler, who was, by no account, a cuddly chap. ("One wants to read Eissler with respect and detachment," writes the ordinarily patient Pulitzer Prize winner Robert Coles, "but his persistent arrogance and rudeness make it hard to do so.")[52] Masson soon hit on a surefire formula: accuse Freud's heirs of concealing information about the founder, which they really were inclined to do.[53] Janet Malcolm told the whole farcical tale in the *New Yorker* and her book *In the Freud Archives*, a story that only sputtered out with the end of a lawsuit long afterward.

Psychoanalysis already had come under heavy fire from the women's movement. Kate Millet condemned Freud as "beyond question the strongest individual counter-revolutionary force in the ideology of sexual politics" while Catherine McKinnon, later Masson's partner, saw pure misogyny pervading psychoanalysis.[54] Peter Swales also alleged that Freud, when not fooling around with a sister-in-law, plotted to murder colleague Wilhelm Fliess.

These lurid accusations were, to say the least, strained. Swales's own psychological tendencies are, as cartoon shrinks mutter, very interesting.[55] In "taking on Freud," Swales writes, "I was taking on the monster that existed in myself. When I came to Freud, when I looked at the man, I immediately knew who he was. . . . My starting point is that all people are devious and sinister, that they're shits."

While there is something to be said for the aforementioned attitude, especially if one finds oneself suddenly in the midst of a vitriolic David Mamet or Sam Shepherd play, it is a stance that doesn't lend itself to fair appraisals. Swales needles Freud for his early-career episode of "cocaine evangelism,"[56] after which Swales unleashes a litany of fanciful denigrations, preceded by puny disclaimers such as "It is conceivable . . . ," "There are a number of possible reasons . . . ," an "in all probability," as well as several more *possibly*s—and all crammed on a single page.[57]

Marianne Krull too berated Freud for shirking child abuse because "his self-analysis could have forced him to accuse his own father of being a seducer, of being perverse."[58] There is no absolutely way to ascertain whether such a charge has merit, but this objection does not interrupt the foes' speculations. In retrospect, it isn't so very difficult to sympathize with the doubtless overprotective attitude of Anna Freud and Kurt Eissler regarding the handling of Freud's correspondence. Overweening fussiness seems wholly justified in view of what transpired when the archives' contents wound up in the hands of a Masson or Swales.

Was Freud a misanthropic elitist? Foes reproach Freud because he thought little of "crowds"—that is, the masses. (One wonders what the foes really say about the hoi polloi at dinner parties or in unguarded moments.) Freud described the masses—awful word—as "lazy and unintelligent" and requiring "guidance by an elite."[59] Yet Freud also urged that the "burden of the instinctual sacrifices imposed on all people needs to be diminished and that compensations should be supplied for those that cannot be removed."[60] Freud likewise lampooned enforced sexual codes that "produce[d] well-behaved weaklings who later become lost in the great mass of people that tend so follow, willingly, the leads given by strong individuals."[61] So it was not in the nature of people to do so (or else why waste one's breath); it was a matter of upbringing.

Why elites should care about anyone but themselves is a question always worth asking, but Freud, the record shows, did care. Freud rather wryly suggested that there were limits to "man's capacity for education" (mostly because of rote indoctrination prevalent even in top schools), which was both a bad and good thing. It was a good thing, you see, if it limited the indoctrination that students underwent. Freud was frankly seditious as to who was at fault: "It need not be said that a culture which leaves unsatisfied and drives to rebelliousness so large a number of its members neither has a prospect of continued existence, nor deserves it."[62] Thomas Jefferson could not have said it better.

Freud was deeply concerned with establishing a rational basis for accommodating necessary cultural demands, one where a "friendly attitude" is taken to the task of reconciling men to civilization in a civilized way. "Think of the distressing contrast between the radiant intelligence of a healthy child and the feeble mentality of the average adult," Freud chided.[63] This drastic difference is imposed by social institutions, which can be reformed. Freud decried a universal "dumbing down" imposed by myopic structures of authority upon institutions from the top to the bottom of the social ladder.[64]

Freud was no snob in the sense of imagining that the "great and the good" (or celebrities, as we call them today) remotely were what they appeared to be.[65] "I have found little that is 'good' about human beings on the whole," he wrote in a note which included wealthier clients. "In my experience most of them are trash . . ."[66] Freud unequivocally evaluated individuals, regardless of neurosis or assets, on their personal merits: "There are healthy people who are not worth anything, and on the other hand, 'unhealthy' neurotic people who are very worthy (*wertroll*) individuals indeed."[67]

Freud's foes seem to go weak at the knees every time they glimpse any upscale person in a white lab coat, whatever the era. In Freud's time a "belligerent somaticism and an acceptance of 'civilized' morality characterized most neurologists," a historian finds, "many of whom by 1900, were listed in the Social register, that new index of American social status."[68] Freud, unlike these cocksure professionals, regarded every normal person—including high personages—as "only approximately normal; his ego resembles that of the psychotic in one point or another, in a greater or lesser degree . . ."[69] This is just not the sort of thing that the upper crust anywhere wanted to hear.

RESISTING RESISTANCE

The dirtiest trick in the Freudian arsenal, foes say, is resistance. Freud argued, on the basis of extensive clinical experience, that an event was forgotten because it was painful and resisted being made conscious so that "a mental conflict occurs, and the symptoms are the result of a compromise"—a tragic circuitousness where repression is undone by a neurotic outbreak. "The expenditure of force on the part of the physician was evidently the measure of a resistance on the part of a patient."[70]

The dastardly deed is that Freud's movement "responded to hostility by deciding that only acolytes were capable of understanding the system."[71] Dissent was "resistance" and treated as "an error that could be corrected only by psychoanalysis: a splendid gambit, still in use," a foe complains. Hence, resistance is a "falsification-evading device," and defined as "the idea that the repudiation of an interpretation of a theory is evidence of its validity, because it shows the desire of the Unconscious of a person not to be unmasked."[72]

Resistance is a clinical term applicable inside the therapy room, and ideally not in theoretical combat, although the latter doubtless occurs. Still, one must appreciate resistance as a tremendous gift to critics who thereby asserted that any critiques aimed at analytic circles were fended off for entirely spurious reasons. Freud, nevertheless, found that the unconscious "conjured up the most evil spirits of criticism against psycho-analysis [and partly] because of the relative inaccessibility of the experiences which provide evidence of it . . . " Freud certainly bemoaned a "contemporary generation of doctors [who have] have been brought up to respect only anatomical, physical and chemical factors . . . they are not prepared to take psychological ones into account."[73] Accounts of the resistance that disquieting new knowledge encounters within scientific communities are not uncommon. The notion that scientists bow politely before superior evidence, especially when their own favorite models are at stake, is profoundly naive.

Werner Heisenberg remarked that once one experienced the clever tenacity with which opponents "react to the demand for a change in the pattern of thought, one can only be amazed that such revolutions in science have actually been possible at all."[74] Max Planck commented, contrary to tepid textbooks, that a "new scientific truth does not triumph by converting its opponents and making them see the light, but rather because its opponents eventually die, and a new generation grows up that is familiar with it."[75] Freud keenly appreciated this trend. "The leading lights of psychiatry really don't amount to much," he comforted Jung, who was smarting from a rough encounter with psychiatrists. "The Future belongs to us and our views; and the young men—everywhere most likely—side actively with us."[76] Resistance is a vexing feature in social sciences where, as the late anthropologist Clifford Geertz kidded on the square, old theories tend less to fade away than to go into second editions. Reductionist models are impossible to banish, for they always have some merit if used prudently. Prudence, alas, is the first virtue that enraptured reductionists heave overboard.

"Human megalomania (after Copernicus and Darwin)," Freud foresaw, "will have suffered its third and most wounding blow from the psychological research of the present time which seeks to prove to the ego that it is not even master in its own house, but must content itself with scanty information of what is going on unconsciously in its mind. We psychoanalysts were not the first and not the only ones to utter this call for introspection; but it seems to be our fate to give it its most forcible expression and to support it with empirical material which affects every individual. Hence arises the general revolt against our science, the disregard of all considerations of academic civility, and the releasing of the opposition from every restraint of impartial logic."[77]

Many inquirers justifiably chafed at the cloying protectiveness of psychoanalytic organizations toward the founder. To the degree defensiveness occurred (and it did), in the long run it worked to the disadvantage of the defenders.[78] Freud was typically prescient when he warned that even an analyst who is "very well able to carry out analysis upon others can behave like any other mortal and be capable of producing violent resistances as soon as he himself becomes the object of analytic investigation"—or, in this case, even when others carry out the task for him.[79]

So the foes' gripe about resistance has merit, but no one needed the foes to point it out. Rieff long ago chided that "built into the therapy, through this notion of resistance, is disavowal of the patient's critical judgment."[80] Unchecked, "resistance" is a facile evasion, a slipping away from scrutiny. The fact that resistance retains explanatory power in clinical practice does not lessen the offensiveness of using it outside that special situation. The idea that only those who are analyzed are entitled to raise questions about the misuse of concepts is absurd. But then again who actually has ever said such a thing?

The concept of resistance, a foe says, means that "the repudiations of an interpretation or a theory is evidence of its validity because it shows the desire of the unconscious of a given person not to be unmasked, is one of the neatest and best known ploys in the armory."[81] Yet historians cite numerous cases where Freud took very seriously valid criticisms from "outsiders." A sharp scientist is aware of how tenuous many finding are, that canonical work is liable to be shredded overnight to confetti (though not belief systems supporting it), and that many problems that the public believes to be solved—such as the origins of mental disturbances—remain great mysteries, despite a myriad of glib newspapers and dull textbooks claiming otherwise.

Frederick Crews is probably the most formidable shock trooper in the anti-Freudian phalanx. Like a choleric ex-cult member, Crews writes proudly of his own "self-deprogramming," which is a rather disingenuous way to describe the event—"reprogramming" is more like it. Here is an indefatigable crusader who shows no skepticism as to the ability of positivist science to illuminate the psychic interior, the human experience, which for him is composed of an uncomplicated blend of empirical events and mental predilections that color and select how we experience events.[82]

Crews resembles the fluid fanatic who "cures" himself of religion by converting from one creed to another. In this case, Crews embraces the allures of scientism, the key features of which Voegelin identified as "(1) the assumption that the mathematical sciences of natural phenomena is a world science to which all other sciences should conform; (2) that all realms of being are accessible to the methods of the science of phenomena and (3) that all reality which is not accessible to the science of phenomena is either irrelevant or, in the most radical form of their dogma, illusionary."[83] Robert Michels nicely summarizes scientism as an "irrational veneration of what appears to be scientific," rather than the discretionary use of "scientific methods as tools."[84]

One can only guess to what extent young Crews brought idealizing tendencies to the Freudian boot camp, and to what degree his drill instructors instilled or exploited these tendencies. No profession is free of dogmatic clowns. Are there fewer in psychoanalysis than in medicine generally? I wouldn't venture to say, but the psychoanalytic method, regardless of imperfect people deploying it, fosters self-reflection and a skepticism of pat answers, and even these days of the profession's stock answers. According to Crews, a self-styled Inspector Javert, his Viennese Jean Valjean is to blame even when his enemies misconstrue him.[85] Crews manages to reprove Freud for Masson's misconceptions on motives for abandoning seduction theory, misconceptions which fueled the baleful recovered memory movement in the 1990s.

Crews bombards fortress Freud: the coot is "pseudoscientific," evokes "irrational loyalty," created a "closed system," and "thumbed his nose at scientific prudence." Psychoanalysis is just an "ingenious witches' brew of speculative neurophysiology."[86] Reading Crews you would think no one before dared to utter a discouraging word about the wise and terrible wizard of Vienna. Freud fostered a "sectarian mentality," which only members of a rabid rival sect fully appreciate. Freudianism "in its most exalted mood verges on outright religious worship," thunders Crews, though one wonders then where is the inquisition, the stake and gibbet, compulsory tithing, and the glowering priesthood with power over life and death?

Freud was no more "chief begetter" of the calamitous recovered memory movement than St. Francis of Assisi launched the Spanish Inquisition.[87] Nonetheless, Freud was "endlessly devious and self-dramatizing," unlike righteous foes.[88] Freud contrived to arrive at "prearranged conclusions," unlike medical modelers who modestly insist all mental disturbances be physical in origin. "Freudians are finding themselves on the defensive," Crews crows, unlike every other period in their existence.[89] Shrinks are very well acquainted with clients who idealize a personage in order afterward to demolish the blemished idol, at least in their own heads. Adroitly bypassed is the truth that we often fear as much or more so than phonies: those rare people who are ethical models, for we might have to summon the energy to live up to them.

What about, ahem, deviation? Freud is blamed by foes for pathologizing homosexuality (and indeed anything but missionary position sex), preaching the joys of cocaine, flouting scientific method, and degrading the female gender. "Freud traced anxiety neurosis, obsession, hysterical vomiting, repressed memories of infantile sexuality, and arguably guilt itself," a book reviewer calmly claims, "to the psyche's confrontation with its primal source of sexual satisfaction—masturbation."[90] Clueless reviewers regularly team up these days with ignorant authors to blame benighted medical attitudes upon Freud rather than upon the medical establishment from which Freud strayed.

Hale tartly points out in a survey of nineteenth- and early-twentieth-century American opinion that "nearly every physician continued to insist that excessive masturbation and sexual intercourse were debilitating and dangerous."[91] A medical text of the era stated that "Semen, if retained, was reabsorbed and invigorated the entire organism." The complaisant high-level quackery pervading medicine was enough to frighten anyone out of their wits. Yet Krull, like Masson, treats Freud's early views on sexual nonconformity as if he alone were nutty enough to promote them.[92] Any assailant on analysis may be sure that no one in the media will dispute him. The conventional wisdom rings as clearly as a Pavlovian bell in a Pavlovian kennel: Freud is a fraud.

Showalter too believes that Freud stirred primal scene memories by hinting to patients what he expected to hear—as if Freud hadn't made Herculean efforts over a lifetime to deal with it.[93] Freud abandoned hypnosis and electrotherapy because suggestion was involved in both: "Psychoanalysis proper began when I dispensed with hypnosis."[94] Grunbaum should be credited as the only foe to affirm that Freud made "brilliant" efforts to overcome this problem, even if the measures are portrayed by him as ultimately inadequate.[95]

The foes' view that Freud "was long the subject of hagiography" is hilariously off the mark.[96] His views on childhood sexuality alone guaranteed scorn in reputable quarters. This slander of the foreign doctor "who decreed that I wanted to kill my father and sleep with my mother," was prelude to the rumpus led by foes against the proposed Smithsonian/Library of Congress exhibition Sigmund Freud: Conflict and Culture, scheduled for 1995.[97] In this spiteful affair objectivity went AWOL. Because Laurence Olivier as Hamlet on screen displayed what was interpretable as an oedipal twitch, the actor was slammed by foes as a slavering Freudian stooge.[98] Foes then made the "modest request" that an anti-Freudian exhibit be included to ensure a "full spectrum of informed opinion."[99]

The curators' predicament was rather like modern creationists approaching a prospective Darwin exhibit and demanding that it incorporate "a full spectrum of opinion," meaning themselves plus Adam and Eve. A full spectrum is always welcome, but a full spectrum is not remotely what Freud's foes are interested in. The Smithsonian, rocked back on its institutional heels, regrouped to mount a show three years later. The curator edited a companion volume—diplomatically incorporating an essay by Grunbaum—and solemnly promised not to "make a case for Freud's influence being positive or negative."[100] But that tap-dancing concession was not nearly enough. The Freud exhibit was denounced as "a predictable tribute."[101]

Even pharmacological fancies can't salvage Freud. E. M. Thornton asserts that Freud exhibited a lifelong cocaine addiction,[102] and as a result, undertook a "messianic obsession" to spread his crackpot gospel. By implied contrast, contemporary biopsychiatrists are, one and all, levelheaded, immaculately ethical professionals.[103] Cocaine is taboo stuff, but physicians who indiscriminately dish out legal drugs are pillars of the community. The preposterous idea that Freud single-handedly suppressed opinion in a medical profession that was at best very wary of him is a bedrock myth to which Thornton resorts.[104]

A British foe insists likewise that "magician or messiah" are the only conceivable poles for organizing debates; Freud spawned an oppressive orthodoxy despite analysis fragmenting into a plethora of schools.[105] Whether analysis is a disciplined organization or a gaggle of squabbling rivals, both states of affairs are conclusive signs of intellectual depravity. An exasperated Freud recalled: "in the course of my work I have modified my views on a few important points, changed them and replaced them by fresh ones—and in each case of course I have made this publicly known. And the outcome of this frankness? Some people have taken no notice whatever of my self-corrections and continue to this day to criticize me for hypotheses which long ceased to have the same meaning for me. Others reproach me for precisely for these changes and regard me as untrustworthy on this account."[106] Ah, but Freud then became a flip-flopper.

WHAT WOMEN WANT

Gloria Steinem dubs Freud the greatest misogynist in recorded history, and speculates on Freud suddenly transforming into a female. Would he not then become sensitive, sensible, and renounce idiotic penis envy?[107] Didn't Freud say that women cannot create lasting art or pull off great accomplishments? Isn't femininity a form of "failed masculinity"? It is easy to forget amid all this indignation that women in Freud's day, as another feminist reminds us, "could not suffer frustration of sexual desire, since they were not supposed to have any."[108] Freud helped to change that social and medical wisdom.

Yet it is Freud, not society, who held women down. One has abundant reasons to doubt even over the last century that physicians alone surpass psychoanalysts in prowoman attitudes, as we see in chapter 4.[109] Indeed, Freud's foes, though not all enamored of feminists, happily invoke them anyway.[110] There is something irresistibly amusing about preening males scampering on stage to rue "the suffering inflicted on women by Freudian condescension, misdiagnosis and blame."[111] One again can only wonder what the women who intimately know the male critics would have to say about their own sterling behavior. Few, one suspects, would survive the malicious scrutiny they train on Freud

Freud's views on women were condescending, but hardly malevolent and far from rigid. Steinem wanted Freud force-marched to see George Sand, who upset all patterns of gender behavior, or to meet U.S. suffragettes at Seneca Falls.[112] They surely would shake him to his senses—unlike Lou Andreas-Salome, Helene Deutsch, Hermine Hug-Helmuth, Melanie Klein, or daughter Anna. Some feminists blamed Freud alone for stoking "women's secondary and inferior relationship to men," as if Freud dictated medical opinion.[113] Another group of feminists, though, finds ample value in psychoanalysis as a "system of ideas whose significance for feminism is that it suggests so much about interaction between social organization and the deepest levels of human sexuality."[114]

Consider the editor of the *Wiener Medizinische Wochenschrift* in Freud's era, who reports a leading medical figure stating that the "aim in life for women was to make themselves interesting: to achieve this purpose they shirked nothing, no matter how unpleasant it was, not even death: *Mulieri ne mortuae quidem credendum est* [not even a dead woman is to be trusted]."[115] Nothing Freud is accused of saying can match this misogynistic gem—a common enough attitude to be expressed without fear of consequences. Forgotten today too is that the sheer bewilderment induced in the average doctor by hysterical disturbances—symptoms often were repulsive—frequently triggered disdain and even nastiness toward the sufferers. Freud's and Breuer's work surely helped to mitigate these unsympathetic attitudes.

Steinem knows for sure that Freud tolerated the many women analysts so long as they were obedient, which is an amazingly condescending attitude toward them. Early European psychoanalytic circles overflowed with talented women, a number of whom openly took Freud to task for his views on gender.[116] If Steinem and her cohort are correct, it is difficult to explain the sharp difference in women in psychoanalytic ranks in prewar Europe and the

United States: 30 percent of émigrés to the United States but 9 percent of all analysts in United States.[117] Steinem winds up trivializing all mental suffering, as when she invokes a letter to Fliess, "quoted by all those struggling against the superficial belief that suffering was inspired by real events, not the deep and important struggles within the psyche."[118] Ah, only real events count. A military physician in 1917 slapping electrodes with alacrity onto shell-shocked soldiers could not have agreed more. Steinem believes that reports of "widespread perversions against children"—the very excesses that other foes revile—must be true. Every hysterical case Freud encountered is attributed to sexual abuse, every single one.[119]

Yes, Freud indulged in hypnosis, employed suggestion, and made serious errors (especially of countertransference) in the treatment room. How do we know? Because Freud told us, just as a fearless "conquistador" would, revealing lapses and wrong turns along the way in service of the larger enterprise. Readers will find little of that modesty in a contemporary science report. What goes down in black and white are results presented in their best possible light, which foes choose to trust. So today, once again, nothing much stems from upbringing; everything originates from genes or biochemistry. The foes who want to rescue us from psychoanalysis are blitheringly determined to plunge us into Victorian medical and scientific mores again.[120] Let us look at their reasoning.

PSYCHOANALYSIS, PSEUDOSCIENCE, AND PSEUDOCRITICISM

Speaking for "science," Hans Eysenck proclaimed long before the recent cluster of foes that psychoanalysis cannot meet the stringent criteria of physical science and, therefore, is unable to prove causality.[121] Ernest Gellner too launched a dogged debunking mission, saying that Freud's movement "remains largely uncharted" even though innumerable studies of varying merit and motive had emerged.[122] This underestimate has the commendable feature of making Gellner, Eysenck, and kindred successors look valiant.[123] Their strategy of nonstop offense has the commendable feature too of distracting attention from the conceits of the scientism they champion. Grunbaum later performed marvelous rhetorical feats to prove the Eysenckian premise he started out with, that positivist methods must be all there is to say sensibly about science.[124]

For Gellner a psychoanalyst is no different from "a gipsy at the fair [who] offers to tell your fortune, and does so, but will not discuss her sources or methods."[125] (Grunbaum invokes shamans and exorcists as relevant comparisons.)[126] Psychoanalysis, alone of all disciplines, is "provocative, calm, arrogantly disdain of dull certainty [and] does possess, if not authority—and it often does claim to have that—at the very least a certain disturbing quality."[127] One trouble is that this pungent account describes the medical profession extremely well. As John Bowlby remarks, Gellner skews his evaluation by fastening on Freudian analysis alone rather than on the phenomena Freud was trying to explain.

Gellner abhors the "unconscious" because it is "a means of devaluing all previous certainties, above all, his assessment of himself."[128] Therefore, it is a self-serving invention to undermine otherwise stable human beings, who possess no unconscious. This peremptory form of reasoning is what Gellner considers scientific. Must something not exist because a positivist cannot measure it with high-tech calipers? As Whitehead chides, if we define out of existence everything that disagrees with our favored model, then we become all-knowing—which is the positivist project, in a nutshell. The double moral of their common story is tacit but clear: Any researcher who is not a positivist invariably is trying to fool you; positivists never fool anyone.

Freud is a hopeless "man of superstition" because he cannot embrace the foes' unduly cramped notion of what constitutes science. "A science cannot be based on subjective interpretations, and the Freudian account of childhood development, with its suggested basis for the development of neurotic symptom, is quite unacceptable," Eysenck judges.[129] Eysenck's declaration only rules out every interesting question in the social sciences, in which explicit recognition of the role of subjectivity otherwise has come to be deemed as much an asset as a liability.

Analysis is supposed to be untestable, subjective, speculative, and unreproducible, and generalizes unrestrainedly from a small number of cases. As Fisher and Greenberg soberly rejoin, the foes demand a level of research testing excellence that is not "commonly found anywhere in the behavioral science literature."[130] The foes say psychoanalysis "assumes that mental activity is causally deterministic." For them, for some undisclosed reason, this cannot be the case. On what grounds do they object to mental activity as causal factor? On what scientific grounds do they prejudge what they find? There is a pretense, or perhaps ignorance, that there has not been a perennial debate in the social sciences about appropriate methods for different subjects.

Freud defended lay (nonmedical) analysts because he feared that medical authorities would distort his framework to suit their appallingly limited intellectual range.[131] American doctors were and are remarkably ill-educated outside their specialties, so it is sometimes hard not to cheer Crews and his cohort as they zero in on a particular shrinks. In analysts' retorts in *The Memory Wars* one occasionally catches a whiff of incense of the priesthood, the cognoscenti, of secrets of the arcana—although the same odors pervade the small worlds of English professors, journalists, physicians, lawyers, and other white-collar crafts. To proclaim that every analyst is venal, arrogant, or clueless is the same as saying that every English professor is a bumbling or cynical clown out of a novel by David Lodge or Kingsley Amis. Some are, most aren't. Probably.

One is struck by the tut-tutting tone of psychoanalysts' replies within *The Memory Wars*.[132] They clearly did not appreciate this was a no-holds-barred fight. Crews's anger stems from feelings of betrayal based on his early misapprehensions of what psychoanalysis can do. He's not the first. What we witness is not an edifice crumbling because of inherent implausibilities (although some surfaced), but another round in the ongoing cultural struggle between neomechanistic thought and humanist inquiry.[133] One beholds resurrections of antagonistic propositions. It is no accident that Bruno Bettelheim, an atheist, entitled a book *Freud and Man's Soul* in recognition of an irreducible, incorrigible, independent spark that Freudians locate within humanity. The biomedical paradigm advocated in Webster's *Why Freud Was Wrong* is no more a novelty today than the "market" model in contemporary economics.[134]

Gellner calls analysis a "technique of salvation" even though all it offers sufferers is, in Freud's infamous words, "ordinary unhappiness." Gellner sagely warns against researchers who "thirst for a pattern," except isn't that what scientists do all the time—find plausible patterns in nature and argue their cases?[135] Gellner ridicules Freud for "persuading the world to accept a certain background theory of knowledge," which is presupposed by the technique which he accuses Freud of lacking the "intellectual sophistication of realizing." Gellner's account of a psychoanalytic theory of knowledge—that after unconscious interferences are cleared, the mind yields unmediated truth—is false. No analyst will credit Gellner's comic book "snap out of it" version of a "cure." Gellner seems to have plucked his impressions of psychoanalysis from *Reader's Digest* or *Vogue* magazine, not the *Standard Edition*.

The psychoanalytic system is ruled by the assumption that our "predicaments are indeed self-imposed," which is true for some, or even a lot of, analysts but has nothing to do with Freud, who took social factors into account. Freud "ran a scientific organization in a manner that bore a fair resemblance to the administration of the mafia or of a Leninist party" even though up to two hundred offshoots of the organization exist today.[136] Gellner ascribes an "idiom of 'maladjustment'" to psychoanalysis, rather than to overarching social forces demanding the adjusting of unruly individuals to their cultural regimes, a condition which Freud addressed ruefully in *Civilization and Its Discontents*.

Gellner applauds empiricism as the great leveler—a completely unproblematic one—because "at its root is the idea that all thing are known in basically the same way, and nothing can have standing greater than the evidence for its existence, and evidence is assembled and evaluated by MEN."[137] And there's the rub. Nature is interpreted by deluded worthies who think of themselves as no-nonsense empiricists. Empiricism, however, is an expression of faith that the universe is orderly, that our senses and our instruments are trustworthy, and that reproducible results extracted from quirky humans are the sole means by which reliable knowledge is attained.[138]

Latour and Woolgar remind us that those nice stories scientists tell about the procedures they follow to elicit experimental truth are often "at odds with the strategies actually employed."[139] Karl Popper implicitly acknowledged this commonplace difference long ago when he divided research into a "context of discovery" (when anything goes) and a "context of justification" (when tests come into play).[140] Empirical tests, of varying merit and applicability, are an indispensable means of checking propositions about how we conduct and experience our lives. But, contrary to Gellner, they are not the only or most apt means of doing so.

"We are in the curious position of using cognitive raw materials, but never seeing them in their raw state," Gellner cagily admits, "for we most emphatically don't invent our experience, but we only see it as and when processed."[141] Absolutely true. As Robinson notes, "the attack on Freud [by Gellner and other foes] is an attack on modernism, on the notion that all human knowledge is subjective and indeterminate."[142] Gellner recoils at this notion. Belief systems "need to be anchored in background assumption, in the pervasive obviousness of an intellectual climate," but Gellner is recasting background conditions to suit his own views. Gellner rightly fears a kind of "cognitive license" conferred on those whom a particular technique had made pure of heart, but this caveat applies to anyone clinging to any scheme of knowledge.[143] If power corrupts, cognitive license distorts. So we need an arbitrator outside the system—but apparently only ones as ill-equipped as Gellner or else Eysenck, who concludes critiques with a plea for the blinkered nag of behaviorism.[144]

Science, as Freud knew, is a human enterprise rife with dead ends, ego trips, fashions, institutional interests, groupthink, and the baneful influence of money. Science also is an ideal. Freud revised his highly contingent theories in light of evidence and experience, according to that ideal. The foes believe that science could or should comprehend us down to the last little manipulable detail. Yet we know that lab rats are driven too crazy by handlers to be reliable representatives even of rodents, let alone the human race.[145] Experiments will go on regardless, as will the search for a gene for this or that condition. "The environment is a tremendous powerful agent in producing alcoholism [and other woes]," a researcher remarks, "but genes are easier to study."[146] The evidence is skimpy but the funding, and the search for a neat answer, is too alluring.[147] Vilify Freud instead.

A scientific paradigm is a model of relations among phenomena that hold for a time and which yields fruitful puzzles for important research.[148] Keep in mind that critics usually ride a hobbyhorse paradigm into battle, but you only tell apart the first-rate critic from the second-rate by whether they try to confront the strongest case their opponents muster. Only Grunbaum does so from atop his hobbyhorse. Freud was keen to prove his theories in terms of reigning medical reasoning, but not so much as to capitulate to unreasonable foreclosure of research.

To understand a major figure you must understand the opponents. The medical model—a physiological monopoly on understanding human motives, actions, and behavior—was the revered means through which medicine interpreted human beings. Nothing matters so much as tracing a "defect" to its doubtless biological source. Failing that, one imputed that a detectable disorder was there somewhere if only one had the wit, or the technical bits, to locate it. This is an investigative strategy, all right, but it isn't the end-all and be-all of science. People, according to this framework, cannot drive other people crazy. Do the savants who foster this belief inhabit the same universe as the rest of us?

A psychoanalyst "has a stake in seeing what the patient says or does in light of theoretical expectations."[149] Yes, and they know it too and can guard against it. Analysts are indeed prey to the same habits of mind that rivals bring to the fray, but psychoanalysis is the only profession in which systematic attempts are made to account for the values, biases, distorted feelings, and emotional tendencies that analysts bring to human encounters. Fisher and Greenberg comment that "no other field devotes so much attention to the study not only of another person's subjectivity so carefully, but one's own."[150] It's nothing less than astonishing to see indignant foes attacking psychoanalysis for what is one of its strongest points, and one in which the foes themselves commonly display a great deficit.

CONCLUSION: STREETLIGHT SCIENCE

Freud's foes lobby for "truths," which, when taken for the whole truth, lead to misleading conclusions. Formal approaches, set up for the convenience of lab experiments, have a seductive appeal, producing a preemptive, false certainty, a "keys under the streetlight" research. There is nothing whatever wrong with searching there so long as you don't confine your search to that spot. Every model is liable to abuse, including the models the critics promote as antidotes but which contain their own intellectual pitfalls. When a skeptic draws the line at his or her own beliefs, or does not recognize them, you know you are in the hands of an ideologue. The signal service that psychoanalysis provides is spurring us to get out of our own way, not to trip over our unconscious (or less conscious) selves, and to recognize the same phenomena in others and get out of their way, or take remedial measures.

What we find in assaults on psychoanalysis is the denigrative, not investigative, method in bilious bloom. Freud is endowed with superhuman influence so that foes can blame psychoanalysis for a "misallocation of resources" by diverting medical research away from neurological investigations.[151] Labs across the Western world apparently were chronically starved for funds that went instead into analysts' pockets. Torrey, incidentally, helped to strip National Institute of Mental Health (NIMH) funds from a group of former patients who met to discuss the "dangers of medication."[152] Eysenck released a study exculpating cigarettes as carcinogenic, connecting lung cancer instead to personality type.[153] One wonders how many of Freud's foes can boast of such stunts.

Absolutely anything can be abused, so psychoanalysis too can be abused. Knowledge must be open to question; the goal is the "ruthless criticism of everything existing."[154] Foes, though, pretend they bravely take on what actually is a weak quarry, unable to strike back, as the medical profession or the pharmaceutical industry certainly can. The foes swarm over what they judge is easy pickings. What they offer in psychoanalysis's stead is a pledge of allegiance to positivism, the procrustean lopping of inconvenient limbs to suit a favored model. Many foes are nothing more than cheerleaders for behavioral therapy, primal screaming, or some other therapeutic brand name.

Top-notch scientists know how provisional knowledge really is.[155] There is no omniscient model, but the lure of finding one never diminishes.[156] Freud declined to claim that psychoanalysis was a cure even for the categories of illness for which he cautiously found it applicable. Even if psychoanalysis's powers of healing are fully granted, it still may not be the most attractive course. Consider the plight of a 1940s American musician, madly in love with his beautiful actress wife, who gave up analysis because it made him choose between a tempestuous time with his wife and levelheaded living.[157] The analyst was right; Artie Shaw's marriage to Ava Gardner didn't last very long. But maybe Shaw was right, for a while, too.

NOTES

1. Sigmund Freud, "An Autobiographical Study," in *Standard Edition of the Complete Psychological Works of Sigmund Freud*, ed. James Strachey et al. (London: Hogarth Press and the Institute for Psychoanalysis, 1954–) 20:50 (hereafter *SE*).

2. See Thomas Kuhn, *The Structure of Scientific Revolutions* (Chicago: University of Chicago, 1962). "Nature will always have to be filtered, simplified, selectively sampled and clearly interpreted to bring it within one map. It is because complexity must be reduced to relative simplicity that different ways of representing it are always possible." David Bloor, "Anti-Latour," *Studies in History and Philosophy of Science* 30, no. 1 (March 1999): 90.

3. More than a third of some 3,400 scientists surveyed admit wrongdoing over 2002–2006, according to a study by HealthPartners Research Foundation. "At a research lab where no one is looking over your shoulder a scientist who ignores anomalous results can produce career-boosting work," said one scientist. "The case of Korean scientist Hwang Woo-Suk regarding embryonic stem-cell cloning is a key case." Only 1.5 percent admitted plagiarism, though. Steve Levin, "Scientists and the Art of Fudging the Truth," *Chicago Sun-Times*, 27 March 2006.

4. On this point see Karl Mannheim, *Ideology and Utopia* (London: Routledge & Kegan Paul, 1936).

5. In child analysis Anna Freud found herself in the same position versus Melanie Klein, tamping down the latter's tendency to "immediate and exclusively symbolic interpretations of a child's acts." Uwe Henrik Peter, *Anna Freud* (New York: Shocken Books, 1985), p. 93.

6. Freud, inadvertently, echoes Carl Jung when saying in his final work that symbolism "disregards all language" and that "investigation would probably show that it is ubiquitous—the same for all people." Freud, "Moses and Monotheism," *SE*, 23:99.

7. Paul Roazen, *Freud and His Followers* (London: Allen Lane, 1976), p. 501.

8. Sigmund Freud, *Civilization and Its Discontents* (New York: Norton, 1961), p. 12. "In my opinion it shows no great confidence in science if one does not think it capable of assimilating and working over whatever may perhaps turn out to be true in the assertions of occultists." Freud, "Dreams and Occultism," in *New Introductory Lectures* (New York: Norton, 1965), p. 49.

9. Freud, who believed he'd die by age sixty-two, self-mockingly wrote a colleague on the occasion of that birthday: "The nice superstition with the sixty-two now finally has to be given up. There is indeed no relying on the supernatural!" Ernst Falzedor and Eva Brabant, eds., *The Correspondence of Sigmund Freud and Sandor Ferenczi* (Cambridge: Belknap Press of Harvard University Press, 1996), 2:281.

10. "The nucleus of what we mean by love naturally consists (and this is what is commonly called love, and what the poets sing of) in sexual love with sexual union as its aim. But we do not separate from this—what in many cases has a share in the name 'love'—on the one hand, self-love, and on the other, love for parents and children, friendship and love for humanity in general. And also devotion to concrete objects and to abstract ideas . . . all these tendencies are expressions of the same

instinctual impulses." Freud, *Group Psychology and the Analysis of the Ego* (New York: Norton, 1965), p. 29.

11. Philip Rieff, *Freud: The Mind of a Moralist* (London: Victor Gollancz, 1960), p. 151.

12. Freud, "Totem and Taboo," *SE*, 13:89.

13. On his wife, see Roazen, *Freud and His Followers*, pp. 70–77. On his first love, see Ernest Jones, *Sigmund Freud: Life and Work*, vol. 1, *The Young Freud 1856–1900* (London: Hogarth Press, 1972), pp. 28–29.

14. Ernest Jones, *Life and Work of Sigmund Freud* (London: Hogarth Press, 1957), p. 85.

15. The enjoyment of a joke is "due to the momentary suspension of the energy expended upon maintaining repression owing to the attraction exercised by the offer of a premium of a pleasure." Freud, "Autobiographical Study," *SE*, 20:112. A bit clunky, but that's it. If you want a bad definition, see Emil Kraepelin's definition quoted in Freud, *Jokes and Their Relation to the Unconscious* (New York: Norton, 1960), p. 11: "The arbitrary connection or linking, usually by way of verbal; association, of two ideas which in some way contrast with each other."

16. See Herbert Butterfield's mordant comments on David Harvey and on Galileo in *The Origins of Modern Science* (New York: Free Press, 1957), pp. 50, 83. Karl Popper implies this is the case in his distinction between "context of discovery" and "context of justification" in his *The Logic of Scientific Discovery* (New York: Harper & Row, 1963).

17. Erik H. Erikson, "The First Psychoanalyst," in *Insight and Responsibility* (New York: Norton, 1964), p. 33.

18. Max Schur, *Freud: Living and Dying* (London: Hogarth Press, 1972), p. 286 (letter to Jung 19 December 1909).

19. Sigmund Freud, *An Autobiographical Study* (New York: Norton, 1963), p. 80n2.

20. Stanislav Andreski, *Social Science as Sorcery* (New York: St. Martin's Press, 1972), p. 20. White coats increased the compliance level of Stanley Milgram's subjects. See his book *Obedience to Authority* (New York: Harper & Row, 1974).

21. Procrustes was a legendary tyrant who either lopped off limbs or stretched visitors to fit the size of his "guest bed," so to speak. He might be called the archetypal control freak.

22. Richard Webster, *Why Freud Was Wrong* (London: HarperCollins, 1995), p. 42.

23. Sigmund Freud, "Anxiety," in *Introductory Lectures on Psychoanalysis* (New York: Norton, 1966), p. 393.

24. "Scientific method involves ruthless objectivity," observes British scientist Susan Greenfield. "That means that the subjectivity of consciousness is anathema to most scientists because it can't be measured. If you can't measure it then it is hard to be very objective about it. But the trouble is that if you just ignore subjectivity, then you are ignoring most of what is important about conscious experience." Jeremy Stangroom, "Conversation with Susan Greenfield," in *What Scientists Think* (London: Routledge, 2005), p. 38.

25. Frank Sulloway claims that Freud has been protected by a vast mythmaking apparatus. Frank J. Sulloway, *Freud: Biologist of the Mind* (New York: Basic Books, 1979), p. 5.

26. Eli Zaretsky, *Secrets of the Soul: A Social and Cultural History of Psychoanalysis* (New York: Knopf, 2004), p. 25.

27. Peter Gay, *Freud for Historians* (Oxford: Oxford University Press, 1985), pp. 3–20. Before the war a majority of his patients were Eastern European and Russian. Jones, *Sigmund Freud*, vol. 2, *Years of Maturity*, p. 15.

28. Joseph Wortis, *Fragments of an Analysis with Freud* (New York: Charter Books, 1954), p. 22.

29. Juliet Mitchell, *Women's Estate* (London: Penguin, 1971), p. 167.

30. On these points see Erich Fromm, *The Greatness and Limitations of Freud's Thought* (London: Jonathan Cape, 1979).

31. See R. D. Laing, *The Divided Self* (London: Penguin, 1965), and before him, Gregory Bateson, "Toward a Theory of Schizophrenia," in *Steps toward an Ecology of Mind* (Chicago: University of Chicago, 1972). On the relation between the two uses of "double bind" theory, see John Clay, *R. D. Laing: A Divided Self: A Biography* (London: Hodder & Stoughton, 1996), pp. 87–91.

32. Hence, we find Crews hailed by a fellow "happy gadfly" for protecting us from "the kind of intellectual thuggery and hypocrisy" wielded by psychoanalytic thought police in our apparently easily intimidated culture. Todd Dufresne, *Killing Freud: Twentieth Century Culture and the Death of Psychoanalysis* (London: Continuum Books, 2003), p. 152.

33. Abdon M. Pallasch, "Sure 'tis Freud That's Crazy," *Chicago Sun-Times*, 11 March 2007, p. 3.

34. "[O]ur imagination is circumscribed by the cognitive resources and limitations of our time and setting." Nicholas Rescher, *The Limits of Science*, 2nd ed. (Pittsburgh: University of Pittsburgh Press, 1999), p. 90.

35. An Irish columnist refers to the remark as something "Freud famously said," in Frank McNally, "An Irishman's Diary," *Irish Times*, 22 June 2008, p. 15.

36. "The Hidden Freud," *Newsweek*, 30 November 1981.

37. "The Explorer," *Time*, 23 April 1956.

38. Zaretsky, *Secrets of the Soul*, p. 3.

39. Terry Johnson, *Hysteria: A Play* (London: Heinemann, 1994). First performed at the Royal Court Theater in London in 1993.

40. Stefan Zweig, *The World of Yesterday* (New York: Viking, 1943), p. 420. A contrasting account of the meeting also is offered in Mark Edmundson, *The Death of Sigmund Freud* (London: Bloomsbury, 2007), pp. 166–68.

41. On "strict Freudians" in New York and their foibles see Janet Malcolm, *Psychoanalysis: The Impossible Profession* (New York: Knopf, 1980).

42. Bruno Bettelheim, *Freud and Man's Soul* (London: Penguin, 1980).

43. Jeffrey Masson, *The Assault on Truth: Freud's Suppression of the Seduction Theory* (New York: Farrar, Straus and Giroux, 1983), p. 189. Also see Masson's *Final Analysis: The Making and Unmaking of a Psychoanalyst* (London: HarperCollins, 1991).

44. Masson, *Assault*, p. 188. "It was my conviction that what Freud had uncovered in 1896—that, in many instances, children are the victims of sexual violence and abuse within their own families—became such a liability that he literally had to banish it from his consciousness" (p. xxx).

45. In this vein, also see Larry Wolff, *Child Abuse in Freud's Vienna: Postcards from the Edge* (New York: New York University Press, 1995).

46. Masson, *Assault*, pp. 10, 134–35.

47. "For many years Fliess was Freud's only audience." Jeffrey Moussaieff Masson, ed., *The Complete Letters of Sigmund Freud to Wilhelm Fliess 1887–1904* (Cambridge, MA: Belknap Press of Harvard University Press, 1985), p. 2.

48. Masson, *Assault*, p. 191.

49. Paul Robinson, *Freud and His Critics* (Berkeley: University of California Press, 1993), pp. 111, 168.

50. Janet Malcolm, *In the Freud Archives* (London: Flamingo, 1984), p. 19. Masson accuses her of dishonest journalism due to her "selective misquotation" of him (p. xviii, introduction to Malcolm, *In the Freud Archives*).

51. Adolf Grunbaum, *The Foundations of Psychoanalysis: A Philosophical Critique* (Berkeley: University of California Press, 1984), p. 50.

52. Robert Coles, *The Mind's Fate* (New York: Little, Brown, 1997), p. 286. Eissler seems to have made a consistent impression on outsiders. Visiting Vienna in 1930 a young American analyst-to-be met Eissler and noted in him "an absence of social criticism and the utter lack of compassion. Did these attitudes represent psychoanalytic values?" Esther Menaker, *Appointment in Vienna* (New York: St. Martin's Press, 1989), p. 68. Anna Freud, for example, "was much more aware of the external realities of life" (p. 97).

53. The story is told with serrated-edge panache by Malcolm, resulting in a lawsuit settled in favor in 1993 but without award of damages—what Freud might call an ambivalent outcome.

54. Roy Porter, "The Assault on Jeffrey Masson," *Contentions* 3, no. 2 (Winter 1994): 13.

55. Malcolm, *In the Freud Archives*, pp. 118, 119.

56. Peter Swales, "Freud's Master Hysteric," in *Unauthorized Freud: Doubters Confront a Legend*, ed. Frederick C. Crews (New York: Penguin Putnam, 1998), p. 23.

57. Swales, "Freud's Master Hysteric," p. 30.

58. Marianne Krull, *Freud and His Father* (New York: Norton, 1987), pp. 57–58.

59. Sigmund Freud, *The Future of an Illusion* (New York: Doubleday, 1953), p. 7. The problem he later indicates is the masses "who are engaged in exhausting labour and who have not enjoyed the benefits of individual education" (p. 19). He suggests the problem is circumstantial.

60. Freud, *Future of an Illusion*, p. 6.

61. Freud, "'Civilized' Sexual Morality and Modern Neuroses," *SE*, 9:197.

62. Freud, "'Civilized' Sexual Morality," p. 16.

63. Freud, "'Civilized' Sexual Morality," p. 84.

64. See Kurt Jacobsen, "Escape from the Treadmill: Education, Politics, and the Mainsprings of Child Analysis," in *World of Yesterday; Vienna 1885–1914*, ed.

Stephen Eric Bronner and F. Peter Wagner (Atlantic Highlands, NJ: Humanities Press, 1997).

65. Joseph Epstein, *Snobbery: The American Version* (New York: Houghton Mifflin, 2002), p. 17. A snob is a "person with exaggerated respect for social position or wealth and a disposition to be ashamed of socially inferior connections. . . . " Cited from *Concise Oxford English Dictionary*.

66. Letter from Freud to Oskar Pfister, 9 October 1918. Reprinted in Jones, *Sigmund Freud* 2:506.

67. Wortis, *Fragments*, p. 68.

68. Nathan Hale, *Freud and the Americans* (New York: Oxford University Press, 1971), p. 56.

69. Freud, "Analysis: Terminable and Interminable," *SE*, 23:235.

70. Sigmund Freud, *An Autobiographical Study* (New York: Norton, 1963), p. 49.

71. Paul Ferris, *Dr. Freud: A Life* (London: Sinclair-Stevenson, 1997), p. xii.

72. Ernest Gellner, *The Psychoanalytic Movement* (London: Fontana, 1985), p. 153.

73. Cited in Rieff, *Freud: The Mind of a Moralist*, p. 9.

74. Werner Heisenberg, *Across the Frontiers* (New York: Harper & Row, 1974), p. 162. Herbert Butterfield finds in most instances it takes two or three generations. See his *Origins of Modern Science*, p. 96.

75. Max Planck, *Scientific Autobiography and Other Papers* (London: Williams & Norgarten, 1949), pp. 33–34.

76. Freud letter to Jung, 1 January 1907. *The Freud/Jung Letters* (London: Hogarth Press and Routledge, Kegan Paul, 1974), p. 10.

77. Freud, "The Sense of Symptoms," in *Introductory Lectures*, lecture XVIII, p. 245.

78. Steve Marcus, *Freud and the Culture of Psychoanalysis* (London: Allen & Unwin, 1984), p. 212.

79. Freud, "Beginning the Treatment," in *Sigmund Freud: Therapy and Technique* (New York: Collier Books, 1963), p. 139.

80. Rieff, *Freud: Mind of a Moralist*, p. 98.

81. Gellner, *The Psychoanalytic Movement*, p. 153.

82. Frederick C. Crews, *Skeptical Engagements* (New York: Oxford University Press, 1986), p. xi.

83. Ernst Voegelin, "The Origins of Scientism," *Social Research* 15 (December 1948): 462–94.

84. Robert Michels, "The Case History," *Journal of the American Psychoanalytic Association* 48, no. 2 (2000): 363.

85. Crews, introductory remarks to Mikkel Borch-Jacobsen, "Self-Seduced," in *Unauthorized Freud*, pp. 43–44.

86. Crews, introductory remarks, *Unauthorized Freud*, p. xv.

87. Crews, *The Memory Wars*, p. 109.

88. Crews, introductory remarks to Mikkel Borch-Jacobsen, "Self-Seduced," in *Unauthorized Freud*, p. xxv.

89. Crews, introductory remarks, *Unauthorized Freud*, p. xxvii.

90. Ian Ranson, "Common Pursuit," review of *Solitary Sex: A Cultural History of Masturbation*, by Thomas W. Lacquer, *Guardian*, 26 July 2003.

91. Hale, *Freud and the Americans*, p. 38.

92. Krull, *Freud and His Father*, pp. 18–20.

93. Elaine Showalter, *Hystories: Hysterical Epidemics and Modern Culture* (London: Picador, 1997), p. 41. "Clearly, Freud was a stubborn, bullying interrogator of hysterical women" (p. 4).

94. Freud, "Resistance and Repression," in *Introductory Lectures* (New York: Norton, 1966), p. 292.

95. Grunbaum, *The Foundations of Psychoanalysis*, p. 283. See his comments on what he calls Freud's "Tally argument" to protect against "epistemic contamination" of the clinical evidence.

96. Showalter, *Hystories*, p. 44.

97. Dinitia Smith, "Revised after Protests: Freud Show Is Back," *New York Times*, 8 July 1998. Swales and Crews even recruited a granddaughter of Freud to their cause.

98. Smith, "Revised after Protests."

99. Richard Pollak, "Sigmund Freud Redux," *Nation*, 7 December 1998, p. 14.

100. Pollak, "Sigmund Freud Redux," p. 14.

101. Pollak, "Sigmund Freud Redux," p. 14.

102. E. M. Thornton, *Freud and Cocaine: The Freudian Fallacy* (London: Blond & Briggs, 1983). Thornton, who writes from a physicalist framework, believes, and it is only a belief, that so-called mind-expanding drugs act only on the brain, not the mind.

103. Thornton, *Freud and Cocaine*, p. 4.

104. Thornton, *Freud and Cocaine*, p. 7.

105. A. C. Grayling, "Sigmund Freud: False Messiah: Scientist or Storyteller?" *Guardian* (review), 22 June 2002, p. 4.

106. Freud, "Psychoanalysis and Psychiatry," in *Introductory Lectures on Psychoanalysis*, p. 245.

107. Gloria Steinem, "Womb Envy, Testyria, and Breast Castration Anxiety," *Ms.*, March/April 1994, p. 1.

108. Elizabeth Young-Bruehl, *Freud on Women: A Reader* (New York: Vintage, 2006), p. xi.

109. Scientists "easily absorb the prejudices of those around them, and many of them are mildly reactionary, and have mild class feelings and race bias, in an unthinking sort of way." Anthony Standen, *Science Is a Sacred Cow* (London: EP Dutton, 1950), p. 26. Also see E. A. Burtt, *The Metaphysical Foundations of Modern Physical Science* (Garden City, NY: Doubleday, 1954), p. 38.

110. For feminist defenses of Freud see Juliet Mitchell, *Psychoanalysis and Feminism* (New York: Pantheon, 1974) and Nancy Chodorow, *Feminism and Psychoanalytic Theory* (New Haven, CT: Yale University, 1989).

111. Crews, *Unauthorized Freud*, p. 75; E. Fuller Torrey, *Freudian Fraud: The Malignant Effect of Freud's Theory on American Thought and Culture* (New York: HarperCollins, 1993), p. 253.

112. Steinem, "Womb Envy," p. 3.

113. Ann Keodt, "The Myth of the Vaginal Orgasm," in *The Radical Therapist*, ed. Jerome Agel (New York: Balantine, 1971), p. 129. "Foreplay is a concept created for male purposes, but works to the disadvantage of many women, since as soon as the woman is aroused the man changes to vaginal stimulation, leaving her both aroused and unsatisfied" (p. 131). There's just no pleasing some people.

114. Jean Stase, "Introduction," in *Women and Analysis: Dialogues on Psychoanalytic Views of Femininity* (Boston: G. K. Hall, 1985), p. 3.

115. Sylvia Zwettler-Otte, *Freud and the Media: The Reception of Psychoanalysis in Viennese Medical Journals* (New York: Peter Lang, 2006), p. 30.

116. See the 1920s essays collected in Karen Horney, *Feminine Psychology* (New York: Norton 1967); and Helene Deutsch, *The Psychology of Women* (New York: Grune & Stratton, 1944), vol. 1.

117. Jacoby, *Social Amnesia: A Critique of Contemporary Psychology from Adler to Laing* (Boston: Beacon Press, 1975), p. 148.

118. Steinem, "Womb Envy," p. 20.

119. Steinem, "Womb Envy," p. 20n.

120. See Deborah Blum, *Love at Goon Park: Harry Harlow and the Science of Affection* (New York: Wiley, 2003).

121. Hans Eysenck, *Decline and Fall of the Freudian Empire* (Hammondsworth, UK: Viking, 1985), p. 14. It was a "a system of thought founded upon an almost complete disregard for empirical facts" (Webster, *Why Freud Was Wrong*, p. 15).

122. Gellner, *The Psychoanalytic Movement*, p. 10.

123. Sulloway claims that he exposes "the myth-making forces at work in the biography of an intellectual who paradoxically dedicated his career to unmasking the myths by which the rest of us live" (*Freud: Biologist of the Mind*, p. 7).

124. Grunbaum, *The Foundations of Psychoanalysis*, pp. 41–42.

125. Gellner, *The Psychoanalytic Movement*, p. 42.

126. Grunbaum, *The Foundations of Psychoanalysis*, p. 54.

127. Gellner, *The Psychoanalytic Movement*, p. 43.

128. Gellner, *The Psychoanalytic Movement*, p. 48.

129. Eysenck, *Decline of the Freudian Empire*, p. 103.

130. Seymour Fisher and Roger Greenberg, *Freud Scientifically Reappraised* (New York: John Wiley, 1995), p. 11.

131. Freud, "The Question of Lay Analysis," *SE*, 20:239.

132. Frederick Crews, ed., *The Memory Wars: Freud's Legacy in Dispute* (New York: New York Review of Books, 1995).

133. See Abraham Maslow, *The Psychology of Science: A Reconnaissance*, 2nd ed. (New York: Maurice Basset, 2000).

134. Webster, *Why Freud Was Wrong*, pp. 180, 454.

135. Gellner, *The Psychoanalytic Movement*, p. 59.

136. Gellner, *The Psychoanalytic Movement*, p. 215.

137. Gellner, *The Psychoanalytic Movement*, p. 108.

138. "Science is base on the belief that the universe is reliable in its operation. And this remains pure assumption, for we can never have proof that the universe is

completely reliable" (Standen, *Science Is a Sacred Cow*, p. 176). Likewise, there is "no reason or evidence to believe in the simplicity of nature." Nicholas Rescher, *The Limits of Science*, 2nd ed. (Pittsburgh: University of Pittsburgh Press, 1999), p. 48.

139. Bruno Latour and Stephen Woolgar, *Laboratory Life: The Construction of Scientific Facts*, 2nd ed. (Princeton, NJ: Princeton University Press, 1986), p. 228.

140. See Popper, *The Logic of Scientific Discovery*.

141. Gellner, *The Psychoanalytic Movement*, p. 91.

142. Robinson, *Freud and His Critics*, p. 12.

143. Robinson, *Freud and His Critics*, p. 94.

144. Eysenck, *Decline of the Freudian Empire*, pp. 197–200.

145. James Meek, "Cage Life May Drive Lab Animals so Insane that Experiments Are Invalid," *Guardian*, 28 August 2001, p. 5. The "sheer boredom of life as a captive cage animal maybe enough to incur brain damage." Their stereotype actions "are a repetitive behavior due to damage to the basal ganglia."

146. Ruth Hubbard, *Exploding the Gene Myth* (Boston: Beacon Press, 1993), p. 101.

147. See Oliver James, *They **** You Up: Surviving Family Life* (London: Bloomsbury, 2002) for a bracing corrective to genetic causation arguments.

148. Thomas Kuhn, *The Structure of Scientific Revolutions* (Chicago: University of Chicago Press, 1962).

149. Fisher and Greenberg, *Freud Scientifically Reappraised*, p. 5.

150. Fisher and Greenberg, *Freud Scientifically Reappraised*, p. 5.

151. Torrey, *Freudian Fraud*, p. 252.

152. Peter Breggin and Ginger Breggin, *The War Against Children* (New York: St. Martin's Press, 1996), pp. 51–52.

153. Roy Porter, *The Greatest Benefit to Mankind: A Medical History of Humanity* (New York: Norton, 1997, p. 712).

154. Karl Marx's letter to Arnold Ruge, Robert Tucker, *The Marx-Engels Reader* (New York: Norton, 1972), p. 7–10.

155. Alas not all are among the best. It seems quite true that "many scientists still regard theoretical laws as convenient prediction devices rather than portrayals of nature." Nick Jardine and Marina Faosco-Spada, "Splendors and Miseries of the Science Wars," *Studies in History and Philosophy of Science* 28, no. 2 (June 1997): 225.

156. For example, "[M]ost historians of science condemn technological determinism, but my MIT colleagues are convinced that it simply is true." Rosalind Williams, "All that Is Solid Melts into Air," *Technology and Culture* 41, no. 4 (October 2000): 649.

157. The episode is related in Anthony Heilbut, *Exiled in Paradise* (Boston: Beacon Press, 1983).

Chapter Two

Birth Pangs

Theory is good but it does not prevent things from existing.

—Jean-Martin Charcot

Viennese fin-de-siècle satirist Karl Krauss is a great favorite of enemies of psychoanalysis for his immortal wisecrack that "psychoanalysis is the disease for which it purports to be the cure."[1] But what snickering critics fail to notice is that Krauss launched his most vitriolic attacks on psychiatry, and did so while it was still in its pure pre-psychoanalytic form.[2] Power misused and knowledge perverted are what really infuriated Krauss, and to confront power one had to deal with the imperious medical fraternity, not a tiny band of marginalized psychoanalysts who themselves were in conflict with that establishment.

So Krauss mocked renowned physicians Julius Wagner von Jauregg (a Nobelist later) and Richard Krafft-Ebing (author of *Psychopathia Sexualis*) for timidly endorsing the institutionalization of princess Louise von Coberg, a woman guilty foremost of loathing her eminently loathsome but royal husband.[3] Medical sages obligingly had discerned that "head scratching"—for a woman suffering psoriasis—suddenly was a sign of "degeneration," a common damning diagnosis. The operational definition of a degenerate, so far as I can discern, was anybody who was not a physician or who could not afford one. The tainted woman required institutional care, as the husband had hoped—and angled—for.

Here a powerful husband beckoned medical experts to act as instruments of the state so as to remove his obstructive spouse. "Nothing," Krauss railed, "is impossible here, in our land of tips and favors." Psychiatrists are "of two kinds, knaves and fools"—erudite flunkies for the well-connected with deep pockets. What ought to incite public outrage, Krauss said, is the shameless structure of complicity linking haughty professionals with wealthy clients. Krauss, never one to place much faith in his fellow man, lamented the widespread "profound stupidity" in Vienna as to people's "inability to see these rigged diagnoses for what they were."[4]

The Coberg case was no shining medical moment, but psychiatry was almost impossible to tarnish inasmuch as one cannot tarnish so badly smudged a thing. Another satirical spirit of the era set the madcap mold for literary ridicule of psychiatric pretensions, presaging Joseph Heller's *Catch-22* when he took aim at a smug circular logic that only raw power fully gets away with. "Oh no, there you go again!" a fictitious plaintive patient replies to a physician. "Now you say that if I have a delusion, I am insane. But you just said that I am insane. In that case my belief is not a delusion, but a correct idea. Therefore I have no delusion. Therefore I am not after all insane. It is only as delusion that I am insane; hence I have a delusion; hence I am insane; hence I am right; hence I am not insane. Isn't psychiatry a magnificent science?"[5]

As historians point out regarding the "psychiatric romanticists" of the eighteenth century, Freud had precursors of whom he knew nothing, largely because they were blotted out by the time young Freud came along. Alexander Haindorf (1782–1862) argued that emotional conflicts can be a primary cause, disturbing the whole organism, a view that was taboo a century later. Friedrich Groos (1768–1852) proposed that the damming up of physiological drives alone can result in mental illnesses, as did Karl Wilhelm Ideler (1795–1860). Other investigators encouraged the devising of a psychosomatic approach to treat the whole personality of sufferers, but they were "eclipsed by the middle of the nineteenth century by a resurgence of organic and clinically oriented psychiatry."[6]

The peculiar beliefs animating, and "desperate cures" conjured by, nineteenth century psychiatry, as documented in chapter 4, defy all parody. Here we set out the context in which Freud devised his audacious approach to the treatment of ills that he too initially saw as only physiological. What reigned during Freud's youth, as again today, was the *nosferatu* proposition that "most mental illnesses were of organic origin [and even] in those cases where no clear somatic illness could be shown, where only a functional deficit was known, one assumed some underlying organic lesion."[7]

This faith attained the stage of common sense within medicine, such that no responsible medical practitioner would dream of questioning it. When Freud arrived on the scene, the medical establishment denied even the possibility of the contribution of social and environmental factors as "causal agents" in serious disturbances such as hysteria and schizophrenia.[8] The patient, Rieff remarks, was regarded as nothing more than an "accidental host of diseases."[9] There were exceptions to, and dissidents against, this strenuously somatic style but these were a small minority, who assembled, for example, around stellar exceptions such as Adolf Meyer and his "dynamic psychiatry" approach in faraway Baltimore.[10]

BIAS AND MEDICAL SCIENCE

Freud had plenty of reasons to complain about charlatans who latched onto the rising interest in psychoanalysis, especially after 1920. All investigative fields are plagued by pests (although boundaries between what is "wild" and what is a worthwhile experiment sometimes can be blurry). Freud saw no alternative to the necessary evil of forming a "headquarters whose duty it would be to announce: All this nonsense is nothing to do with psychoanalysis."[11] As numerous classic texts in social science testify, organizations, once established, are often inherited by mediocrities who prize control over the original purposes. Yet, even more dangerously, there are credentialed practitioners who sincerely con patients, each other, and themselves as to the state of their uncertain or patchy knowledge.[12] "Wild analysis" had its robust and prolific counterpart in "wild surgery."

What Freud confronted was the medical model's "doctrine of the specific etiology"—a single cause, usually a pathogen, for any illness. "The medical model, since it is based on a conception of physical rather than social events," Scheff explains, "fractures the figure-ground relationship between behavior and context, leading almost inevitably to a bias of seeing suspect behavior as meaningless."[13] Like society, Scheff goes on to say, the psychologist may well find it easier to locate source problems in the captive person of the patients than in the less easily controlled and investigated processes that occur in the world outside.

Responding to critics, Freud recalled that

> like other neuro-pathologists I was trained to employ local diagnoses and electro-prognosis, and it still strikes me myself as strange that the case histories I write should read like short stories and that, as one might say, they lack the serious stamp of science. I must console myself with the reflection that the nature of the subject is evidently responsible for this, rather than any preference of my own. The fact is that local diagnosis and electro-prognosis lead nowhere in the study of hysteria whereas a detailed description of the mental processes, such we are accustomed to find in the world of imaginative writers enables me, with the use of a few psychological formulas, to obtain at least some kind of insight into the course of that affliction.[14]

Freud's foes ever since have enjoyed sniping at regrettable instances where an organic disease had been overlooked in favor of a psychosomatic explanation. But the opposite tragedy is no less dreadful and a more frequent occurrence. Even from the sobered vantage point of the late 1930s, a humane psychiatrist recited a terrible litany of recent or ongoing medically approved butcheries: "Appendices are cut out in instances of psychogenically determined abdominal pain. Tongues are clipped with the expectation that this will remedy stuttering or faulty articulation. Circumcisions are done as a means terminating enuresis or masturbation. Tonsils are removed for a variety of reasons, or no reason at all."[15] The list, as chapter 4 demonstrates, is a dismayingly long and shocking one. Yet these physicians meant well, didn't they?

Freud, according to implacable foes, did not. Indeed, the founder himself is accused of being something of a "wild analyst." Freud indeed violated many of his own caveats, though usually, upon examination, with good reason. Mediocrities stick to "the rules," never questioning their applicability in special cases or under changed conditions or after the input of new knowledge to which they pay no attention. Idiots and sociopaths violate rules as they please but any truly first-class mind weighs the circumstances against the guidelines when deciding whether to make discrete exceptions.

These exceptions ranged from treating a family member (his daughter, Anna) to giving "real world" advice to patients who asked for it to inviting them to his house socially.[16] A patient could sit up on the couch "depending on how he adjusted the pillows," his dog was usually present at sessions, and he smoked all the time. He "chattered" at sessions, treated quite a few people for free, and shook hands in Viennese fashion with patients before and after sessions; the "orthodox analysts acknowledged that Freud, at his best, treated every patient as an exception."[17] Max Schur, his personal physician, warmly recalls Freud's "undiminished interest in the lives of those to whom he felt close" and "his ability to place an interest in other before his own needs, an utterly genuine attitude which had nothing in it of the polite gesture."[18] Schur mentions Freud's "wonderfully expressive eyes" and unflinching devotion to truth in all matters. Freud, unfortunately (and fatally), could do no creative work without smoking. He "was able to retain in daily life not only the utmost self-control, but a serenity and dignity which had an impact on everyone." Freud also showed "wonderful flexibility which permitted him to communicate with people of all walks of life."[19] Freud is not the glowering visage that adorns the covers of so many of his enemies' books jackets.

WAYWARD BEGINNINGS

Freud was born May 6, 1856, in Freiberg in Moravia, about 150 miles northeast of Vienna. His family moved three years later to Vienna, capital of an increasingly fragile Austro-Hungarian empire, where he grew up. His father, whom Jones describes as a "Micawber-like" man of "gentle disposition," was a wool merchant and textile manufacturer; the mother was a "lively personality" who "retained to the last her gaiety, alertness and sharp witted intelligence."[20] "I have found that people who know they are preferred by their mother give evidence in their lives of a peculiar self-reliance," surmised Freud, his mother's "meiner golden Sigi," "and an unshakeable optimism which often seem like heroic attributes and bring actual success to their possessors."[21] Freud admired Napoleon for demolishing the potent remnants of feudalism in Central and Eastern Europe, and identified wholeheartedly with Oliver Cromwell's loathing of hereditary privilege.[22] Dreyfus became a political hero too.

Raised in a secular middle-class Jewish family, Freud became a lifelong atheist but, in cultural affairs, was a proud though far from militant Jew. "Rest assured that, if my name were Oberhuber," Freud wrote a colleague, referring to discreet forms of anti-Semitism rampant in high circles, "in spite of everything my innovations would have met with less resistance."[23] Jewishness may also have made its impact insofar as it distanced Freud from a Vienna medical establishment that still thought of Jews as hereditarily suspect.

Gilman describes a class-ridden and racist "world of science which Freud entered as a student, within which he formulated the basics structure of psychoanalysis, and which he later attempted to negate with his advocacy of analysis."[24] Gilman emphasizes that Jews intrinsically were implicated in popular theories of degeneracy—including a specific "racial smell"—so that Freud hardly would have embraced it, although some other Jews accepted the theories, or else excepted Jews from them.[25] Freud, though, later referred ruefully, and perhaps skeptically, to his own family's possible "neuropathic taint" via troubled cousins.[26]

"As early as my school [gymnasium] days I was always in vehement opposition to my teachers, was always an extremist and had to pay for it."[27] Freud recalled "that through the whole of this time there ran a premonition of a task ahead, till it found open expression in my school-leaving essay as a wish that I might during the curse of my life contribute something to our human knowledge."[28] No one who underwent this intense rote educational experience had very fond memories of it, except for lifelong friends they made.[29]

The multitalented Freud, concerned to curb his own speculative tendencies, initially aimed to become a research biologist. After acquiring a medical degree in 1881, he scribbled a skein of highly specialized papers at Ernst Brucke's laboratory. Yet "after forty-one years of medical activity," an elderly Freud reflected, "my self-knowledge tells me that I have never really been a doctor in the proper sense." He instead exulted that "the triumph of my life lies in my having, after a long and roundabout journey found my way back to my earliest path."[30] What he felt most acutely all his life was "an overpowering need to understand something of the riddles of the world in which we live." One such riddle was (and is) women. Making a riddle of them doubtless was an advance on his youthful attitude of condescending suspicion, typical of his class, gender, and era.[31]

Freud freely admitted "that the great poets knew and gave expression to all the problems he was struggling so painfully to uncover."[32] Freud in 1912 paid sincere tribute to writer-playwright Arthur Schnitzler as a fellow explorer "of the underestimated and much maligned erotic."[33] Still, Freud shied away from Schnitzler, as well as from Nietzsche and Schopenhauer, as being too kindred as inquisitive spirits at the same time that he credited their influence. Anyone engaged in research will appreciate the motive—to avoid having the work of likeminded folks "contaminate" one's own thoughts. However, wherever Freud's work can be shown to be anticipated in any way by contemporaries then, according to foes, he rode an easy current of fashionable research. Where, however, medical authorities opposed him, Freud the fanatic was pursuing weird lines of implausible thought. Contrary to Sulloway or Ellenberger, Freud never claimed to have discovered the unconscious, but only took well-deserved credit for placing the exploration of it on a scientific basis.

Freud was a rebel in all things, except lifestyle, which has not won him much sympathy in an era that celebrates rebelliousness in lifestyle only. His major achievement—greater than his "self-analysis"—was to break away from pure neurology to devise the radical depth-psychology that he would dub in 1896 "psycho-analysis." Freud thereby antagonized disdainful gatekeepers whose duty is to impose high costs on dissidents at minimal cost to themselves. The man who "disturbed the asleep of the world" by exposing the instinctual underlife of it, also was never confident that healing was the best asset psychoanalysis offered. He judged psychoanalysis to be most therapeutically useful for relatively well-integrated patients, although disciples (some brilliantly and successfully, others less so) extended analysis to more seriously afflicted people.

In close relations Freud evidently was not the shrewdest judge of his colleagues, as his much-storied ruptures with Breuer, Fliess, Jung, Stekel, Adler, and others attest. Freud enjoyed good jokes, collected antiquities, championed children, and relished good cigars.[34] He saw his own life and the history as psychoanalysis as "intimately interwoven," which could hardly been otherwise.[35] Freud's controversial self-analysis blazed a trail into the dicey terrains of Oedipal conflict, the unconscious, and dreams.

Under prominent physicians Pierre Janet and Jean-Martin Charcot in Paris in the mid-1880s he studied hysteria and learned how hypnosis could induce physical paralysis.[36] In Charcot's tentative formulation, "ideas, which may or may not be physico-chemical processes, can influence organic processes and play an important role in the formation of hysterical symptoms."[37] Allowing speculative space for psychological causation in mental disturbances was a radical step. It also was daring to drop the snobbish assumption, as Charcot did, that "lower orders were too primitive in their emotional and nervous apparatus to suffer from the 'diseases of civilization'"—such as hysteria.[38] Charcot grafted "greater causal latitude to the role of the emotions" but he never brought sexuality to the fore as an etiological consideration.[39] Freud recalled returning to Vienna and being derided for his audacious contention that hysteria was not necessarily organic. "[An] old surgeon, actually broke out with the exclamation: 'But my dear sir, how can you talk such nonsense?' Hysteron [*sic*] means the uterus. So how can a man be hysterical?"[40]

In 1886 Freud returned to Vienna to marry Martha Bernays and settled into specialization in nervous diseases so as to support a growing family. Freud, bruisingly, had encountered the jealous gatekeepers. Neither the medical establishment nor Freud were particularly impressed with the other. His highly controversial period of isolation and exclusion ensued. Showalter, meanwhile, says Freud blamed neurasthenia (neurosis) on masturbation and nocturnal emission.[41] That Freud, at an early stage, held opinions that resonated with conventional medical beliefs of his era is a fact conveniently glided over. Freud, as we shall see, soon relinquished these prejudicial ideas while the average medical practitioner came around much more slowly, if at all.

Treating "nervous" patients, Freud had two "weapons," hypnotism and electrotherapy. (Vienna phone books from the 1920s show he described himself as a physician who treated "nervous diseases.") The latter, promoted by a leading light in neuropathology, proved useless, which "helped to rid me of another shred of the innocent faith in authority from which I was not yet free."[42] Freud found, though, that suggestion stirred encouraging results. He turned to hypnosis and, after enjoying his "miracle worker" status for a while, he discovered its chief drawback: short-term efficacy. But, more important, Freud had gotten unforgettable glimpses into the "powerful mental processes, which nonetheless remained hidden from the consciousness of men."[43] Freud, however, bridled at hypnotic etiquette. "I can remember even then feeling as muffled hostility to this tyranny of suggestion when a patient showed himself unamenable was met with the shout: 'What are you doing? Vous vous contre-suggstonnez!' I said to myself that this was an evident injustice and an act of violence. For the man certainly had a right to counter-suggestions if Poppel were trying to subdue him with suggestions."[44] Freud suspected there were greater depths than hypnosis so far had reached—sexual ones.

Freud formed a research rapport on hysteria with Dr. Josef Breuer, some years his elder, and in 1895 they published an initially obscure work, *Studies on Hysteria*. Peter Swales, a doughty foe, pinpoints a protofeminist moment here in that Breuer and Freud laud patient Anna O. (Bertha Pappenheim, who was Breuer's patient) as a highly intelligent and gifted woman from whom they learned a great deal, proving, contrary to many medical bigots "that hysteria of the severest type can exist in conjunction with gifts of the richest and most original kind."[45]

Breuer and Freud's warm admiration for the talented Viennese teenager departed markedly from the typical patriarchal medical attitude. Breuer, however, did not quite wrench himself free from all the medical niceties of the day, stipulating at the outset that Anna O. "may be regarded as having had a moderately severe neuropathic personality, since some psychoses had occurred among her more distant relations."[46] The exquisite period zeal involved in ritually ascribing a "moderately severe" condition to a link to "distant relatives" is well worth pondering if you want a flavor of the "scientific" fears of the era. Still, the case of Anna O. put psychology—of which Freud would regard psychoanalysis to be a branch—on "a radical new footing."[47] Breuer was surprised to find that when patients such as Anna O. openly discussed their symptoms they seemed thereby to dissolve these physical woes in a catharsis, or "abreaction."

In a grudging admission lately a Crews compatriot reckons Anna O., "because of her 'belated return to health,' probably "hadn't been suffering from organic brain damage that some observers have hypothesized" after all.[48] Freud's foes thereby have managed with alacrity to align themselves with moralistic diagnoses of the age where only plainly somatic distress deserved attention. Hans Eysenck is not too shy to conjecture from afar (much further than Freud was from Little Hans or Daniel Schreber) that Anna O. suffered from tubercular meningitis.[49] We are not likely to fully appreciate that hysteria then often was regarded as a "form of malingering," and, as frustrated doctors beheld it, even an odious one.[50]

The decisive turn came in Freud's 1888 paper on hypnotism: "We possess no criterion which enable us to distinguish exactly between a mental process and a physiological one, between an act occurring in the cerebral cortex and one occurring in the subcortical substance; for 'consciousness,' whatever that may be, is not attached to every activity of the cerebral cortex, nor is it always attached in an equal degree to any particular one of its activities; it is not a thing which is bound up with any locality in the nervous system."[51] Freud rejected the common sense dogma of his compatriots. Crews, nevertheless, persists in groundless claims that Freud "failed to learn Bernheim's more important lesson that hypnosis is essentially compliance with instructions, not the genuine eliciting of a prior state on the subject's part."[52]

Freud found that hypnosis operates "like a cosmetic, whereas psychoanalysis was 'like surgery.'" Hypnosis uses "suggestion in order to forbid the symptoms; it strengthened the repressions but, apart from that, leaves all the processes that have led to the formation of the symptoms unaltered."[53] That impact alone would not lift a crippling symptom, effect a cure, or tell one anything about the formation of the problem. Freud would not settle for a fairground attraction cure. "From being in love to hypnosis is evidently only a short step," Freud noted. "The respects in which the two agree are obvious. There is the same humble subjection, the same compliance, the same absence of criticism, toward the hypnotists as towards the loved object."[54] Most incisively, he found that his clients were, to some degree, complicit in their symptoms: "I felt I had filled up a gap in medical science, which in dealing with a function of such great biological importance, had failed to take into account any injuries beyond those caused by infection or gross anatomical lesions."[55] Breuer declined to follow Freud into the disreputable precincts of the sexual etiology of neuroses.[56]

Breuer could not bring himself to deviate from the medical model stipulation that material causes ultimately underlay mental maladies.[57] According to Sulloway, "Breuer's inability to follow Freud completely on this issue is simply a measure of Freud's own growing fanaticism about it."[58] Breuer complained to August Forel in a 1907 letter about Freud being "given to absolute and exclusive formulations," but neither Breuer nor Sulloway mention horrific acts that Forel was performing at the time, and with establishment approval.[59]

Freud's foes elevate Breuer to the status of defiant hero, a black sheep returned to the safe, sane, grazing flock. Breuer shied away as Freud delved into the explosive issue of sexuality, found that "symptoms had a meaning," and deduced that suppressed impulses find substitute expressions in neuroses.[60] Freud encountered a "damming up of an affect" in clients and hypothesized that a psychical "economic factor" was at work in which the "same symptom was a product of a quantity of energy which would otherwise have been employed in some other way."[61] Here Freud employs the hydraulic metaphor that shaped the early design of psychoanalytic theory.

Yet catharsis, which he always credited as "Breuer's catharsis," helped only temporarily to relieve this "affliction of reminiscence." Abandoning hypnotism (and, earlier, electrical stimulation), partly because of daunting outbursts of "transference love" (patients fell in love with their therapist, which made life very difficult on one occasion for Breuer), Freud sought another method, which eventually evolved into the couch and free association.[62] Awareness did help and, in some cases, "abreaction" amounted to a cure. But more often "abreaction recedes" and must be replaced by "the work the patient had to do recollection, repetition, and working through." Symptoms, Freud stressed, "have a sense and are related to the patient's experience."[63] Crazy people were not incomprehensible, not if one delved into the experiential origins of their symptoms.

Here is where Freud went unforgivably off the rails so far as biomedical opponents reckon, taking seriously the heresy that "hysterics suffer mainly from reminiscences." In his blast at Freud's handling of the Anna O. case, Borch-Jacobsen, like the best medical minds of the nineteenth century, argues that hysteria "is not a real illness, as we know, and its features vary according to the medical theory that frames it."[64] He counts post-traumatic stress disorder (PTSD) and multiple personality disorder under the same dismissive category. They aren't "illnesses," by definition. Nothing that lacks a physical cause makes one measurably ill, unless perhaps someone invents a thermometer to measure anxiety or a stethoscope to detect angst. This is the serene scientific mind at work, and this stern bias was what Freud was up against.

FREUD, FLIESS, AND FANTASY

"For more than ten years after my separation from Breuer I had no followers," Freud complained. "I was completely isolated."[65] Did Freud, as foes accuse, romanticize his period of "splendid isolation" in which he developed psychoanalysis as a method? Stefan Zweig, for one, sees Freud's position in Vienna during this period as that of "an obstinate and difficult hermit."[66] But Ernest Jones is probably correct to say that when Freud "spoke later of ten years of isolation, one must understand that this referred purely to his scientific, not to his social, life."[67] In a letter to Fliess on August 1, 1890, for example, Freud lamented, "I still feel quite isolated, scientifically dulled, lazy and resigned."[68]

Ellenberger scoffs at the notion of psychoanalysis encountering strong opposition in its early going, and he likewise questions whether Freud was isolated.[69] Fellow foe Sulloway, taking a different denigratory tack, speaks of Freud's "increasingly self-imposed isolation."[70] Freud griped in his introduction to *The Interpretation of Dreams* that "it received the least attention from the so-called 'research workers of dreams' who have thus afforded a brilliant example of the aversion to learning anything new so characteristic of the scientists. . . . The few reviews which have appeared in the scientific journals are so full of misconceptions and lack of comprehension that my only possible answer to my critics would be a request that they should read the book over again—or perhaps merely that they should read it!"[71] It has long been known that *The Interpretation of Dreams* was not shunned to the degree Freud felt it was.

Going further, Zwettler-Otte combed through Viennese journal archives from 1895 to the Anschluss to find that Freud was not quite as ostracized as he imagined, at least not in medical journals.[72] There his reception was plainly mixed, ranging from the "hostile indifference" Freud cited to "fascinated interest and appreciative open-mindedness"[73]—and with a "highly ambivalent reception" for *Studies on Hysteria*. But Freud's foes' assertion that Freud enjoyed a positive initial reception is "equally untenable," Zwettler-Otte finds.[74]

The recurrent criticism of reviewers was that Freud, however interesting his work may have been, paid too little attention to "constitutional factors and overemphasized sexuality"—hardly a welcoming posture toward psychoanalysis.[75] The medical community was offended by Freud, Masson admits, and indeed "Freud was at odds with the entire climate of German medical thinking."[76] So "as long as Freud believed in seduction, he would have to reject the conventional explanations of mental illness in terms of heredity (la famille neuropathique, as the French called it)."[77] Helena Deutsch, a physician, attested that the atmosphere in Wagner-Jauregg's clinic (where she worked) was so hostile to Freud that she had no alternative but to resign her position there.

"Almost all my women patients told me they had been seduced by their father," Freud reported. "I was driven in the end to recognize that these reports were untrue."[78] At first Freud thought that every hysteria (conversions of emotional conflict into physical symptoms) was rooted in actual physical abuse. Robinson emphasizes that "Freud never gave up the belief that at least some neuroses originated in real experiences of seduction during childhood."[79] Freud, after dropping the theory, nonetheless pointed to the "gruesome frequency of sexual abuse of children by teachers and servants merely because they have the best opportunities for it." Still, the statements of the patients, which he at first readily accepted, eventually "broke down under the weight of [their] own improbability and contradiction in definitely ascertainable circumstances."[80]

Showalter concedes that Freud "took the crucial step of actually listening to hysterical women and paying serious attention to their stories," which contributed to his initial crediting of all their stories in every particular.[81] Freud soon discovered that hysteria was better understood as a defense against unconscious libidinal drives than a response to real abuse, which he never denied happened. Freud had laid out his "seduction theory" in 1893 in a letter to Fliess (successor to Breuer as key confidante) and in 1896 delivered an ill-received public lecture—Julius Wagner-Jauregg, among many physicians, deemed it a "scientific fairy tale"—on abuse-based "etiology of hysteria." The following year Freud said he no longer believed it, although it took eight more years before he openly repudiated the seduction theory in *Three Essays on Sexuality*.

Here is where Freud commits the "crime" his foes say he never admitted, which was admitting that he was wrong. Instead it was most often "phantasies that my patients made up on which I myself had perhaps forced upon them."[82] So Freud remains condemned for the most decisive instance in which he shed original formulations. Freud spoke of "more a feeling of victory than defeat" in doing so.[83] In a letter dated September 21, 1897, Freud stated, "I no longer believe in my theory of neurotica [theory of the neuroses] . . . the father, not excluding my own, had to be accused of being perverse for the framework to work . . . such widespread perversions of against children are not very probable."

In 1914 he recollected:

> Influenced by Charcot on the traumatic origin of hysteria, one was readily inclined to accept as true and aetiologically significant the statements made by patients in which they ascribe their symptoms to passive sexual experiences in the first years of childhood—to put it bluntly, seduction. When this aetiology broke down under the weight of its own improbability and contradiction in definitely ascertainable circumstances, the result at first was helpless bewilderment. One had no right to despair because one has been deceived in one's expectations; one must revise those expectations. If hysterical subjects trace back their symptoms to traumas that are fictitious, then the new fact which emerges is precisely that they create such scenes in phantasy, and this psychical reality requires to be taken into account alongside practical reality.[84]

After acknowledging the immense difficulties of distinguishing between "the facts upon which [these] tales of the prehistoric are based" and fantasies based partly on stories told by persons in the child's environment, Freud reckoned that "people's childhood memories" are consolidated only at a later period, usually at the age of puberty, and that this involves a complicated process of remodeling analogous in every way to the process by which a nation constructs legends about its early history.[85] So Freud "questioned whether we have any memories at all from our childhood, memories relating to our childhood may be all that we possess."[86] How then did accusations of false memory arise? The foes say it took Freud nine years to admit the seduction error, edging from that pat diagnosis to a fantasy-based etiology of hysteria. This criticism evokes the old joke about snooty ladies complaining about the bad restaurant food—and such small portions. Freud shouldn't have changed the seduction etiology, but it took him nine years to do so.

Calling this reassessment a cop-out, as foes do, is absurd. His new position—leading to formulation of the "Oedipus complex"—was hardly more popular among medical colleagues. As Erikson observes, the acknowledgement that children were damaged from other than direct physical harm also happened to ignore "the exploitation of the child's immature emotions by parent and grandparent for the sake of their own petty emotional relief, of suppressed vengefulness, of sensual self-indulgence and [that] sly righteousness must be recognized," too.[87] Borch-Jacobsen admits that Freud had beheld not reliable "memories" but "reproductions of the infantile sexual scene," but charges that these scenes stem not from his clients but from meddling Freud himself.[88]

Yet critiquing Freud in majestic detachment from the historical scenes in which he moved only breeds gross distortions of medicine as it actually was practiced. Inquiring into nineteenth-century medical attitudes in America, for example, Cardyn finds that physicians, not unlike European counterparts, were more avid to keep social relations stable than to speak out about the "evidence of a high degree of marital rape and abuse they encountered constantly."[89] She cites physicians saying that a physically healthy woman cannot be raped, that 99 percent of women claiming rape are liars, and that a child of six or under cannot be raped. But, obligatorily, Cardyn lays blame at Freud's door anyway. Because he didn't stick to seduction theory, "a certain scientific momentum" was lost—even though Freudianism "ultimately served to facilitate the emergence of more sophisticated psychodynamic approaches to the problem of sexual traumatization in women and girls."[90]

Freud knew that his insight into infantile sexuality and murderous wishes toward parents and siblings would upset this audience no less than his seduction theory. At the same time Freud—who was not alone in this endeavor—was casting humanity into a basic uncertainty about the nature of emotional reality. Freud burrowed down to the basic ambivalence in all human relations, even the most intimate and loving ones. The next step was setting out the dynamics of the Oedipus complex. He abandoned hypnosis for free association to elicit unforced "material." Medicine cannot encompass all the fields of knowledge that were needed to unlock the mysteries of certain mental maladies, and so Freud inexorably moved into, and tapped, the realms of psychology and philosophy.

"As a young man I knew no longing other than that for philosophical insight, and I am now in the act of achieving this by steering from medicine to psychology," Freud wrote Fliess on April 2, 1886. Fliess, Freud later wrote appreciatively, was "my first audience," even if not a fully appreciative one. It was in this fascinating correspondence that Freud formulated, and reformulated, embryonic notions of psychoanalysis, such as his view that love, along with hunger, is an instinctual or motive force, and that (almost) nothing in our mental life is purely accidental. The infamous Emma Eckstein episode was an instance of a distraught Freud scrambling, guiltily, for grounds to excuse a major error—a near-fatal hemorrhage—committed by a close colleague. This sort of thing happens more often among the medical fraternity than we are ever likely to learn about.

Freud gradually split from Fliess over different estimates of the role of psychic conflict as a factor in precipitating neurosis. Freud already stood accused of flights of fancy, unanchored in anything tangible. But Fliess himself brimmed with theories regarding "nasal reflex neurosis" and the periodicity of biological events, theories that seem daft today but were much closer than Freud to the somatic orthodoxy of the era. Fliess was an "unflinching reductionist," and one who was determined to derive the higher-order "achievement of human development, including their psychical ones, from their lower, physiological determinants."[91] Fliess hardly was someone with whom Freud was going to remain chums forever.[92] Still, Freud appreciated the friendship while it lasted, and indeed it is instructive in how carefully one must approach the clinical deployment of psychoanalytic terms that Freud speaks of "homosexuality" (male-to-male friendship, in colloquial terms) regarding Fliess, a relationship that even foes say was devoid of any sexual implication.[93]

In 1892 Freud linked neurasthenia to coitus interruptus, commenting that "a sexually neurasthenic man makes his wife not so much neurasthenic as hysterical."[94] Without reliable and easy contraception, Freud foresaw spreading neuroses and diseases.[95] Anxiety neuroses threatened both parties in coitus interruptus. Many problems that Freud treated were not foremost intrapsychic ones, but originated in and were imposed by the social system, toward which Freud, weighing the costs, took an increasingly critical attitude. Freud viewed most neuroses as preventable but incurable so long as nutty social taboos held sway.

Meanwhile Fleiss, in a notorious incident, diagnosed that Freud's young patient Emma Ekstein required nasal surgery. "Women who masturbate are generally dysmenorrhal," Fliess somehow figured. "They can only be finally cured through an operation on the nose if they truly give up this bad practice."[96] Fliess hypothesized that a peculiar swelling under the nose indicated masturbation. The knife was the answer. Eckstein, whom Freud foolishly referred to Fliess, underwent the operation and suffered a series of rounds of profuse bleeding that Fliess at first attributed to "nasal reflex neurosis" and to attention-seeking. Physicians never needed psychoanalysis to dream up similar excuses.

Upon investigation, half a meter of gauze was pulled from Eckstein's nose.[97] It is extremely difficult for anyone to read Freud's next letter to Fliess without detecting self-reproach and anger. "So this is the strong sex," was Eckstein's own rebuke to Freud, who quavered at the sight of her blood, he reported. How many physicians would have repeated such a gibe at their own expense? "So we had done her an injustice; she was not at all abnormal," Freud wrote, ruing "how my intention to do my best for this poor girl was insidiously thwarted and resulted in endangering her life." Yet endangering the lives of patients was something the most distinguished doctors routinely did and with little sign of self-criticism so long as what they did was reckoned in the realm of best practice, which could never be wrong and therefore they could never be held liable.

Freud clearly does his best, as many a colleague would, to lighten the responsibility of his hitherto trusted friend without excusing him altogether for the mishap. While most foes approach the case as if Freud maliciously teamed up with Fliess to injure the young woman, Masson at least acknowledges the "ambivalence in the letter."[98] Freud deeply admired Eckstein for her fortitude and was "very fond" of her: "I am really very shaken to think such a mishap could have arisen from an operation that was purported to be harmless."[99] Anyone imagining that dignified doctors of the era were never conscience-stricken about their own occasionally and sometimes consistently wayward practices is very much mistaken.

Fliess's nose theory emanated from the batty atmosphere of physical fundamentalism at large in medical circles. One consequence was the devaluing of emotional pain and its consequences by deciding it wasn't "real" because it was not physical. Freud's much-maligned dealings with Eckstein or Anna O. or Dora nowhere approach the myriad of lobotomies, leucotomies, electroshocks, and other invasive procedures ordered for people who physicians were dead certain were suffering from physical ailments.

In October 1900 Freud warily began treatment with teenaged Dora (Ida Bauer), which lasted about three months. Dora, who consciously and reasonably equated Freud both with her father and his amorous friend (Herr K), avenged herself on them all by terminating treatment, judges a feminist analyst.[100] Dora's despicable father, for his own purposes, asked Freud "to bring her to reason," as Erikson reminds. Dora's father was having an affair with Frau Bauer and in tacit exchange offered his own nubile daughter to her husband, Herr K. Dora was in analysis against her will. The analytical situation was thoroughly compromised from start.

Although "early feminist readings see only Freud's misogyny," other feminists note, "it is too easy and ultimately unproductive . . . to point simply to Dora's victimization by Freud's overarching interpretations, to see Dora as a feminist heroine."[101] Marcus reminds us that Freud was just coming to grips with the trickiest of analytic phenomena—transference and countertransference—at the time.[102] Dora and Freud then engaged in impressive verbal sparring matches, all points of which of which impartial foes award to her. Yet judging how Dora developed in later years, as Freud's physician records of meeting her in middle age, it is hard to dispute that Freud offered valid insights into her inner life, or that he and other analysts learned a great deal from reflections on the encounter, especially about countertransference.[103]

Freud characterized the clitoris as an "atrophied penis" and will never be forgiven for it.[104] Yet Freud also scolded readers that "women in general are said to suffer from so-called physiological weak-mindedness; i.e., a poorer intelligence than the man's. The fact itself is disputable, its interpretation doubtful" and he attributes it to the "harshness of social prohibitions that inhibit women from fully using their minds."[105] In a skeptical spirit Freud said that what "constitutes masculinity or femininity is an unknown characteristic which anatomy cannot lay hold of."[106] He always cautioned against "underestimating the influence of social customs, which similarly force women into passive situations. All this is still far from being cleared up."[107] Passivity of this kind takes a lot of activity, he added.

"Intellectual training," Freud conjectured, may make women "depreciate the feminine role for which [they are] intended." Freud did offer his fallible reasons for why "women have but little sense of justice," that their "social interests are weaker than those of men," and "their capacity for sublimation of instincts is less."[108] Yet this malicious misogynist dismissed any hint that girls are less intelligent than boys and, if anything, suggests the contrary, arguing that "little girls are more intelligent and livelier than boys of the same age." His poignant story of the caretaker's daughter and the landlord's daughter depicts how class origin and social interests combine to inhibit one girl and not the other, who is "sacrificed to the Ideal of feminine purity and abstinence."[109] The intrepid explorer of the intrapsychic regions, unlike many foes and disciples, never forgot the interplay of these realms with the external world.

By 1896 Freud gave up trying to cast his research in neurological terms and trying to be contained by them. From the moment Freud veered into psychology and addressed it as primary, most doctors saw him as a lost cause, or pursuing one. If you believe a certain way of seeing reality, and accordingly are committed to certain methods for sifting phenomena as the only reliable path, then deviants are discarding what you know deep down is the one and true science. This act raises hackles and contempt. Sulloway strangely denies, nonetheless, that Freud ever made a break with "neurological reductionism."[110]

Freud said he always regarded being a physician as a detour from his genuine vocation.

> A man like me cannot live without a hobbyhorse, without a consuming passion, without—in Schiller's words—a tyrant. I have found one. In its service I know no limits. It is psychology, which has always been my distant beckoning goal and which now, since I have come upon the problems of neuroses, has drawn so much nearer. I am tormented by two aims: to examine what shape the theory of mental functioning takes if one introduces quantitative considerations, a sort of economics of nerve forces, and, second, to peel off from psychopathology a gain for normal psychology [and] a satisfactory theory of neuropsychiatric disturbances is impossible if one cannot link it with clear assumptions about normal mental processes.[111]

THE BREAK WITH MEDICAL DOGMA

In 1895 Freud scribbled his "Project for a Scientific Psychology," which was a sincere attempt to devise a "psychology that shall be natural science, that is, represent psychical processes as quantitatively determinate states of specifiable material particles."[112] Many, if not all, of Freud's foes reckon that that moment was the last moment that he was on the right track, if ever he was. Indeed, Grunbaum's intricate and wonderfully wrongheaded critique is built entirely on the premise that the "Project" ought to have been Freud's animating objective throughout his career.[113] Yet Freud in that paper saw that "no attempt" at explanation can show "how it is that excitating processes in the (co) nerves bring consciousness along with them."[114] The sheer inadequacy of "the physiological terms then available" led him to strike out to create an autonomous psychology, Marcus writes.[115]

Freud was a reluctant "paradigm-buster" who initially hoped his explorations of a scientific psychology would find physical correlates or causes for everything knocking about in the human psyche. Yet if this extreme view were correct, we human beings do nothing, everything is being done to us—by genes, by germs, or by our milieu. How could this abject passivity be accurate if Freud also found repeatedly in his research that experience and environment, filtered through one's psyche, "caused" not only behavior but accompanying physiological reactions? The arrows of causation went both ways and they did not always fly in straight lines either.

The *Standard Edition* editor justifiably concludes that Freud abandoned the project, insofar as it assumed that physical preceded and explained "the fact of consciousness," when he had to conclude that it obviously doesn't. "Where do qualities originate?" Freud wondered. "Not in the external world. [For out there] there are only "masses in motion." Neurology's favorite word, as Oliver Sacks has noted, is "deficit," denoting an impairment or incapacity of neurological function.[116] In the nineteenth century Broca famously had begun mapping mental functions to specific areas of the brain. Freud's neglected short book on aphasia, however, found that mapping was too simple and that all mental performance possessed an intricate internal structure.[117] The simplicity of explanation for which neurologists were striving so single-mindedly obscured far more than it revealed.

Freud lectured brilliantly at the University of Vienna for almost a decade beyond the normal point when a professor extraordinarius title should have been awarded. The title was withheld partly because of his Jewishness, partly because of his controversial status, and partly because he declined to lobby for the promotion he richly deserved. Freud, though displeased about a "break with my strict scruples," knew how the system worked and finally allowed influential friends to intervene for him.[118] Virtually the day after the conferral, Jones reports, people who previously looked askance at Freud practically curtsied to "Herr Professor," his patient roster lengthened, and he could charge more.[119] That is how it was and, of course, still is.

The "Project" rapidly dwindled for lack of a credible foundation. By World War I Freud openly mocked the standard attribution of major psychiatric problems to heredity as "a very general and remote aetiology."[120] He repudiated degeneration as "a judgment of value—a condemnation instead of an explanation."[121] Freud likewise rebuffed the "impatient contempt with which the medical profession of an earlier day regarded the neuroses, seeing in them the unnecessary results of invisible lesions."[122] Here is a potent professional attitude, masquerading as a scientific stance, that he cracked up against constantly and knew all too well for what it was. Jung informed Freud in 1907 of attending a psychiatry conference in Amsterdam where a speaker's remark that he detested any "doctor of the Freudian persuasion" was greeted with "huge applause."[123]

Freud after 1909 ceased to refer to masturbation as a cause of neurosis and ceased to refer to it at all after 1912. His first reference to such causation was in "Obsessions and Phobias" in 1895. Masturbation, like any practice judged morally repugnant, was thought to be a cause of diseases from dyspepsia to acne.[124] Indeed Freud, like a sound physician absorbing the state-of-the-art truths and errors of his discipline, subscribed for a while. Freud relinquished this notion while most physicians, who go unmentioned by the foes, continued to peddle this punitive view.

Freud also was savaged for attempting a "distant" analysis in the Schreber case. Freud wrote about Schreber based on records, not clinical material. Yet the case, even if one grants the critiques, can be read in a way congenial to Freud. Schreber suffered crippling paranoiac symptoms as a result of chronic abuse by his physician father, whose own medical approach was "purely biological." The father thrust the naughty son into a wide assortment of painful mechanical apparatuses. As investigator Eric Santler realized, the medical paradigm of the era sanctified any action aligning with it. The brain was but "a network of channels and relays" in which "personhood dissolved into systems of information transfer."[125] Those physicians who embraced this paradigm, Santler says, "were provided with explicit reassurance of their own moral innocence—indeed, moral virtue—at the very moment when the interests . . . effectively lost their remaining integrity."

Crews, anxious caricaturist, contends that "To be a good classical Freudian is to hold, first, that all children entertain highly explicit sexual designs on at least one parent."[126] Yet as Freud took great pains to explain, the concept of what is sexual "goes lower and also higher than its popular sense. This extension is justified genetically; we reckon as belonging to 'sexual life' all the activities of the tender feelings . . . even when these impulses have become inhibited in regard to their original sexual aim or have exchanged this aim for another which is no longer sexual."[127] Here Freud insists on the ambiguity, and ambivalence, pervading human relationships. Rieff agrees with Fromm that "power is the father of love, and in love one follows the parental example of power, in a relation that must include a superior and a subordinate."[128]

Educational reform seemed to Freud a sensible social route for alleviating, if not eliminating, the unhappy consequences of harsh social mores regarding sexuality. "Hitherto, education has only set itself the task of controlling, or it would often be more proper to say, suppressing the instincts," Freud wrote. "The results have been by no means gratifying."[129] His daughter Anna and a circle of second-generation analysts started a vigorous movement of experiment in application of psychoanalytic principles to the treatment of childhood disturbances and to the enlightened conduct of education. Willi Hoffer recalls in his early training that Freud himself, from the beginning, always encouraged analysts to think of how to minimize or prevent "the traumatic effects of education."[130]

CONCLUSION

Freud was "a child of his times," to be sure, but he also compiled, as defenders like Roazen note, a radical critique of the moral order of his times.

Freud found it "impossible to side with conventional sexual morality" because society's morality called for a "bigger sacrifice than it is worth."[131] Sexuality as an act or panoply of biological acts is "tension-releasing"—that is all. By itself, as an isolated activity, devoid of emotional aspect, sex is little more than the two-dimensional rutting of Breughel's pug-ugly peasants on canvas.

Freud is no reductionist. Sex does not end there, or it rarely does. Affection, deriving from the infant's gratitude to protective parents, is the primary form of love and it occurs "prior to sensual feeling." Sensuality and affection, as Freud is neither first nor last to observe, must be united for love to matter in adult life. So seriously did he take this point, one suppressed in his hypocritically puritanical time, that he at first tended to trace all neuroses to disturbances in sexual life. It was not a foolish place to start.

Freud was forced by his findings to "overthrow the whole neurological framework," which could not account for the fact of consciousness.[132] No dogmatic neurologist of the era would forgive him for discovering a strange unruly mental domain outside the piano keyboard model they assumed they would find, and which they assumed would exhaust all useful knowledge about humanity. Here was an early example what Frosh calls a "social construction of individuality, including the permeation of subjectivity by interpersonal and social-structural"—only here it was a social construction of neurological knowledge among a community of practitioners caught in the same systemic error together.

Freud knew that it took a trusting relation with the therapist to enable the patient to face repressed material and work it through. And, added Freud, "besides all this, one may sometimes make a false inference, and one is never in a position to discover the whole truth."[133] So the task then is simply to discover in respect to a senseless idea or a pointless action the past situation in which the idea was justified and the action served a purpose.[134] Here was a remarkable advance in the treatment of human suffering. "We must not forget that the relationship between analyst and patient is based on a love of truth," Freud enjoined, "that is, on an acknowledgement of reality, and that it precludes any kind of sham or deception."[135] Given how much of commercial society is built on sham and deception, Freud was bound to have a hard time of it.

NOTES

1. Hans Eysenck echoes the verdict in *Decline of the Freudian Empire* (Hammondsworth, UK: Viking, 1985), p. 50. Also see Thomas Szasz, *Anti-Freud: Karl*

Krauss's Criticism of Psychoanalysis and Psychiatry (Syracuse, NY: Syracuse University Press, 1976). Szasz dismisses all Freud scholars as "Freud apologists" (p. xii).

2. Edward Timms, *Karl Krauss: Apocalyptic Satirist* (New Haven, CT: Yale University Press, 2005). Krauss "acknowledged that psychoanalysis might have 'scientific value'—adding that one would be inclined to take it more seriously if it were not compromised by 'so much fraud'—a comment not directed at Freud himself" (p. 178).

3. Krafft-Ebing in *Psychopathia Sexualis* produced what contemporary eyes regard as a mixed bag of views ranging from opposition to spanking (due to sexual excitation) to his belief that many people were "hereditarily tainted."

4. Krauss, cited in *The Age of Madness*, ed. Thomas Szasz (New York: Anchor, 1973), p. 128. Krauss, like Freud, was distrustful of Americans who "loved everything they haven't got, especially antiques and the soul."

5. Frigyes Karinth, "The Sick and the Mad," in *The Age of Madness*, ed. Szasz, p. 167.

6. Franz Alexander and Sheldon T. Selesnick, *The History of Psychiatry* (New York: Mentor Books, 1966), pp. 188–89.

7. Sander Gilman, *The Case of Sigmund Freud: Medicine and Identity at the Fin de Siecle* (Baltimore, MD: Johns Hopkins University Press, 1993), pp. 15–16.

8. Joseph Schwartz, *Cassandra's Daughter: A History of Psychoanalysis in Europe and America* (New York: Viking, 1999), p. 96.

9. Philip Rieff, *Freud: The Mind of a Moralist* (London: Victor Gollancz, 1960), p. 6.

10. Nathan Hale, *Freud and the Americans* (New York: Oxford University Press, 1971), p. 17.

11. Sigmund Freud, *The History of the Psychoanalytic Movement* (New York: Collier Books, 1963), p. 76

12. On bogus doctors in medicine see Harry Collins and Trevor Pinch, *Dr. Golem* (Chicago: University of Chicago Press, 2005), pp. 35–60.

13. Thomas Scheff, *Being Mentally Ill* (New York: Aldine Publishing Company, 1984), p. 174.

14. Freud, "On the Psychical Mechanism of Hysterical Phenomena: Preliminary Communication," *SE*, 2:160.

15. Leo Kanner, *Child Psychiatry*, 3rd ed. (Springfield, IL: Charles Thomas, 1972), p. 49.

16. Paul Roazen, *Meeting Freud's Family* (Amherst: University of Massachusetts Press, 1993), p. 28.

17. Roazen, *Meeting Freud's Family*, p. 29.

18. Max Schur, *Freud: Living and Dying* (London: Hogarth Press, 1972), pp. 408, 446.

19. Schur, *Freud: Living and Dying*, p. 413.

20. Ernest Jones, *Sigmund Freud: Life and Work*, vol. 1, *The Young Freud 1856–1900* (London: Hogarth Press, 1972), p. 3.

21. Sigmund Freud, *The Interpretation of Dreams* (Hammondsworth: Penguin, 1953), p. 398.

22. Carl Schorske, *Fin-De-Siecle Vienna: Politics and Culture* (New York: Vintage, 1981), p. 89.

23. Freud letter to Karl Abraham, cited in Roazen, *Freud and His Followers*, p. 49.

24. Sander Gilman, *Freud, Race and Gender* (Princeton: Princeton University Press, 1993), p. 6.

25. Sander Gilman, *The Case of Sigmund Freud: Medicine and Identity at the Fin-de-Siecle* (Baltimore, MD: Johns Hopkins, 1993), pp. 7, 31.

26. Jones, *Sigmund Freud*, p. 19.

27. Jones, *Sigmund Freud*, p. 215.

28. Freud, "Some Reflections on Schoolboy Psychology," *SE*, 13:241–42. Thanks to Sylvia Zwettler-Otte for drawing my attention to this essay.

29. "I am only able to live in conditions of that leave my spirit and imagination completely free: and so it is that the memory of my years in prison is actually less hateful to me than the recollection of the slavery and fear to which my sensitive boyish soul was subjected through the ostensibly honourable discipline in the small square white school-house down in the town." Thomas Mann, *Confessions of Felix Krull, Confidence Man: The Early Years* (New York: Knopf, 1955), p. 37.

30. Freud, "The Question of Lay Analysis," postscript, *SE*, 20:253.

31. In a Letter to Silberman, an early friend (27 February 1875), young Sigmund warned that "a woman, let alone a girl, has no inherent ethical standard." Freud in this instance probably was jealous, as Grosskurth infers. Phyllis Grosskurth, *The Secret Ring: Freud's Inner Circle and the Politics of Psychoanalysis* (Reading, MA: Addison-Wesley, 1991), p. 27.

32. Schur, *Freud: Living and Dying*, p. 207.

33. Schorske, *Fin-de-Siecle Vienna*, p. 11.

34. Schur, *Freud: Living and Dying*. "Freud used to point out that when a patient could recognize this humorous aspect of a situation, accept a joke or make one himself about it, this indicated a shift to the dominance of the ego" (p. 449n7).

35. Freud, "Autobiographical Study," postscript, (1935), *SE*, 20:71.

36. Freud, "Autobiographical Study," p. 22.

37. Cited in Alvin Rosenfeld and Elsa G. Shapiro, *The Somatizing Child: Diagnosis and Treatment of Conversion and Somatization Disorders* (New York: Springer-Verlag, 1987), p. 8.

38. Mark S. Micale, "Jean Martin Charcot and les nevrosees traumatiques: From Medicine to Culture in French Trauma Theory of the Late Nineteenth Century," in *Traumatic Pasts: History, Psychiatry and Trauma in the Modern Age, 1870–1930*, ed. Mark Micale and Paul Lerner (Cambridge: Cambridge University Press, 2001), p. 117.

39. Micale, "Jean Martin Charcot," pp. 123, 126.

40. Freud, "Autobiographical Study," pp. 24–25.

41. Elaine Showalter, *Hystories: Hysterical Epidemics and Modern Culture* (London: Picador, 1997), p. 120.

42. Freud, *An Autobiographical Study*, p. 26.

43. Freud, *An Autobiographical Study*, p. 28.

44. Freud, *Group Psychology and the Analysis of the Ego*, pp. 25–26.

45. Peter Swales, "Freud's Master Hysteric," in Frederick C. Crews, ed., *Unauthorized Freud: Doubters Confront a Legend* (New York: Penguin Putnam, 1998), p. 26.

46. Breuer, "The Case of Anna O," in *Studies on Hysteria* by Sigmund Freud and Josef Breuer (London: Penguin, 1974), 3:73.

47. See Jones, *Sigmund Freud*, 1:264ff.

48. Mikkel Borch-Jacobsen, "Anna O: The First Tall Tale," in *Unauthorized Freud*, ed. Crews, p. 11.

49. Eysenck, *Decline of the Freudian Empire*, p. 32.

50. Charles Bernheimer and Claire Kahane, eds., *In the Case of Dora* (London: Virago Press, 1985), p. 5.

51. Freud, "Hypnotism and Suggestion," in *Sigmund Freud: Therapy and Technique*, pp. 38–39.

52. Crews, *Unauthorized Freud*, p. 5.

53. Freud, "The Analytic Method," in *Introductory Lectures*, p. 450.

54. Freud, *Group Psychology*, p. 58.

55. Freud, *Outline of an Autobiography*, p. 42.

56. Freud, *Outline of an Autobiography*, p. 42.

57. Freud, *The History of the Psychoanalytic Movement*, p. 16.

58. Frank J. Sulloway, *Freud: Biologist of the Mind* (New York: Basic Books, 1979), p. 89.

59. Sulloway, *Freud: Biologist of the Mind*, p. 85.

60. Freud, "Autobiographical Study," p. 34.

61. Freud, "Autobiographical Study," p. 36.

62. "I was modest enough not to attribute the event to my own irresistible personal attraction." Freud, *Outline of an Autobiography*, p. 46.

63. Freud, "The Sense of Symptoms," in *Introductory Lectures*, p. 257.

64. Mikkel Borch-Jacobsen, *Remembering Anna O: A Century of Mystification* (New York: Routledge, 1996), p. 83.

65. Sigmund Freud, *Freud, An Outline of Psychoanalysis* (New York: Norton, 1963), p. 82; *History of the Psychoanalytic Movement*, p. 54.

66. Stefan Zweig, *The World of Yesterday* (New York: Viking, 1943), pp. 419–20.

67. Jones, *Sigmund Freud*, 1:365.

68. Masson, *The Complete Letters of Sigmund Freud to Wilhelm Fliess*, p. 27.

69. See Henry F. Ellenberger, *The Discovery of the Unconscious* (New York: Basic Books, 1970).

70. Sulloway, *Freud: Biologist of the Mind*, p. 478.

71. Sigmund Freud, *The Interpretation of Dreams*, 1938, p. 186, cited in Seymour Fisher and Roger Greenberg, *Freud Scientifically Reappraised* (New York: John Wiley, 1995), p. x.

72. Sylvia Zwettler-Otte, *Freud and the Media: The Reception of Psychoanalysis in Viennese Medical Journals* (New York: Peter Lang, 2006), pp. 7–10. Also see her *Freud in Der Press: Rezepzion Sigmund Freud und der Psychoanlyse in Osterreich 1895–1938*.

73. Zwettler-Otte, *Freud and the Media*, pp. 9, 21.

74. Zwettler-Otte, *Freud and the Media*, p. 22.

75. Zwettler-Otte, *Freud and the Media*, p. 28.

76. Jeffrey Masson, *The Assault on Truth: Freud's Suppression of the Seduction Theory* (New York: Farrar, Straus and Giroux, 1983), pp. 136, 137.

77. Masson, *The Assault on Truth*, p. 137.

78. Freud, *New Introductory Lectures*, p. 106.

79. Paul Robinson, *Freud and His Critics* (Berkeley: University of California Press, 1993), p. 168. "The sexual abuse of children is common enough and often results in neurosis," Freud later wrote in *An Outline of Psychoanalysis*.

80. Freud, *Three Contributions to a Theory of Sexuality* (New York: E. P. Dutton, 1962), pp. 13–14.

81. Showalter, *Hystories*, p. 38.

82. Robinson, *Freud and His Critics*, p. 173.

83. Jeffrey Moussaieff Masson, ed., *The Complete Letters of Sigmund Freud to Wilhelm Fliess, 1887–1904* (Cambridge, MA: Belknap Press of Harvard University Press, 1985), p. 265.

84. Fliess 21 September 1897, in Freud, *The History of the Psychoanalytic Movement*, p. 171.

85. Freud, "Notes on a Case of Obsessional Neurosis," *SE*, 10:206n.

86. Freud, "Screen Memories," *SE*, 3:322.

87. Erik H. Erikson, "The First Psychoanalyst," in *Insight and Responsibility* (New York: Norton, 1964), p. 33.

88. Borch-Jacobsen, "Self-Seduced," in *Unauthorized Freud*, ed. Crews, p. 51.

89. Lisa Cardyn, "The Construction of Female Sexual Trauma in Turn of the Century American Mental Medicine," in *Traumatic Pasts: History, Psychiatry and Trauma in the Modern Age, 1870–1930*, ed. Mark Micale and Paul Lerner (Cambridge: Cambridge University Press, 2001), p. 196.

90. Cardyn, "The Construction of Female Sexual Trauma," p. 198.

91. Sulloway, *Freud: Biologist of the Mind*, p. 177.

92. Sulloway, "The Rhythm Method," in *Unauthorized Freud*, ed. Crews, p. 61.

93. Masson, *Complete Letters of Sigmund Freud to Wilhelm Fliess*, pp. 3–4.

94. Masson, *Complete Letters of Sigmund Freud to Wilhelm Fliess* (8 February 1893), p. 42.

95. Masson, *Complete Letters of Sigmund Freud to Wilhelm Fliess*, p. 44.

96. Masson, *Complete Letters of Sigmund Freud to Wilhelm Fliess*, p. 57.

97. Masson, *Complete Letters of Sigmund Freud to Wilhelm Fliess* (8 March 1895), p. 117.

98. Masson, *Complete Letters of Sigmund Freud to Wilhelm Fliess*, p. 119.

99. Masson, *Complete Letters of Sigmund Freud to Wilhelm Fliess*.

100. Janet Sayers, *Freudian Tales: About Imagined Men* (London: Random House, 1997), p. 2.

101. Bernheimer and Kahane, *In the Case of Dora*, p. 25.

102. "He does not like Dora very much. He does not like her negative sexuality, her inability to surrender to her own erotic impulses. . . . He does not like her endless

reproachfulness. . . . it was largely a negative countertransference—an unanalyzed part of himself." Steven Marcus, "Freud and Dora," in *In the Case of Dora*, ed. Bernheimer and Kahane, pp. 89, 90.

103. See Felix Deutsch, "A Footnote to Freud's 'Fragment of an Analysis of a Case of Hysteria,'" in *In the Case of Dora*, ed. Bernheimer and Kahane.

104. Freud, "The Dissection of the Personality," in *New Introductory Lectures*, p. 60.

105. Freud, *Future of an Illusion*, pp. 85–86

106. Freud, "Femininity," in *New Introductory Lectures*, XXIII, p. 101.

107. Freud, "Femininity," in *New Introductory Lectures*, XXIII, p. 102.

108. Freud, "Femininity," in *New Introductory Lectures*, XXIII.

109. Freud, "The Psychology of Women," in *New Introductory Lectures*, p. 270.

110. Sulloway, *Freud: Biologist of the Mind*, p. 491.

111. Letter to Fliess, 25 May 1895, Masson, *Complete Letters*, p. 129.

112. Freud, "Project for a Scientific Psychology," *SE*, 1:295.

113. Adolf Grunbaum, *The Foundations of Psychoanalysis: A Philosophical Critique* (Berkeley: University of California Press, 1984), pp. 86–87.

114. Freud, "Project," *SE*, 1:311.

115. Steve Marcus, *Freud and the Culture of Psychoanalysis* (London: Allen & Unwin, 1984), p. 62.

116. Oliver Sacks, *The Man Who Mistook His Wife for a Hat* (London: Picador, 1985), p. 1.

117. Sacks, *The Man Who Mistook His Wife*.

118. Schorske, *Fin-de-Siecle Vienna*, p. 184.

119. Jones, *Sigmund Freud*, 1:374.

120. Freud "Psycho-Analysis and Psychiatry," in *Introductory Lectures*, p. 254. "It will be expected in the none too distant future that a scientifically based psychiatry is not possible without a sound knowledge of the deeper-lying unconscious processes of mental life."

121. Freud, "The Sense of Symptoms," p. 260.

122. Freud, "Analysis; Terminable and Interminable," in *Therapy and Technique*, p. 233.

123. Jung letter to Freud, *The Freud/Jung Letters*, p. 11.

124. Sander Gilman, *Sexuality* (New York: John Wiley, 1995), pp. 198, 206.

125. See Eric L. Santler, *My Own Private Germany: Daniel Paul Schreber's Secret History* (Princeton, NJ: Princeton University, 1996), p. 71. Also William Niederlander, *The Schreber Case: Psychoanalytic Profile of a Paranoid Personality* (Hillsdale, NJ: Analytic Press, 1984).

126. Crews, introductory comment to Frank Cioffi, "Was Freud a Liar?" in *Unauthorized Freud*, ed. Crews, p. 34

127. Freud, "Wild Psycho-Analysis," *SE*, 11:222–23.

128. Rieff, *Freud: Mind of a Moralist*, p. 153

129. Freud, "Analysis of a Phobia in a Five year Old Boy," *SE*, 10:146.

130. Willi Hoffer, "Psychoanalytic Education," in *The Psychoanalytic Study of the Child*, Vol. 1 (1945), p. 299.

131. Freud, "Transference," in *Introductory Lectures*, p. 434.

132. Strachey in Freud, *SE*, 1:293.

133. Freud, "Observations on 'Wild' Psychoanalysis," in *Therapy and Technique*, p. 94.

134. Freud, "Sense of Symptoms," in *Introductory Lectures*, p. 270.

135. Freud, "Analysis: Terminable and Interminable," in *Therapy and Technique*, p. 266.

Chapter Three

Psychoanalysis versus Cultural Lesions

But we can't bother with the biologists. We have our own science.

—Freud[1]

Free association was a curious therapeutic innovation, hardly a device ordinary physicians were likely to stumble upon or, if so, bother to examine. After rejecting hypnosis and suggestion, Freud by happenstance began to work out a relatively democratic method that "exposes the patient to the least amount of compulsion."[2] One day a patient said "in a definite grumbling tone that I was not to keep asking her where this of that comes from, but to let her tell me what she had to say," he remembers. "I fell in with this . . ."[3] Habermas rightly portrayed this serendipitous shift as a liberatory achievement, if not quite, as Grunbaum cavils, the awarding of a "cognitive monopoly" to the patient.[4] Foucault too recognized, guardedly, the essential element of dignity and respect for the whole person that was implied by this form of treatment.[5] An analysis was in every case to become a mutual adventure—not good footing in which always to pull rank.

Patient and therapist together decipher the meaning of symptoms and sift through emergent "material" for telling clues, although of course the collaboration could not be perfectly egalitarian. One party, after all, is engaged to help to heal the other, but cannot do it alone by peremptorily prescribing a pill or a diet or ice-pick surgery. It remained true, as Freud said, that ultimately "analysis is not a chivalrous affair between equals."[6] Erikson echoed this admonition when he attested that the process can be rough because of the unusual candor demanded and the raw feelings that are stirred: "We must learn to do to another what helps him fulfill his potential even as it helps us to fulfill ours . . . This is love but it is not always loving in its expression. It can call for ruthless indignation, and it may hurt."[7]

But psychoanalysis ushered the patient into nearly equal dialogue with analysts, who had to relinquish a self-image as faultless medical guides. In dream analysis alone several layers of meaning needed to be sorted and sifted. "The interpretation of dreams is the royal road to a knowledge of the unconscious activities of the mind," but just what repressed wish was a particular dream a disguised fulfillment for?[8] A therapist is flummoxed unless inquiring into idiosyncratic associations for the dreamer. Those pop psychology books with predesignated interpretations for dream scenes are not Freudian field manuals. Wending one's way intelligibly through many emotional ravines and back alleys during the turbulent course of an analysis is trickier still.

"It is the analyst's ability to face the danger of the unconscious as well as the bewilderment of the primary process which enables him to go along continuously and actively with the thought process of the analysand," Richard Sterba testifies.[9] "It gives the patient the feeling of being protected by the holding presence of the analyst." Psychoanalysis, Freud learned, "always brings to the surface the worst that is in man."[10] The therapist encounters the transference of the anguished patient—the cumulative sound and fury of misdirected anger—and works it out painfully and painstakingly in a new setting so that it transforms into something lucid and liberating.[11] Or that is the case if all goes more or less well, which isn't always the outcome.[12]

Transference, as Zaretsky notes, is primarily about one's relation to authority—although one can have transference feeling to siblings too.[13] Gabbard succinctly calls transference a way "to replicate the past in order to rectify it."[14] Transference, which permeates all relationships, is the "most powerful resistance," which does not always have the chance to be worked through.[15] If not, the therapist no longer is a "holding presence" but can instead become identified literally with emotional figures from the past—and messy problems of all kinds ensue.[16] Free association was never conceived of as a direct route to unproblematic crystalline clear truth. Direct routes already were blocked or obscured through repression and a cluster of defenses, hence the resort to free association to dodge and feint around some of these barriers some of the time. The psyche's sentries aren't always alert.

The goal for a patient in analysis is to awaken to his or her formative experiences and to the insidious hold they still exert. The therapist works with the developing transference, and against resistance, to dispel the images that the patient superimposes on the analyst (and others) via a medley of internalized fantasies and a repertoire of defenses buttressing them.[17] Eventually, these potent mirages lose power as we "realize we were immersed in a drama" whose figures, however real their effect is, were mere spirits.[18] Precious little in this treacherous terrain is clear and straightforward. Inasmuch as the idealization or demonization of the therapist is the means through which patients break the spell that significant figures exert, a psychoanalyst only half-humorously calls transference a "cure of idolatry, by idolatry."[19]

Yet Freud, Grunbaum says, believed in the "uncontaminated nature of free association,"[20] which is a position so far from the truth as to almost not be worth correcting. Freud also is accused by every foe except Grunbaum of staying oblivious to suggestion in therapy even though psychoanalysis, as it grew, was premised explicitly on heightening awareness of the analyst's influence and using this awareness as a valuable tool—transference and countertransference—to flush out or, in a secular sense, exorcise old haunts.[21]

Analysts are so accustomed to distorted renditions of their work that they often shrug their shoulders.[22] Unfortunately, shrugging plays into the hands of the foes in a literal-minded culture that takes a lack of response for admission of guilt or inability to rebut. The art of interpretation undeniably is crucial in analysis. (Positivists cherish the illusion that that they are not themselves interpreters, cutting and pasting reality to suit their own purposes.) In the zigzag course of free association the patient transfers emotional configurations from key figures—usually parents—onto the therapist. The analyst usually then begins to offer interpretations; free association otherwise might be interminable.[23] It is this intense emotional engagement with the projection screen that the therapist has become that draws patients forward. And it is through the interpretation of the transference that an analyst lures the patient out from the shadow play inside her psyche and into the light.

WHAT DOES FREUD WANT?

The foes claim that Freud merely sought to adjust troubled patients to a gruesomely imperfect society—just like the pre-Freudian psychiatric profession as a whole. Strangely, one is hard put to find any radicals among the foes (perhaps the libertarian Szasz counts), despite their loud lamentations for all those stillborn dissenters moldering in analysts' waiting rooms. While there is truth to this accusation regarding the way a domesticated brand of psychoanalysis became incorporated into American psychiatry, as noted further below, it is quite a stretch to blame Freud for it.

The therapeutic objective of Freud's psychoanalysis is straightforward, even if it is a complex thing to accomplish: "To strengthen the ego, to make it more independent of the super-ego, to widen its field of perception and enlarge its organization, so that it can appropriate fresh portions of the id. Where id was, there ego shall be," Freud exhorted. "It is a work of culture not unlike draining the Zuider Zee."[24] The unruly id and the harsh superego both have to be brought to heel by a savvy ego, yielding a human being more in charge of formerly unconscious impulses. Freud later revised his views to recognize a more active ego relating to other psychic components—a revision elaborated afterward in "ego psychology" by his daughter, Erik Erikson, Heinz Hartmann, and others. (Some schools of psychoanalysis, such as the Kleinians, would put forward other therapeutic objectives.)

From this healthy point the alert clients can do what they see fit in the social sphere, as far as circumstances allow anyway. In a plea for secular education Freud writes: "So long as a man's early years are influenced by the religious thought-inhibitions and the loyal one derived from it, as well as by the sexual one, we cannot really say what he is actually like."[25] So Freud, the maligned misanthrope, sees justification for hope. The utopian moment is a limited one but it is desirable: "Thus by withdrawing his expectations from the other world and concentrating all his liberated energies on this earthly life he will probably attain to a state of thing in which life will be tolerable for all and no one will be pressed by culture anymore."[26]

Contrary to hackneyed caricatures, Freud never viewed human beings only as hapless playthings of internal undercurrents.[27] "Turn your eyes inward, look into your own depths, learn first to know yourself!" Freud urged. "Then you will understand why you were bound to fall ill; and perhaps you will avoid falling ill in the future."[28] What Freud injected into every patient's plight, no matter how overwhelming, was an element of, and a therapeutic demand for, responsibility. Without this ingredient of volition, even in the making of what the patient thought was the best of an undeniably awful situation, there was no real way to help patients to work their way out of the patterns they adopted.

Freudian psychoanalysis was no pallid philosophy celebrating victimhood either. The daunting circumstances of one's upbringing are hardly one's fault but in order to get a grip one had to see how one decided to deflect the pain one encountered. As one begins to acknowledge split-off parts of oneself, one awakens from destructively protective habits in which one wrapped oneself. Hysteria, Freud recognized, may have been as much a reaction to the acquisition of "a false self, than to sexuality alone, since sexuality is itself a sign of liveliness."[29]

Far from spewing obscure jargon Freud, winner of the Goethe Prize for his limpid prose style, wanted ego, id, superego, and all other key terms to be translated into everyday words, rather than the fusty Latin ones they became in translation.[30] So naming the unconscious the *it* (*das es*) was to express how this force felt, like an it, apart from the "you" or "me." The term *id* was a scientific confection imposed by translators intent on medicalizing the vocabulary in the quite vain hope that it would facilitate the reception of psychoanalysis into medicine.

This translational bent entailed repercussions one cannot go into exhaustively here. But Schur, for example, is one of legions who protest that *instinctual drive* is a better translation of German *Trieb* than *instincts*, which implies an innate behavior pattern rather than a tendency or motivating force—and which has profound implications for the way one characterizes the human condition.[31] The battle cry of analysis, in any translation, remains, "Where id was, there ego shall be."[32] Self-knowledge does not always lead to total mastery or complete cure but it does improve one's ability to steer through one's problems. Attaining this self-knowledge, unfortunately, may require going over the same ground many times. "I began to think," a shrink writes half in jest, "that when psychoanalysis worked, it did so by boring the symptom to death."[33]

Freud coaxed the study of neurosis (or "nervous diseases") out of the precinct of a one-dimensional form of "science and into the world of the humanities, because a meaning is not a product of causes but a creation of the subject."[34] Freud stressed this aspect so much so that Lomas allows that at times Freud sees "meaning where he should be seeing mechanism, i.e., the inevitable consequences of psychic dissociation which are quite outside the scope of the person's will, regardless whether the latter is considered to be conscious or unconscious." If so, an "interpretation" won't matter. One doesn't need foes to point this out; plenty of "insiders" were acutely attentive.[35] This valid criticism, incidentally, is the opposite of the customary knock that Freud was too mechanistic.[36]

The tripartite schema—id, ego, and superego—is famous. The ego's relation to the id might be compared with that of "the rider to his horse."[37] So "the ego, driven by the id, confined by the superego, repulsed by reality, struggles to master its economic task of bringing about harmony among the forces and influences working in and upon it, and we can understand how it is so often we cannot suppress a cry: "Life is not easy." On the same page, Freud writes: "Its intention is indeed to strengthen the ego, to make it more independent of the superego, to widen its field of perception and enlarge its organization, so that it can appropriate fresh portions of the id." Depth psychology, Kahn nicely puts it, "is an attempt to convert the most important unconscious forces from enemies into allies."[38]

The ego is first of all a "body ego" from which we derive our everyday sense of ourselves. Freud formulated the oral stage of early infancy, the anal stage, the phallic stage (ages three to five), a latency period from five to ten, and from puberty onward the genital stage. Fixations at different stages yield different symptoms and character structures. The Oedipal complex arises because the child wants to monopolize the mother yet needs the love of both parents. This predicament gets resolved in the male through the castration complex (motivated by a mixture of fear of and love for the "rival" father). That Freud made little room for cultural modifications of character structure is a standard criticism of him from analytical loyalist Bronislaw Malinowski to Erich Fromm to Geza Roheim and is worth debating.

Repression of instinctual wishes triggers substitute gratifications in the form of neuroses as the repressed returns in unrecognized and harmful ways. Repression also breeds guilt and aggressiveness, which can be turned inward. What is repressed will not be ignored. The therapist's couch is the digging site for explorations into stricken psyches. Free association is the means by which to delve for disguised clues, and the forming of a transference is the "battle-field." Resistance is ingenious, ranging from fits of rage to, in the "Wolf Man's" case, "obliging apathy."[39]

Lou Andreas-Salome records Freud saying in a lecture that retrieving something from the unconscious is done "swiftly, like a diver snatches something from the abyss" because we "have access to the unconscious only thorough pathological material: the conscious waking mind will put up resistance . . . and drawing it up into sphere of scientific observation."[40] There are other ways of reaching unconscious material—and not all of it by any means pathological—but in this and other kinds of delvings Freud did not pretend an interpretation "is anything more than a conjecture which awaits examination, confirmation or rejection," to be worked out to see how it accords with the rest of the evidence, of which the experience of the patient forms an essential part.[41] Freud cited as a sign of accuracy an intensification of symptoms when a patient denied the truth of a "construction." Here is a sticking point in the Freud wars, for positivists like Grunbaum do not see or decline to see external means by which to count interior experience as evidence.[42] Indeed, the prescriptive upshot of Grunbaum's critical enterprise, which jettisons "the mystique of self-reflection" and other mental detritus, is a tacit endorsement of rat-lab behaviorism, for nothing else fits his criteria.

FREUD AND UNCERTAINTY

Did Freud believe that insight alone constituted a cure?[43] Freud initially detected a causal connection between insight into the roots of an attitude or behavior and the depth and permanence of a cure. But Freud by the 1930s, if not earlier, distanced himself from any necessary link between them. Revelations did not banish personal hobgoblins. As he said as early as 1910, the "pathological factor is not his ignorance in itself but the root of his ignorance in his inner resistances," which are not overcome very easily. Nonetheless, "only the further course of an analysis enables us to decide upon the correctness of usefulness of our constructions," Freud advised.[44]

Freud is castigated for the false memories that foes have of his work. "Having diagnosed a case of neurasthenic neurosis with certainty and having classified its symptoms correctly, we are in a position to translate the symptomatology into aetiology; and we may then boldly demand confirmation of our suspicions from the patient. We must not be led astray by initial denials, if we keep firmly to what we have inferred, we shall in the end conquer every resistance . . . "[45] Of course, Freud did no such thing because he appreciated the fact that cumulative contrary evidence does not constitute "resistance." In their book on the repressed memory controversy Loftus and Ketchum focus on the role of poorly trained therapists—from which they except psychoanalysts. They find that "the clinician cannot tell the difference between believed-in fantasy about the past and created memory about the past. Indeed there may be no structural difference between the two," which is why Freud gave up seduction theory.[46]

Suggestion is an abiding analytic concern. Glover tries to turn the "power of suggestion" accusation around, saying "all psychotherapies, other than psychoanalysis, were pure suggestion, merely substituting one symptom for another in 'successful cases.'"[47] Wallerstein bluntly calls psychoanalysis a "battle against suggestion," which relies for its successes "on the strong transference authority of the analyst."[48] The point of psychoanalysis is to influence the patient so as to enable healing (though even some analysts will demur). Why not? In 1912 Freud admitted that suggestion mattered: "by suggestion, however, we must understand . . . the influencing of the person by means of the transference phenomena which are possible in his case."[49]

Another therapeutic danger is that the analyst may alert the patient to events or patterns he or she has repressed when these events or patterns are really only part of the necessary components to the total treatment, "which require emotional readiness by the patient as well as good relations with the therapist to help him weather the repercussions of unpleasant revelation."[50] Freud stressed "working through" and the danger of forcing prematurely insights upon fragile patients.[51] Freud was worried too about the "Barnum effect" of patients accepting "bogus interpretations as correct interpretations of their personalities," a phenomenon which drove the false memory uproar.[52] Subjects feel real "relief when they hit upon a plausible but incorrect explanation for their feelings," Freud knew, but he warned that the patient's approval does not validate the correctness of interpretation.[53] By 1937 Freud concluded: "Quite often we do not succeed in bringing the patient to recollect what has been repressed. Instead of that, if the analysis is carried out correctly, we produce in him an assured conviction of the truth of the construction which achieves the same therapeutic result as a recaptured memory."[54]

"An analysis ends when the patient releases his transference neurosis—when he finally accepts the analyst is not, not, not going to fulfill the wishes the patient had as a child towards the parents, that it is just not going to happen," Malcolm writes. "He must find fulfillment of those wishes in his work and in his other relationships."[55] What has changed is that "more context" has been added so that the client can figure out where he is and where he stands. Inherent in Freud's approach is a compassionate view of humankind—a methodic encouragement of the sense that "there but for the grace of kindly circumstances go we." (And perhaps we go into realms of the taboo or frowned upon all the time anyway, as one might infer from the sordid history of righteous televangelists.) "Everyday experience has shown that most of these transgressions, at least the milder ones, are seldom wanting as components in the sexual life of normals who look upon them as upon other intimacies," Freud said. "In no normal person does the normal sexual aim lack some designable perverse element, and this universality suffices in itself to prove the inexpediency of an opprobrious application of then name perversion."[56] Those who pretended otherwise or blinded themselves to these quirks were doing humankind no service.

Freud had no time for prigs, squeamishness, hypocrisy, and finger-pointing.[57] At a time when revulsion was the proper response to "perversion," Freud declared that homosexuality "scarcely deserves the name."[58] Freud used the terms perversion and perverse as clinical, rather than moral, categories—which for most people are impossible to keep separate. (Clinical terms must be approached with great care—Max Schur, for example, described Freud's surgeon as an "obsessive" man in the best, sublimated sense of the word.)[59] "There are men and women who are often, though not always, irreproachably fashioned in other respects, of high intellectual and ethical development, the victims of only this one fatal deviation,"[60] Freud famously advised a concerned mother.

Freud deplored the fact that homosexuality was deemed "a congenital sign of nervous degeneration" and he repudiated degeneration as a diagnostic term, which did not endear him further to the medical profession.[61] Gay people "often have no marked deviation from the normal in any other way and are found to include distinguished and ethical individuals," Freud found, "and it originates from a variety of causes." One hardly could uncover a more humane or well-judged opinion regarding sexual proclivities. Homosexuality was listed as a disorder in the *Diagnostic and Statistical Manual*, and was only dropped in 1973 after a great deal of agitation, for a compromise diagnosis for gays who are unhappy about being gay, sexual orientation disorder.[62] Presumably, it applies to heterosexuals who are unhappy about being heterosexual too.

Was Freud a crude determinist? Erikson dismissed as "originology" the "habitual effort to find the 'cause' of a man's whole development in his childhood conflicts." By this, Erikson "meant to say that beginnings do not explain complex developments much better than do the ends, and originology can be as great a fallacy as teleology."[63] Linked to this fallacy is that of "traumatology," which focuses only on the deformative or formative shocks that shape character, and devalues the "fabulous restorative energy of youth." Although "what a man adds up to must develop in stages," there is "no stage [that] explains the man." Erikson saw these faults arising from misunderstandings of psychoanalysis. Freud emphasized the conscientious search through childhood origins for trauma, but neither the capacity for emotional growth nor the capacity for injury ended there.

To adversaries who see psychoanalysis as obsessively sexual, Freud rejoined that psychoanalysis "has never forgotten that there are instinctual forces as well which are not sexual. It was based on a sharp distinction between the sexual instinct and the ego-instincts, and, in spite of all objections, it has maintained not that the neuroses are derived from sexuality but that their origin is due to a conflict between the ego and sexuality."[64] Fromm allows that "Freud never saw the individual as an isolated being," as do many foes, but believes that Freud never saw that "the primary phenomenon is not the family but the structure of society that creates the character of the needs for its proper functioning and survival."[65] But Fromm, so often enthrallingly perceptive, is simply wrong.

Freud, as Gay observes, "recognized that ego and superego are continuously enmeshed with outside forces"—that is, family, politics, and religion.[66] A "mind-body dualism" is present, but a porous line exists between mind and body in Freud. Brown notes that in his last work Freud said therapy "depends on the patient's capacity for rising superior to the crude life of the instincts. The libido seeks objects in the outside world—so how can there be dualism?"[67] This comic-book dualism is inherent in the medical model. Contrary to Webster, it was somatic psychiatrists who cleaved to the mind-body split inasmuch as they had no proof that lesions caused the conditions they observed.[68] Hence, the mind was portrayed as "immortal, immaterial substance" that was "forced in this world to operate through the medium of a material instrument, the brain."[69] The failure to observe physical lesions could be explained by claiming that existing instruments and techniques were simply too crude to detect the very subtle changes involved.[70] Does the word resistance ring a bell here, describing what doctors were doing despite lack of evidence?

"The patient who puts up a resistance is so often unaware of that resistance," Freud wrote. "Not only the fact of that resistance is unconscious to him, but its motives as well."[71] It certainly is a potentially self-serving formulation, except it does happen. Have foes never encountered anyone in whom it is obvious that the pain of a memory prevents it from coming to awareness? Or met someone who denies truths that challenge their fragile worldview? No one can be allowed to get away with attributing resistance to anyone else unchallenged, but no one is entitled either to dismiss resistance as an operating factor in conflicts. The medical profession, with honorable exceptions, denied that psychological trauma exerted physiological harm, and did so to the detriment of its patients. Psychoanalysts, and historians, have grounds on which to call this phenomenon resistance, or worse.

In 1920 Freud testified to a government committee of inquiry that doctors "were glossing over the facts" when they claimed applications of electric shock to "malingering" soldiers during the war were mild ones, argued that psychological therapy was far superior, and created an uproar when pointing out an inherent clash for physicians between military priorities and the best interests of the patient.[72] And it is hardly surprising that in a slaughterhouse climate in which 9 million were killed and 21 million wounded that Freud reconsidered the role of aggression, and its (lack of) repression, in motivational drives. In *Beyond the Pleasure Principle*, just after the war ended, Freud depicted aggression ("death instinct") as partly independent of the libido and as a source of neurosis too, and he highlighted the tendency to repeat bad experiences; that is, repetition compulsion, which comprised misguided attempts to gain mastery over past traumas. Psychoanalysis wasn't all about sexual impulses.

The hypothesis that every malady has a physical cause, or correlate, is an entirely reasonable one that is worth exploring, but that is all it is, a hypothesis. The finest practitioners are prudently aware of this point, their own limitations, and of the mix occurring between physical and psychological causes and symptoms in many illnesses.[73] The "true believers" and the public at large are not so aware, and the critics exploited this from the beginning. The lesions that doctors speculated were scarring the cranium were, in a sense, cultural lesions. The key point is that, as Wallerstein puts it, "the stimulus that reaches the individual does not register directly but are first internally reconstituted in such a way as to give them personal, even idiosyncratic meaning" so there "is no direct of necessary connection between one's social condition and one's subjectivity."[74] The individual was no blank slate but instead actively "remixed," as it were, external events according to internal impulsions, needs, and temperamental predilections. This point was extremely plain to Freud and was just as extremely unwelcome to a generation intoxicated by the promise of achieving certainties in both inner and outer space.[75]

Appignanesi and Forester therefore portray psychoanalysis as "an account of the cultural generation of human sexual subjectivity" that rejects a glib view that "sees people as merely the passive transmitters of social and cultural goals."[76] Freud and his fractious followers "interposed psychic reality between the subject and the social order, thus making possible the pursuit of the feminist project of revealing the construction of the subject, without necessitating a mirroring relation." Feminists, for whom the foes show such tender concern, oppose a "direct, unmediated, and uncontested translation and transference of patriarchal values."[77]

PALEO-CRITIQUES

From the start, as Zwettler-Otte reminds us in her foray into Freud's formative period, critiques of psychoanalysis abounded—centered on his sexual "obsessiveness" (versus the critics' own obsessive avoidance of the subject), his daring departure from physical explanations (when they saw nothing else), and his alleged lack of scientific rigor (versus, in retrospect, their own scientific rigor mortis).[78] Innocent readers might imagine from reading the current crop of opponents that their critiques are bold and new and unanswerable. Nothing could be more mistaken. The opposition never slackened over ensuing decades, even as psychoanalysis enjoyed a gain in legitimacy. Zwettler-Otte treats the fiercest critics among Freud's contemporaries—Albert Moll, Emil Raimann, and a host of others—with admirable evenhandedness, and her highly recommended account need not be repeated here.

A typical entry in a surge of postwar jeremiads, though, is Emil Ludwig's *Doctor Freud*, which bewailed the "spreading grip of pat, psychoanalysis-born phrases."[79] In 1947, as Freud's work won grudging acceptance in the United States, Ludwig complains that "If [Richard] Wagner was a German peril, then Freud was an American one. In no other country do his teachings so greatly influence the thought of a people."[80] Low blow, there. The fact is, Ludwig asserts, "that the march of the laboratory and microscope have by far outdistanced the old Freudian gropings."[81] Ludwig concocts his dyspeptic screed during a lull in the sanctioned barbarism that reigned so long in psychiatric asylums. A parade of myths and misrepresentations get trotted out, to be replayed by the Masson-Crews generation in the fulsomeness of time.

Freud, who loved hiking, "had no feeling for scenic beauty" (a different matter than the mystic "oceanic feeling").[82] The author of a book on jokes and the unconscious, and a connoisseur of Jewish jokes who was a dab hand at wheeling them out to illustrate a point, was "a man without any humour."[83] Freud, Ludwig accuses, was a "stranger to children" despite all the abundant evidence of Freud's kindness and compassion—and his encouragement of his daughter and a whole cohort of talented analysts in their work with youngsters.[84] The next defamatory tactic, widely employed among foes, is to concede condescendingly that Freud had a point here or there but that his "guiding idea became an obsession, his method a compulsion,"[85] which is not unlike the case with just about every other instance of an investigator modeling human behavior.

"No one disputes the productive originality of Freud's early work," admits Ludwig.[86] But how dare Freud move beyond racy insights about unconscious influences into, heaven forfend, child sexuality and, most repellent, the Oedipus complex. The critic, be assured, cannot recall personal hostility toward his or her father nor a desire to monopolize Mom, so the Oedipal struggle can't be universal. "There are no genuine tender feelings," Ludwig moans. "Everything has its origins below the waist."[87] This archetypal rant forms the Apostle's Creed of anti-Freudians, impregnable beliefs no evidence or reasoned argument sways. There's nothing wrong with a scientist placing her bets on a particular model in full appreciation of its partial but hopefully useful character. A problem arises only when a model is made the only access to knowledge. Foes are right to cite those instances when psychoanalysts are guilty of slipping into doctrinaire drivel. Foes, however, are dishonest if they imply psychoanalysis cannot help but do so and that it is the only paradigm that ever succumbs.

One quickly gets the flavor of the medley of muddled themes that foes embrace. Maurice Natenberg in *Freudian Psycho-Antics* aims to "dispel the dim shadow of the psychoanalytic séance."[88] Poor Natenberg underwent over a hundred sessions, he says, with an orthodox analyst and "gave up a financially ruinous enterprise" which for some individuals even more gullible than he constitutes "intellectual and emotional slavery."[89] Wielding the word "resistance" is, as Natenberg so presciently says, "wielding a subjective blackjack."[90] "The notion that we resist realizations which endanger our self-image is a crucial aspect of the psychoanalytic structure" as Roazen notes, but that insight cuts no ice with a disappointed analysand who wants a refund.[91] Natenberg rails on and on about those fees. One sympathizes but by no means does one unhappy patient vitiate a profession, or else medicine would have been extinct sometime in the thousands BC.

Jump ahead to the early 1960s and we find Cushman in *Freud—A Man Obsessed* denouncing Freud for approving of homosexuals, who infernally get a "clean bill of health."[92] Throughout this literature whatever annoys the writer is exactly what Freud, the projection screen, is guilty of. It goes on like this as one leafs through one anti-Freudian screed after another. The precedents are all too plentiful. "By May 1920 opposition to psychoanalysis in official medical circles in Budapest had grown to the point that [Sandor] Ferenczi was expelled from the medical societies. Freud congratulated him ironically for his public distinction."[93] Ernest Jones too faced an uphill task in London, facing much hostility—though some of it was of his own making.

A "dispassionate evaluator" is one who reviles Freud.[94] Academic enemies of Freud are dismayed that "everything depends on the unconscious as source of motivation." The rub for them "is the evidence for unconscious mentation is at best ambiguous, and there is no rigorous empirical way of testing claims about it."[95] So, accordingly, we must abandon scientific interest in any phenomenon for which we have no adequate test. This is a staggering move for anyone who poses as being versed in the realities of science. Thus the foes convert self-imposed inabilities or incapacities, their own weaknesses, into a bludgeon against Freud and all "untestable" phenomena. This is a strange scientific attitude, if by science we mean a search for knowledge and not a "streetlight science," searching for keys only where a certain beam falls.

Here was the view that Freud had to shake off to make any progress charting the inner depths. Positivism exerted an extraordinarily strong attraction for those seeking not a key to hidden knowledge but a rulebook for plowing a narrow rut of reality. All reductionist strategies come at the price of some distortion. Good scientists know this and consciously factor it in but mediocrities infest every field. This stultifying view is what came under severe challenge during Freud's life, and not just in Vienna.[96] Is the cost in knowledge foregone worth the cost of the knowledge gained? Does one mind the cost one's prohibitions impose on the wider field of knowledge?

Ignored is the classic German distinction of *geisteswissenschaften* (roughly social sciences) and *naturwissenschaften* (natural sciences), for which different methods are judged appropriate to deal with different subject matters, although the boundaries even here seem arbitrary at times. A rampant "physics envy" arose just when the hard sciences were themselves beginning to look more questionable regarding empiricism and its adequacy. Someone—as well as something, like a quark—who changes under observation because of observation is a discomfiting datum. The therapist, or scientist, has some impact on what he or she beholds. Freud, for instance, was concerned with good reason that Ferenczi's personalized style leads to seductiveness, but allowed that "sometimes one has to be both mother and father to the patient" and that "you do what you can."[97] But, Roazen points out, Freud wanted to be sure that this warm approach did not mean some "personal gratification for the analyst but was in the interest of the patient."[98]

ALL THOSE SCHISMS

"I of course belong to a race which in the Middle Ages was held responsible for all epidemics and which today is blamed for the disintegration of the Austrian empire and the German defeat," Freud wrote to novelist Romain Rolland after World War I. "Such experiences have a sobering effect and are not conducive to make one believe in illusions. A great part of my life has been spent [trying to] destroy illusions of my own and those of mankind."[99] Imposing new illusions was not Freud's solution to old ones.

Yet the "subtext of psychoanalytic history," Grosskuth believes, "is the story of how Freud manipulated and influenced his followers and successors."[100] Freud, an out-of-control "guru," demanded total submission by craven followers. One's first question is, has any pioneering figure handled the transmission of their insights through an organization any better than did Freud? The circle around him was inevitably rife with ambition as well as obsequiousness, iconoclastic sprits as well as father-figure seekers, penetrating intellects as well as mere followers.

In 1912 George Groddeck, self-described "wild analyst," published a novel ridiculing analysis, but five years later he admitted to Freud that he really hadn't understood it. (Zwettler-Otte relates the story of an opponent who likewise admitted this fault to Freud, but not publicly.)[101] Groddeck, who would contribute to the understanding of the concept of the id, remained in the fold. He hadn't taken steps that entailed forming a competing group. Exactly what could Freud have done? Exiled him to Elba or to the wilderness? For those—Adler, Jung, Rank, Stekel—who broke away it was, as Freud bitterly remarked, the making of their careers.[102] Freud could not have stamped out schisms if he tried; he could only protect the core of psychoanalytic explanation within his organization. Labeling Freud's response excommunication is overdoing the ecclesiastical imagery.[103] Rival groups were free to form as they pleased. "Above everything else, while [Otto] Rank did not state it openly," Grosskurth writes, "the fact of the matter was that Rank wanted to replace the Oedipus complex with the birth trauma—and everyone realized that."[104] Given this brutally blunt challenge what else exactly was Freud supposed to do?

Never trust a fawning disciple either; there's always something else going on underneath. Wilhelm Stekel declared, "I was an apostle of Freud who was my Christ"—yet severed his ties to the movement.[105] Freud is accused of establishing the Vienna Psychoanalytic Society in 1908 because he was "disturbed by democratic unruliness" rather than by the shoddy or diametrically opposed formulations emerging in other quarters. Freud seems to have taken critiques well if they were sound and if they were expressed within, in practice, the rather wide margins of psychoanalytic debate.

During a key reformulation of psychoanalytic dynamics,[106] Lou Andreas-Salome, who kept up links with several camps, was "surprised how readily [Freud] acquiesced to a view of neurosis conflict between libido and ego instead of proceeding unilaterally from the libido. When I commented it read otherwise in his books he said, 'My latest formulation.' And that corresponds with my general impression: that the theory is by no means hidebound, but is adjusted to further findings, and, further, that this man is great simply in that he is a man of research advancing quietly and working tirelessly. Perhaps the 'dogmatism' with which he is reproached derived from the necessity to establish guidelines in the course of the tireless advance, if only for the sake of his fellow-workers."[107]

Freud thought psychoanalysis as most applicable to the "transference neuroses," having found that "paranoiacs, melancholics and sufferers from dementia praecox remain on the whole unaffected and proof against psychoanalytic therapy."[108] Freud estimated that a positive transference was very unlikely in cases of schizophrenia and paranoia. But eventually practitioners—from Harry Stack Sullivan and Freida Fromm-Reichmann through R. D. Laing and many others—with an interest and, better yet, an aptitude for work with severe cases did explore them and usually to some benefit, if not always to the point of cure. Carl Jung was drawn to Freud because he saw the power of his apparatus of insight, of what it revealed of the vast mythic underworld of human personality. Freud also gave his guarded blessing to child analysis because his daughter Anna became involved in these unusual therapeutic explorations.[109]

Anna Freud cited the radically distinct conditions under which analysis for children operated: "The situation lacks everything which seems indispensable in an adult: insight into illness, voluntary decision, and the wish to be cured."[110] Utopian-minded educators at the time "raised the hope that it was possible to raise conflict-free people, if only disturbing influence—in particular those of family and environment—were eliminated, or rectified early enough through child psychoanalysis." She explained that these were unrealizable.[111] Why? Because human beings, most especially children, still have anxiety-creating inner drives to reckon with.

In 1911 Alfred Adler departed with nine of thirty-five members of the Psychoanalytic Society, due to his diminution of the sexual drive to stress instead of the "will to power." The Adlerians resigned "to protest Freud's autocratic control," charges a foe, and not because they had a separate therapeutic brand to bring to market. Turning away from the unconscious and sexuality, the Adlerians "in the name of individual psychology, take the side of society against the individual. What must be faulted is not society's hostile frustration" of the neurotic, but the neurotic's "failure to adapt to society."[112] Personal animus played its part in deepening the rift between Freud and Adler, whose ideas he regarded as "parasitic" at best. A sense of betrayal, justified or not, is an event that no one, not even Freud, can fully arm themselves against, or stand above. Adler's short-term therapy, attention to the present-day ego's problems, and his issue of "mastery" are long since integrated into modern psychoanalytic practice.

Adler also was a socialist who was attentive to the influence of environment. Yet Freud too wrote: "the recognition of our therapeutic limitations reinforces our determination to change other social factors so that men and women shall no longer be forced into hopeless situations."[113] Freud knew that psychoanalysis is "not suited to the study of actual events," but rather to the "inner world" transformation of events into experience. These two factors were less of a bind for clinicians than a matter of finding their own balances. Psychoanalysts could do what they liked in their civic lives, given their clinical knowledge and an appreciation of its limitations, but as a professional body they were no political vanguard.

Later, the synonymous use of power and sexuality was accepted within Freudian analysis inasmuch as this parallelism clearly was inherent in Freud's notions anyway. Jung can be faulted for the same implications in his work. Still, until the final break, and despite Jung's shying away from the centrality of sexuality too, Freud picked him as president of the International Psychoanalytic Association, albeit for mixed if explicit motives: Jung was brilliant, an eminent psychiatrist, and a rebuff to all those who derided psychoanalysis as a "Jewish science." The implications of Jung's more mystically oriented explorations were conservative too—privileging inner world over external events—although they needn't have been.

The psychoanalytic movement seethed with creative internecine conflict and also with the narcissism of small (and, yes, sometimes great) differences. Freud advised Ferenczi that, ideally, scientific "differences are tolerated within the organization unless personal behavior such as Stekel's or Adler's makes these impossible."[114] As Jung finally ditched libido theory for a more airy élan vital, Freud was forced to respond in 1913 in what was by definition a doctrinaire way. Jung was out. In the 1930s Freud wrote of Jung's search "exclusively in present-day motives and in expectations of the future" for neurotic motives that this version "may be a school of wisdom; but it is no longer analysis."[115] After breaking away Jung claimed, belittlingly, that Freud declined to share private details when they compared dreams on a journey together because Freud said he dare not "risk" his authority.

"Since this was written many years after the event described one should accept this story with considerable caution, because if Freud indeed lost his authority for Jung entirely at that time," a reviewer notes, "then Jung's many expressions of deep respect in his letters to Freud during the following years would have been a fraud."[116] After the split Sabine Speilrein, whom Jung treated shabbily during an affair, "tried to convince both Jung and Freud that they had much more in common in theory than they had supposed." Freud was working out the behavior codes as he goes along. Recall that in a tight community dealing with a limited pool of affluent patients that a lot of confidences were spilled and spread.

METAPSYCHOLOGICAL ERRANDS

The metapsychological works (*Totem and Taboo*, *Civilization and Its Discontents*, *Moses and Monotheism*, and so on) were Freud's "own business," with no need for practitioners to sign on to them in all their speculative particulars. Here is where he gave, as Jones put it, "his speculative daemon freer rein than ever before."[117] Is there really a death instinct? Was Moses was an Egyptian or not? Did Freud literally believe in the *Totem and Taboo* scenario of parricidal sons and their tyrant father as laying the basis for the pact of civilization? "Civilization has been attained through the renunciation of instinctual satisfaction, and it demands the same renunciation from each newcomer in turn," Freud certainly asserted, and throughout "an individual's life there is a constant replacement of external by internal compulsion."[118] To say his "just-so" story of the origins of the Oedipal complex is true is to mistake the metaphorical illustration for an empirical claim.

These volumes are audacious expeditions—provocations—from which one still can learn much even or especially when disagreeing. For example, Freud wrote in *Moses and Monotheism* that nothing that has been "repressed enters consciousness smoothly and unaltered; it must always put up with distortions which testify to the influence of the resistance (not entirely overcome) arising from the anticathexis, or to the modifying influence of the recent experience or to both."[119] So, again, contrary to the foes' depiction of Freud, there are no pure memories.

Freud stubbornly held to what are regarded as wayward opinions. Who does not? His own physician chides Freud for the fallaciousness of "archaic heritage assumptions, his Lamarckian belief in transmission of belief," and his "comparison of archaic heritage with animal instincts [does] not stand up."[120] On the other hand the "hopeless pagan" who wanted to live without illusions shrewdly understood that "if you want to expel religion from European civilization, you can only do it by means of another system of doctrines; and such a system would from the outset take over all the psychological characteristics of religion—the same sanctity, rigidity and intolerance, the same prohibition of thought."[121] For all that, Freud believed in the primacy of the emotionally informed intellect, which aimed to overcome a narrow understanding of science too. None of these metapsychological adventures vitiates Freud's standing as a scientific explorer of the inescapable inner world that some critics imagine they do not inhabit.

One far from metapsychological point is worth making. The high cost of classical analysis makes it prohibitively expensive for many, such that it has functioned almost as a status symbol and a class-restricted therapy.[122] But in the Red Vienna period after World War I and up to Hitler's takeover, "the Vienna Ministry of education and School administration were not so hostile to psychoanalysis as the city's medical and psychiatric circles were."[123] So Freud heartily encouraged the use of free clinics and the offer of reduced rates to enable access for ordinary income earners to psychoanalysis.[124] By the 1930s it was typical for analysts to treat one-fifth of their patients for free.[125] The higher fees they charged foreigners were redistributed locally.[126] Class exclusivity was no part of Freud's intention.

FREUD AND AMERICANIZATION

"I do not know if you have detected the secret link between [the essay on] Lay Analysis and the [Future of an] Illusion," Freud wrote a trusted associate. "In the former I wish to protect analysis from the doctors and in the latter from the priests. I should like to hand it over to a profession which does not yet exist, a profession of lay curers of souls who need not be doctors and should not be priests."[127] "Freud's subversiveness is derived from his concepts and not from his stated political opinions," Jacoby points out. "This disjunction is absolutely crucial to recognize."[128]

Freud fretted that the medical profession whose hegemony he so doggedly challenged would kill all that was professionally seditious about his own work. That is one reason why he championed the role of "lay analysts" in the profession, for nonmedical analysts were less likely to be as narrow in their intellectual and emotional growth as were doctors, and far more "experimental" and eclectic in their insights, and brought more material to work with into the fray on the couch. Freud's so-called secret ring of six practitioners (Karl Abraham, Max Eitengon, and Ernest Jones, and Ferenczi, too, were physicians) included Hans Sachs, a lawyer, and Otto Rank, who had a doctorate in literature—a considerable representation.[129]

From his 1909 Clark University visit onward, Freud brought a promising curative method to a profession whose most perceptive members understood they were experiencing dead ends in the treatment of mental disorders. Freud, though, distrusted the enthusiasm he suddenly encountered.[130] Training was the key issue. The medical society's demand for "more stringent qualifications" translated into a homogenization of the kinds of people who undertook the training and the training itself, which was a worrisome development. In effect, the cobras insisted on monopolizing the training of mongooses, or vice versa.

Americans were deeply hostile to nonmedical analysts and an "analytic civil war ensued in the 1930s" ending with the compromise inclusion of already credentialed European analysts.[131] California grudgingly permitted entry of lay analysts of the supremely high caliber of Siegfried Bernfeld, Ernst Simmel, and Otto Fenichel. Physicians or not, these European émigrés, many socialists and social democrats, kept their political heads down as vulnerable guests in their new country. "It is important to realize that the Freudians of the first and second generations were primarily cosmopolitan intellectuals," Jacoby reminds us, "not narrow medical specialists."[132] In the medical American ingestion of psychoanalysis, the "Freudian notion of an essential antagonism between the individual and a repressive society, between pleasure and reality, is dismissed; rather, society is the best friend of the individual who is innately inferior and uncertain."[133] In 1950 Los Angeles split into two institutes over the lay analysis question. Less than 10 percent of analysts in the American Psychiatric Association in 1938 were nonmedical, and the numbers thereafter dropped.

These suspect analysts and the somatic psychiatrists, after all, were going to compete for scarce resources, although the latter always got the lion's share.[134] The complaints made about medical funding of psychoanalytic projects were not because psychoanalysts hogged all the resources—about 7 percent of NIMH money between 1943 and 1973—but because any penny for analysis was thought by somatic psychiatrists an unconscionable waste. In Britain too there also was strong opposition to lay analysts, led oddly enough by Freud loyalist Ernest Jones. What numbers are we dealing with? Overall, there were "1,400 practicing analysts in the world in 1957, perhaps 14,000 people in analysis and no more than 100,000 who completed treatment." In the 1930s there were fewer than five hundred practicing psychiatrists in United States, which grew to sixteen thousand by the mid-1960s with eleven hundred certified psychoanalysts.[135]

Surveying the self-satisfied upper-middle-class psychiatric scene in the 1970s, Paul Roazen, among others, was amazed at the utterly incongruous use of Freud's work to justify the status quo. "No one seems very eager to identify with the Freud who ignored everything that had been said or written before, who dared to try to understand what had previously been considered utterly meaningless," Roazen remarked. "Freud wrote and thought shocking things."[136] Rieff earlier lamented that, as opposed to the widely read and deeply cultivated mavericks who filled the psychoanalytic ranks in the first two generations, that given the kind of people who seek medical degrees, "intelligent 'normals' are now flooding the field and they are, characteristically, without analytic talent."[137]

In 1980 the advent of the biopsychiatrically authored *Diagnostic and Statistical Manual of Mental Disorders, Third Edition* (DSM-III) signaled the de facto expulsion from psychiatry of psychoanalytic influence, although analysts belatedly were allowed token input, then disregarded. By that juncture, anyway, "three fifths of psychoanalysts already used medication with some patients."[138] The depressing downshift that psychoanalysis underwent in the Babbitry-ridden American milieu is concisely captured in Jacoby's observation that Freud's advice for a fulfilling life, "to love and to work" (and to enjoy it), was translated by Karl Menninger in his Topeka outpost as the need to attend briskly to "the business of making love and the business of making a living."[139]

A FREUDIAN SAMPLER

Spiteful intrapsychoanalytic conflicts are legendary, forming incendiary markers along the trail. Few analysts, one infers, fully approved of one another.[140] After Adler and Jung, the next major breakaway is the neo-Freudian or "cultural interpersonal" school of Karen Horney and Harry Stack Sullivan, which arose to affirm the cultural relativity of Freud's concepts.[141] Freud allegedly "mistook cultural phenomena for biological-instinctual phenomenon."[142]

Sexuality may not be so strongly repressed in different societies or in the same society over epochs. "All the observations will hold true for a certain society," Freud clearly saw, "if the society changes, then the phenomena will be different."[143] Perhaps too the fundamental problem Freud identified was repression not of sexuality but of truth.[144] Freud himself noted this connection in "Civilised Sexual Morality," where he remarked that those souls too timid to question sexual mores are "scared away from any form of thinking."[145] Likewise, if there is a basic "conflict between conscious and unconscious strivings" within us, as Freud argued, latter-day analysts ventured to identify different kinds of conflicts that they argued were more prevalent in their time and place. Still, one should not make the mistake of assuming that critics are correct just because they came along a little later.[146]

The countercritique of the neo-Freudians is they encourage "the myth of the autonomous ego . . . autonomous from bodily drives, and conflicts among them, and between them and society."[147] "If Freud may be accused of biologizing the ambivalences by which all societies are constituted, the post-Freudians may sociologize them too much," Rieff finds.[148] "We are not unhappy because we are frustrated, Freud implies; we are frustrated because we are, first of all, unhappy combinations of conflicting desires." One must add to Rieff that, for Freud, we also are unhappy because social arrangements do not grant the means or the leeway for essential gratifications.

Here is a long and bitter debate that need not be reiterated in all details here. For our part, we side with Jacoby's verdict that the revisions of Adler, Horney, Fromm, and Sullivan "sustained by the myth of Freud as authoritarian in theory and person, have been marked by a monotonous discovery of common sense."[149] The point, for Jacoby, is "not orthodoxy versus revision but the content of the change" and "what's new is not necessarily better or even different." Nonetheless, all the foregoing revisionists are worth reading for their enlightening contributions to therapy, if not perhaps to theory. The revisionists often enough displayed wider educations in humanities and the social sciences than did orthodox analysts of later generations, which was a useful spur.[150]

The Kleinians, on the other hand, insist on the primacy of "instincts" and focus on an interior world of phantasy, splitting, and projections. The Kleinians are most influential in Britain, forming a sharp point of the triangular analytic competition between themselves, the (Anna) Freudians, and a so-called Middle Group. Games, petty games, inevitably get played. R. D. Laing, for instance, was refused training analysis supervision by Melanie Klein, who believed his first (Middle Group) analyst could not have analyzed him properly.[151] Haughtiness seems a quality that analysis is as likely to stoke as to tamp down. (There is, as therapists have grumbled privately, no *DSM* category, and no sure cure, for being an a—hole.) Klein, a critic writes, assumed "that the problems stem from infancy where an 'excess of aggression' either innate or in response to frustration is experienced . . . and is blind to the life circumstances of the patient." But, Lomas continues, "there is no reason both the intrusion of the environment and the projection of undesired emotional states should not combine in the production of symptoms."[152] For Klein, by the way, penis envy was "displaced envy of the breast."[153] The ego-psychologists of Hartmann and Erikson, the cultural relativists, Kohutian "self" psychologists, and many others appeared or erupted on the primal scene.

The pattern of mental disturbances too may change with circumstances, pressures, and social attitudes over time. The "civilized sexual morality" that Freud sardonically decried a century ago is almost absent in urban industrialized society. The problem facing therapists in the postwar era has been less hysteria than schizoid features: "the problem of persons who are detached, unrelated, lacking in affect, tending toward depersonalization, and covering up their problems by means of intellectualizations and technical formulations."[154] Still, a first- or second- generation analyst would recognize immediately the panoply of basic "problems of living" that the vast majority of neurotic or otherwise troubled patients bring to therapists today. Still, the super-rich, whom F. Scott Fitzgerald thought were very different from you and me, are different than they used to be, according to recent reports from their therapists who find these clients often are too narcissistic, powerful, and aggressive to reach at all in our era of upward concentration of wealth.[155]

In the postwar era the object relations school, echoing neo-Freudian concerns, emphasized "the relational context of development, not biological drives that determine all behavior" so that the quality of relationships available to the person lay down the basic psychic structure which provide a "template for later relationships."[156] John Bowlby fair-mindedly regarded object relations as an advance but one which still is "a scientific rendering of human intimacy."[157] To this day there is no agreement between the rival schools about what is a symptom and what is its source. Taking sides in these fascinating debates before examining them meticulously is terribly foolish since a great deal can be learned from the best practitioners in every school. One simply cannot comprehend psychoanalysis without becoming thoroughly versed in these internecine conflicts. Without question too, though, psychoanalysts in feuding schools in the past have been guilty of treating their own particular approaches as if they were catechisms.[158] These debates, though, properly are grist for those who haven't damned all of psychoanalysis.

In an era besotted with high-tech drugs the rhetorical strategies wielded by Freud's critics have proved extremely effective: (1) hitch a ride on the zeitgeist—fashionable middle-class creeds of the moment; (2) generate an outpouring of contradictory charges against the target; (3) ally with the dominant group but carefully portray it as the underdog; (4) spin out a highly selective and truncated history; (5) plant insinuations that your opponents are inveterate yarn spinners who simply cannot be trusted; (6) use a single fact to support a generalization, that is, treat the exception as the rule; (7) present one special and, by itself, retarded form of reasoning as pure common sense; (8) manipulate testimony and documents to provide foils or support, as needed, for your argument; (9) elevate your targets to an impossibly idealized stature they never enjoyed in their lifetime in order to make their ascribed faults look all the worse; (10) and dismiss any vindicating or mitigating evidence. All these slippery tactics have been deployed against Freud and his followers.

Pioneering is risky and thankless work, except posthumously. A pioneer is the last vocation to take up if one wants a quiet and secure life. Freud was engaged in overturning, not embroidering, the dominant paradigm, and therefore roused opposition that was as subtle as it was fierce. What Kuhn calls "normal science"—in the absence of internal critics attentive to anomalies—can be an extraordinarily ruthless thing, as any dogma is. In the light of the standard knowledge of the era a reckless lobotomist like Dr. Walter Freeman afterward can still be given the benefit of every imaginable doubt while Freud is allowed none.[159] Freeman's psychosurgical jihad in New Jersey is even deemed excusable "because there is persuasive evidence that at times he acted in the best interest of his lobotomized patients, given the limitations of the medical environment he worked in."[160]

So too was the extenuating case with the famous Dr. August Forel despite a seamy, even ghastly, side to his celebrated work in Switzerland.[161] The lesson is so long as you steadfastly display no curiosity about phenomena outside your narrow patch you are safe from criticism. The clinching reason why orthodox medical men are given a pass is because at any given time and place the vast majority of practitioners, by definition, adhere to whatever the standard is and so they identify with those who also operate within the code, no matter how senseless or hazardous it turns out to be. That is why favored models survive far longer than the evidence should allow.

The cancer came back in 1936. Freud had endured some two dozen jaw surgeries over the years and now was in constant pain. The grim period images that the foes like to use for book covers derive from this time, of a man wearing a lower jaw prosthesis he could not keep comfortably fitted. Freud managed to exit Vienna two months after the Anschluss, the German Nazi takeover in March 1938. He died from his spreading jaw cancer in London, September 23, 1939. His personal physician Max Schur spoke of treating him through many difficult and painful procedures, which Freud bore "with his usual grace and patience."[162]

CONCLUSION

Freud's medical counterparts, implicitly lionized by Crews and company, viewed Freud's hysteria patients quite literally as degenerates, or potential degenerates. The impression that Freud's foes propagate is that the medical fraternity was comprised of nothing but warmhearted humanitarian heroes. Yet it was these wary medical colleagues, not Freud, who excelled at reinforcing "feelings of worthlessness and oppression by dependence and authority and sub-hypnosis suggestion." Instead, for Freud, through his trial-and-error development of free association, the "transference angle became a road to wisdom: the truth could cure the patient only insofar as the doctor had faced the corresponding truth in himself."[163] Freud refused to treat his patients in the peremptory manner that the medical mores of the day encouraged. This is commonplace. Descartes thought animals had no feelings. Southern U.S. planters thought slaves had no feelings. Many doctors thought crazy people had no feelings and some of them still think certain crazy people do not have feelings. And so it goes, according to the convenience of the more powerful figure in any relationship.

"I have always felt it as a gross injustice that people refused to treat psychoanalysis like any other science," Freud complained.[164] Why should he be reproached for incomplete or insufficient "hard data" when "a science based on observation has no alternative but to work out its findings piecemeal and to solve its problems step by step? Clear fundamental concepts and sharply drawn definitions are only possible in the mental sciences insofar as the latter seek to fit a department of facts into the frame of a logical system. In the neutral sense, of which psychology is one, such clear-cut general concepts are superfluous and indeed impossible."[165]

Freud was an irrepressible rebel, a true enlightenment intellect and consequently a moral force too. Unlike foes, Freud confronted his own prejudices, questioned his own training, and moved boldly into this very daunting and ill-understood realm of gnawing fears and desires. A pathetic schoolboy philosophy understanding of what constitutes genuine science and its bare-bones positivist applications are the basis for the most ferocious critiques leveled at his work. The foes, though, have built their own foundations on a metaphorical landfill packed with intensely toxic and tragic waste.

NOTES

1. Joseph Wortis, *Fragments of an Analysis with Freud* (New York: Charter Books, 1954), p. 80.
2. Freud, *An Autobiographical Study*, p. 70.
3. Quoted in Paul Roazen, *Freud and His Followers* (London: Allen Lane, 1976), p. 99.
4. See Jürgen Habermas, *Knowledge and Human Interests* (Boston: Beacon Press, 1971), p. 261, and Adolf Grunbaum, *The Foundations of Psychoanalysis: A Philosophical Critique* (Berkeley: University of California Press, 1984), pp. 22–23.
5. Foucault writes of Freud freeing "the patient from the existence of the asylum" via his reformulated physician-patient relationship, which remained, in Foucault's view, imperfect if much improved. Michel Foucault, *Madness and Civilization* (New York: Vintage, 1973), p. 277.
6. Wortis, *Fragments of an Analysis with Freud*, p. 53.
7. Richard I. Evans, *Dialogue with Erik Erikson* (New York: E. P. Dutton, 1970), p. 48.
8. Freud, "The Interpretation of Dreams," *SE*, 5:608.

9. Richard Sterba, *Memoirs of a Viennese Psychoanalyst.* (Detroit: Wayne State University Press, 1982), p. 123.

10. Sigmund Freud, *The History of the Psychoanalytic Movement* (New York: Collier Books, 1963), p. 71.

11. Robert Caper, "Psychic Reality and the Interpretation of Transference," *Psychoanalytic. Quarterly* 66:18–31, p. 21.

12. "Transference is a universal tendency active whenever human beings enter into a relationship with others in such a way that the other also 'stands for' persons as perceived in the pre-adult past: he thus serves the re-enactment of infantile and juvenile wishes and fears, hopes and apprehensions, and this always with a bewildering mixture of affects—that is, the ratio of loving and hateful tendencies which under certain conditions alter radically. This phenomenon plays a singular role in the clinical encounter, and not only in the dependent patient's behavior toward the clinician but also as part of what the clinician must observe in himself; for he too can transfer onto different patients a variety of unconscious strivings which come from his infantile past." Erik Erikson, *Gandhi's Truth: On the Origins of Militant Nonviolence* (New York: Norton, 1993), p. 74.

13. Eli Zaretsky, *Secrets of the Soul: A Social and Cultural History of Psychoanalysis* (New York: Knopf, 2004), p. 9.

14. Glen O. Gabbard, *Love and Hate in the Analytic Setting* (Northvale, NJ: Jason Aronson, 1996), p. 186.

15. Freud, "The Dynamics of Transference," *SE*, 12:101–2.

16. Gabbard, *Love and Hate*, p. 288. Here is a recipe for huge problems, if analysis terminates in the midst of it: "The therapeutic work did succeed in lessening the moralizing and idealizing defenses and in easing the stifling rigidity of the symbiotic character disorder. Indeed the traumatized, annihilated true self began to emerge with all its raw, infantile power, lust and rage, but while it was still identified with the aggressor in a very primitive way" (p. 234). A "transference psychosis" can ensue.

17. Janet Sayers, *Freudian Tales* (London: Random House, 1997), p. 211.

18. Sayers, *Freudian Tales*, p. 212.

19. Adam Phillips, "Psychoanalysis and Idolatry," in *On Kissing, Tickling and Being Bored: Psychoanalytic Essays on the Unexamined Life* (London: Faber & Faber, 1993), p. 130.

20. Adolf Grunbaum, "Made-To-Order Evidence," in *Unauthorized Freud: Doubters Confront a Legend*, ed. Frederick C. Crews (New York: Penguin Putnam, 1998), p. 77.

21. Robert Michels, review of Frederick Crews's *The Memory Wars*, *Journal of the American Psychoanalytic Association* 44, no. 2 (1996): 575.

22. Not everyone is oblivious. "We are dealing with a carefully orchestrated and well-organized effort to suppress psychoanalytic ideas," the editors of the *Journal of the American Psychoanalytic Association* note. Michels, review of Crews's *The Memory Wars*, p. 367.

23. Clara Thompson, *Psychoanalysis: Evolution and Development* (New York: Grove Press, 1950), p. 233.

24. Freud, "Dissection of the Personality," in *New Introductory Lectures*, p. 71.

25. Freud, *Future of an Illusion*, p. 84.

26. Freud, *Future of an Illusion*, p. 89.

27. One finds groundless denigration creeping into psychoanalytical works. James Grotstein says Freud only "valued the truth of the drives," was "probably an hysteric" who polarized everyone, given to hyperbole, vulnerable to slights, and "irritable, self-conscious and subject to introspections (in the sense of being preoccupied with oneself) rather than truly gregarious, considerate or loving." James Grotstein, foreword to *Carl Goldberg, The Evil We Do: The Psychoanalysis of Destructive People* (Amherst, NY: Prometheus Books, 2000), p. 13.

28. Freud, "A Difficulty in the Path of Psychoanalysis," *SE*, 17:143.

29. Peter Lomas, "Psychoanalysis Freudian or Existential," in *Psychoanalysis Observed*, ed. Charles Rycroft (London: Constable, 1966). Rycroft, *Psychoanalysis Observed*, p. 139.

30. See Bruno Bettelheim, *Freud and Man's Soul* (London: Penguin, 1980).

31. Max Schur, *Freud: Living and Dying* (London: Hogarth Press, 1972), p. 293n11.

32. Freud, "Dissection of the Psychical Personality," in *New Introductory Lectures*, p. 71.

33. Michael Kahn, *Basic Freud* (New York: Basic Books, 2002), p. 188.

34. Lomas, "Psychoanalysis Freudian," p. 141.

35. Lomas, "Psychoanalysis Freudian." Lomas cited Paul Federn as such a physician—but there were many others.

36. Thompson, *Psychoanalysis: Evolution and Development*, p. 43. The so-called cultural Freudians argue that Freud "did not envision people in terms of developing powers and as total personalities. He thought of them much more mechanistically—as victims of the search for the release of tension."

37. Freud, *New Introductory Lectures*, p. 69.

38. Kahn, *Basic Freud*, p. 202.

39. Freud, *The Wolf Man* (New York: Basic Books, 1971), p. 157.

40. Lou Andreas-Salomé, *The Freud Journal* (London: Quartet Books, 1987), pp. 32, 33.

41. Freud, "Constructions in Analysis," *SE*, 23:265.

42. Grunbaum, *The Foundations of Psychoanalysis*, p. 271.

43. "For him the analyst was always right, the patient inevitably wrong." Phyllis Grosskurth, *The Secret Ring: Freud's Inner Circle and the Politics of Psychoanalysis* (Reading, MA: Addison-Wesley, 1991), p. 40.

44. Freud, "Constructions in Analysis," *SE*, 23:265.

45. Freud, "Sexuality in the Aetiology of Neuroses" (1898), in *SE*, 3:269.

46. Elizabeth Loftus and Katherine Ketchum, *The Myth of Repressed Memory* (New York: St. Martin's Press, 1994).

47. Robert Wallerstein, *The Talking Cures* (New Haven, CT: Yale University Press, 1995), p. 7.

48. Wallerstein, *The Talking Cures*, p. 7.

49. Freud, "The Dynamics of Transference," *SE*, 12:106.

50. Freud, "Wild Psycho-Analysis," *SE*, 20:225–26.

51. Freud, "Remembering, Repeating and Working Through," *SE*, 12:147–56.

52. See Jon Henley, "Victims of False Paedophilia Case Tell French MPs of Ruined Lives," *Guardian*, 19 January 2006. Thirteen victims tell of lives ruined by false accusations by a woman who ultimately admitted she made up the charges.

53. Freud, "Construction in Analysis," *SE*, 23:262.

54. Freud, "Construction in Analysis," pp. 265–66.

55. Janet Malcolm, *Psychoanalysis: The Impossible Profession* (New York: Knopf, 1980), p. 52.

56. Sigmund Freud, *Three Contributions to the Theory of Sex* (New York: E. P. Dutton, 1962), p. 24.

57. By contrast, as Sulloway points out, Richard Kraft-Ebbing, who was friendly with Freud, used Latin for risqué terms in *Psychopathia Sexualis* (1886). He also accepted "hereditary taint" theories of the cause of homosexuality and perversions, as a man "by no means free from the prejudices of his times"—blaming them also on "excessive masturbation in early youth." Perversions included sadism, masochism, fetishism, and so on. Sulloway, *Freud: Biologist of the Mind*, pp. 28, 248.

58. Freud, *Outline of an Autobiography*, p. 65.

59. Schur, *Freud: Living and Dying*, p. 362.

60. Freud, "The Sexual Life of Human Beings," in *Introductory Lectures*, p. 304.

61. Freud, *Three Contributions*, p. 4.

62. Rachel Cooper, "What Is Wrong with the DSM?" *History of Psychiatry* 15, no. 5 (2004): 7.

63. Erikson, *Gandhi's Truth*, p. 98.

64. Freud, "Development and Regression," in *Introductory Lectures*, p. 351.

65. Erich Fromm, *The Greatness and Limitations of Freud's Thought* (London: Jonathan Cape, 1979), pp. 60, 61.

66. Peter Gay, *The Naked Heart: The Bourgeois Experience, Victoria to Freud* (New York: Norton, 1995), p. 9.

67. Norman Brown, *Life Against Death* (New York: Vintage, 1959), pp. 52, 54.

68. Webster portrays analysis as "a disguised continuation of the Judeo-Christian tradition," as if that is necessarily a bad thing (p. 5). But, as Bakan has argued, it probably owed far more to the Kabbalah. See David Bakan, *Freud and the Jewish Mystical Tradition* (New York: Shocken Books, 1965).

69. Scull, *Madhouses, Mad Doctors and Mad Men* (Philadelphia: University of Pennsylvania Press, 1981), p. 159.

70, Scull, *Madhouses, Mad Doctors*, pp. 160–61.

71. Freud, "Dissection of the Psychical Personality," in *New Introductory Lectures*, p. 96.

72. See Jones, *Sigmund Freud: Life and Work*, vol. 3, *The Last Phase* (London: Hogarth, 1957), pp. 23–25.

73. Oliver Sacks, *The Man Who Mistook His Wife for a Hat* (London: Picador, 1985), p. 19.

74. See Robert Wallerstein, "Psychoanalytical Perspective on the Problem of Reality," *Journal of the American Psychiatric Association* 21 (1973): 7; and Zaretsky, *Secrets of the Soul*. "Stimuli that come to the individual from the society or culture

were not directly ingested but first were dissolved and reconstituted in such a way as to give them personal even independent, meaning." Accordingly there is no "direct connection between one's social condition and one's subjectivity" (p. 7).

75. Young regards Freud as a "'psychophysical parallelist' who saw no need to connect mind processes and brain processes." Robert M. Young, "Freud: Scientist and/or Humanist," *Free Associations* 6 (1986): 24.

76. Lisa Appignanesi and John Forrester, *Freud's Women* (New York: Other Press, 2001), p. 461.

77. Appignanesi and Forrester, *Freud's Women*, p. 461.

78. See Sylvia Zwettler-Otte, *Freud and the Media: The Reception of Psychoanalysis in Viennese Medical Journals* (New York: Peter Lang, 2006), pp. 18–60.

79. Emil Ludwig, *Doctor Freud: An Analysis and a Warning* (New York: Hellmann, Williams & Company, 1952), p. 17.

80. Ludwig, *Doctor Freud*, p. 19.

81. Ludwig, *Doctor Freud*, p. 21.

82. Ludwig, *Doctor Freud*, p. 18.

83. Ludwig, *Doctor Freud*, p. 306.

84. Ludwig, *Doctor Freud*, p. 310.

85. Ludwig, *Doctor Freud*, p. 311.

86. Ludwig, *Doctor Freud*, p. 31.

87. Ludwig, *Doctor Freud*, p. 82.

88. Maurice Natenberg, *Freudian Psycho-Antics: Fact and Fraud in Psychoanalysis* (Chicago: Regent House, 1953), p. 7.

89. Natenberg, *Freudian Psycho-Antics*, p. 51.

90. Natenberg, *Freudian Psycho-Antics*, p. 53.

91. Roazen, *Freud and His Followers*, p. 13.

92. Martin D. Cushman, *Freud—A Man Obsessed* (Philadelphia: Dorrance & Company, 1967), p. 143.

93. Grosskurth, *The Secret Ring*, p. 94.

94. A. C. Grayling, "Sigmund Freud: False Messiah: Scientist or Storyteller?" *Guardian* (review), 22 June 2002, p. 4.

95. Grayling, "Sigmund Freud," p. 4.

96. See the discussions of psychoanalysis in light of the quantum revolution in physics in H. Stuart Hughes, *Consciousness and Society: The Reorientation of European Social Thought, 1890–1930* (New York: Knopf, 1958) and in Floyd Matson, *The Broken Image: Man, Science and Society* (New York: George Braziller, 1964).

97. For all his reputed compassion, though, Ferenczi, like Jones, opposed homosexuals becoming analysts while "Vienna was much more tolerant."

98. Paul Roazen, *How Freud Worked* (Northvale, NJ: Jason Aronson, 1995), p. 192.

99. Quoted in Schur, Freud: Living and Dying, p. 350.

100. Grosskurth, *The Secret Ring*, p. 35.

101. On Emil Raimann and Freud, see Zwettler-Otte, *Freud in the Media*, pp. 76–79.

102. See also Paul Roazen, *Brother Animal: The Story of Freud and Tausk* (New York: Knopf, 1969).

103. Roazen, *Freud and His Followers*, p. 197.

104. Grosskurth, *The Secret Ring*, p. 52.

105. Grosskurth, *The Secret Ring*, p. 36.

106. Freud changed basic concepts about symptom formation and the role of anxiety in normal and abnormal development in his essay "Inhibitions, Symptoms and Anxieties." ("The Problem of Anxiety: Inhibitions, Symptoms and Anxieties," 20 *SE*, pp. 77–174).

107. Andreas-Salomé, *The Freud Journal*, p. 37.

108. Freud, "Transference," in *Introductory Lectures*, p. 439.

109. "To rid the child of anxiety proved an impossible task. Parents did their best to reduce the child's fear of them, merely to find that they were increasing guilt feelings, i.e., fears of the child's own conscience. Where in its turn, the severity of the superego was reduced, children produced the deepest of all anxieties, i.e., the fear of human beings who feel unprotected against the pressure of their drives." Anna Freud, *Normality and Pathology in Childhood* (London: International Universities Press, 1965), pp. 7–8.

110. Anna Freud, *The Writings of Anna Freud* (New York: International Universities Press, 1974), p. 6.

111. Appignanesi and Forester, *Freud's Women*, p. 214.

112. Grosskuth, *The Secret Ring*, p. 42.

113. Russell Jacoby, *Social Amnesia: A Critique of Contemporary Psychology from Adler to Laing* (Boston: Beacon Press, 1975), p. 126.

114. Grosskurth, *The Secret Ring*, p. 56.

115. Freud, "Dissection of the Psychical Personality," in *New Introductory Lectures*, p. 143.

116. Bruno Bettelheim, "A Secret Symmetry," in *Recollections and Reflections* (London: Thames & Hudson, 1990), pp. 74–75. "As so often in psychological matters, highly personal matters eventually determined theoretical positions, something the psychoanalyst should be first to recognize" (p. 77).

117. Jones, *Sigmund Freud: Life and Work*, vol. 2, *Years of Maturity* (London: Hogarth Press, 1955), p. 479.

118. Sigmund Freud, *Civilization and Its Discontents* (New York; Norton, 1961), p. 282.

119. Freud, "Moses and Monotheism," *SE*, 23:94.

120. Schur, *Freud: Living and Dying*, p. 473.

121. Sigmund Freud, *The Future of An Illusion* (New York: Doubleday, 1953), p. 55.

122. Three-quarters of Freud's clients are reckoned to warrant the word "wealthy." Joseph Schwartz, *Cassandra's Daughter: A History of Psychoanalysis in Europe and America* (New York: Viking, 1999), p. 99.

123. Elisabeth Young-Bruehl, *Anna Freud: A Biography* (New York: Macmillan, 1988), p. 64.

124. Freud, "Lines of Advance in Psychoanalytical Psychotherapy," *SE*, 17:167.

125. Elizabeth Ann Danto, *Freud's Free Clinics: Psychoanalysis and Social Justice* (New York: Columbia University Press, 2005). Analysis was "available to students, artists, craftsmen, laborers, factory workers, office clerks, unemployed people, farmers, domestic servants and public school teachers" (p. 2).

126. Danto, *Freud's Free Clinics*, pp. 96–97.

127. Letter from Freud to Oskar Pfister, 25 November 1928, cited in Schur, *Freud: Living and Dying*, p. 403.

128. Jacoby, *Social Amnesia*, p. 25.

129. Grosskurth, *The Secret Ring*, pp. 3–6.

130. Nathan Hale, *The Rise and Crisis of Psychoanalysis in the United States* (Edgewater, NJ: Replica Books, 2001), p. 77.

131. Hale, *Rise and Crisis*, p. 126.

132. Russell Jacoby, *The Repression of Psychoanalysis* (Chicago: University of Chicago Press, 1986), pp. 10, 146–48.

133. Jacoby, *Social Amnesia*, p. 23.

134. Hale, *Rise and Crisis*, p. 252.

135. Franz Alexander and Sheldon T. Selesnick, *The History of Psychiatry* (New York: Mentor Books, 1966), p. 24.

136. Roazen, *Freud and His Followers*, p. 40.

137. Philip Rieff, *The Triumph of the Therapeutic* (London: Chatto & Windus, 1966), p. 106.

138. Hale, *Rise and Crisis*, p. 339.

139. Jacoby, *The Repression of Psychoanalysis*, p. 158.

140. "Anna [Freud] was very cool toward both Erik Erikson and Helene Deutsch." Roazen, *Meeting Freud's Family*, p. 104. One can fill in the blanks of these names with new names almost until exhausting the pantheon.

141. Thompson, *Psychoanalysis: Evolution and Development*, p. 15.

142. Thompson, *Psychoanalysis: Evolution and Development*, p. 34.

143. Wortis, *Fragments*, p. 60. Also see the interview with the elderly Wortis in Todd Dufresne's *Against Freud: Critics Talk Back* (Palo Alto, CA: Stanford University Press, 2007), pp. 9–25. Wortis, despite the volume title, hardly sounds like he opposes Freud.

144. Jules Henry, *On Sham, Vulnerability and Other Forms of Self-Destruction* (London: Allen, Lane, 1973), p. 25.

145. Freud, "'Civilised' Sexual Morality and Modern Neuroses," *SE*, 3:199. Freud also remarked that "the thirst for knowledge seems inseparable from sexual curiosity" in "Analysis of a Phobia in a Five Year Old Boy," *SE*, 12:100.

146. Jacoby, *Social Amnesia*, p. 10.

147. Jacoby, *Social Amnesia*, also see Marcuse's postscripted critique of cultural neo-Freudians in his *Eros and Civilization*.

148. Philip Rieff, *Freud: The Mind of a Moralist* (London: Victor Gollancz, 1960), p. 339.

149. Jacoby, *Social Amnesia*, p. 11.

150. See the comments on the disciplinary narrowness of orthodox psychoanalysts in Rieff, *The Triumph of the Therapeutic*, pp. 103–6.

151. John Clay, *R. D. Laing: A Divided Self* (London: Hodder & Stoughhton, 1996), p. 68.

152. Lomas, "Psychoanalysis Freudian or Existential," in Rycroft, *Psychoanalysis Observed*, p. 139.

153. Julia Segal, *Melanie Klein* (London: Sage, 1997), p. 21.

154. Rollo May quoted in Alexander Lowen, *Betrayal of the Body* (New York: Macmillan, 1967), p. 3.

155. Eric Kongsberg, "Therapists to the Elite," *New York Times*, 7 July 2008.

156. Stephen Frosh, *The Politics of Psychoanalysis*, 2nd ed. (London: Macmillan, 1999), p. 4.

157. Karl Figlio and Robert M. Young, "Interview with John Bowlby," *Free Associations* 6 (1986): 37.

158. Schwartz, *Cassandra's Daughter*, p. 224.

159. Jack El-Hai, *The Lobotomist: A Maverick Medical Genius and His Tragic Quest to Rid the World of Mental Illness* (New York: John Wiley & Sons, 2005), p. 3.

160. El-Hai, *The Lobotomist*, p. 4.

161. Berhard Kuechenhoff, "The Psychiatrist August Forel and his Attitude toward Eugenics," *History of Psychiatry* 19, 2 (2008). Forel, an arch-eugenicist, bragged about removing ovaries from a fourteen-year-old girl whose mother and grandmother had been prostitutes and from an older woman who entered the clinic with a chronic cough diagnosed as evidence of hysteria (p. 220).

162. Schur, *Freud: Living and Dying*, pp. 493, 526. Also on Freud's last days, see Peter Gay, *Freud: A Life for Our Time* (New York: Norton, 1988), pp. 648–51.

163. Erikson, *Gandhi's Truth*, p. 245.

164. Freud, "An Autobiographical Study," *SE*, 20:100.

165. Zoology and botany did not start from correct and adequate definitions of an animal and a plant; to this very day biology has been unable to give any certain meaning to the concept of life. Physics itself, indeed, would never have made any advance if it had had to wait until its concepts of matter, force, gravitation, and so on had reached the desirable degree of clarity and precision. The fundamental concepts or most general ideas in any of the disciplines of science are always left indeterminate at first and are only explained to begin with by reference to the realm of phenomena from which they were derived; it is only by means of a progressive analysis of the material of observation that they can be made clear and can find a significant and consistent meaning. Freud, "An Autobiographical Study," *SE*, 20:100, pp. 99, 100.

Chapter Four

Medicine Men and Invisible Wounds

From this tree [of heredity] a child inherits
Everything he does and says
All his faults and all his merits
All his stigmata, such as
Temper tantrums, enuresis
BMR, Ph, IQ
Tendency to cold and sneezes
and dislike of Irish stew
Sunken arches, refractile error
Thumbs in mouth and bitten nails
Daily horrors, nightly terrors
Cruelty to kitten's tails.[1]

A psychiatrist recalls training at Johns Hopkins University in the 1940s where he encountered a tutor "whose principal pedagogic pleasure seemed to be to hold "clinical conferences" in the children's outpatient department to "demonstrate" in the presence of its distressed family as well as before her increasingly disbelieving and indignant students that some deprived and mistreated child was a "hopelessly constitutional inferior who would always be a hopeless burden on society."[2] The author knew of exceptions such as the "gently avuncular" Austrian-born psychiatrist Leo Kanner, but the tutor's view was all too typical. What is problematic is not so much that experts operate on the basis of the best they "know" under the historical circumstances, but that they do so without doubt. The tutor's counterparts today are just as sure of their shaky ground. From that ground springs the fabled tree of the instructive ditty above, quoted by the aforementioned Kanner.

This chapter sets the perennial assault on Freud in the context of the state-of-the-art medicine of his era. The medical, or somatic, model promotes to this day the creed that a traceable toxin or physical trauma is needed to create an authentic mental illness. Freud's foes invariably decline to apply to medical authorities the stringent standards they inflict on this reviled Viennese renegade. With few exceptions, Freud's contemporaries interpreted mental difficulties as indisputable signs of "degeneration" too. If Freud ever displayed "invincible arrogance," one need have ventured no further than the nearest ward to find scores of physicians who surpassed him at it.[3] This is the materialist medical culture that one passionate Freud foe characterizes as bandying a "belief in mysterious, apparently unconscious, forces."[4] This odd statement may be true, but only insofar as those unexamined and unconscious beliefs propel the psychiatric canon.

Doctors, steeped in a puritanical climate, were inclined to attribute a multitude of maladies to sexual nonconformity. Who dared to risk their reputations to defend masturbation, noncoital sex, or any other sexual trespass? Indeed, this equating of taboo practices with mental illness itself contributed to crippling anxieties, as Freud recognized. Any physicians "skeptical of the relationship between self-abuse and insanity all too often became the pariahs of their profession."[5] From the mid-nineteenth to the early twentieth century there was a virtual scientific obsession, now forgotten, with the "sanctity of male semen," proposing that any "expenditure" at all weakened the frail male.[6] Even nocturnal emissions led to physical woes and moral hell. Eminent practitioners were convinced. Freud's foes, had they lived at the time, would have backed them, for the foes always invoke what they imagine to be the sagacious medical opinion of the day.

"It is doubtless true that an anatomical lesion of some kind does in each case exist and the classification of diseases as organic and functional is but a concession to our ignorance," a prominent doctor judged in a 1905 issue of the *American Journal of Insanity* (later the *American Journal of Psychiatry*).[7] A functional neurosis, incidentally, is one that is "is known only by its symptoms," despite which these physicians knew where the real problem must lie. The investigators ritually proclaim at the outset that explanation of the nature of mental problems "shall be found in harmony with the true principles of general pathology . . . These are essential requirement for the progress of psychiatry."[8] That's that.

The medical article of faith is that the human mind "cannot be diseased, because there is nothing upon which disease can fasten."[9] So "sooner or later, so-called mental diseases must be recognized as simply states of mind, which exist by reason of disease processes in some one or more of the organs of the body." The insane "as citizens of our great country, have an inborn right to liberty and the pursuits of happiness," another authority says. If this "right can be restored to them by the use of the knife, we would be remiss in our duty not to use it."[10] That's logic—and self-interest and specialist blinders—remorselessly at work.[11] There was no limit to what thoroughly modern medicine confidently explained. The *Encyclopædia Britannica* in 1910 defined "writer's cramp, thusly: an affliction of the central nervous system," most often resulting from "a history of alcoholism in the parents or some neuropathic heredity."[12]

Scan Henry Goddard's popular eugenic tract *The Kallikaks* and it is clear that it never occurred to the author that environment exerts any influence on anyone. The one-note explanation for all the familial foul deeds he decries is "bad stock"; environment matters insofar "as they themselves, because of their different characters, changed that environment."[13] "There is every reason to believe that criminals are made and not born," is the stolid refrain.[14] Here the Puritan conscience—unchecked and (mostly) unconscious—contrives to crucify a former Revolutionary War soldier for the "havoc caused by one thoughtless act" of sexual intercourse—thereby peopling the countryside with a splatter of "defective degenerates."[15]

Goddard says it is a pity that castration and ovariectomies are "regarded as mutilation," musing "while there is no rational basis for this feeling [that the] average man acts not upon reason, but upon sentiment and feeling . . . "[16] One might like to dismiss this guff as the prattle of a callous clown, but the "the trouble is that on close inspection there was virtually no psychiatrist who did not at one time express an opinion favorable toward eugenics."[17] As late as his 1908 case study of "Little Hans," a boy scared of horses, Freud felt he had to defend the lad against the looming medical charge that he was "degenerate."[18]

Statistical studies conclusively "proved" eugenics, none surpassing Francis Galton's impressive numerological displays of the genetic inferiority of just about everyone outside his immediate social circle. Proof is readily at hand because statistics too often, like dreams, are barely disguised wish fulfillments, an invitation to engage in the manufacture of cozy social fictions. Sander Gilman reminds us that for fin de siècle medical science Jewish racial differences unequivocally were plain to see, that "Jewish pathologies were statistically evident."[19] Here is the august medical profession against which readers must assess the struggles, mistakes, and achievements of Freud.

BEYOND THE PALE

Crews shamelessly tries to identify Freud with the "discredited crackpots of the 1870s who had treated hysterical women through gynecological mutilation."[20] The trouble with Crews's maneuver is that those crackpots were the cream of their profession, and their supercilious attitudes never vanished. While one historical investigator characterizes the whole sordid history of eugenics, with justice, as "widespread academic fraud combined with almost limitless corporate philanthropy to establish the biological rationale" for their own prejudiced ends, the real problem is that there was a frightfully thin line between what was considered arrant fraud and what was exemplary science.[21]

Why is there such a powerful pull toward externalist explanations? And why did Freud come to resist it?[22] For one thing, Freud never felt any predilection to be a physician: "I was moved rather by a sort of curiosity, which was, however, directed more towards human concerns than toward natural objects."[23] Freud testifies that in the mid-1880s as a young researcher, utterly innocent of psychological knowledge of the neuroses, he studied nervous diseases. Freud self-mockingly notes that his subsequent explanation of headaches as stemming from a certain physical source brought reproof even from some colleagues: "By way of excuse I may add that this happened at a time when greater authorities than myself in Vienna were in the habit of diagnosing neurasthenia as cerebral tumour."[24]

Freud later tellingly noted that his "medical conscience" was pleased that he found sexuality had not only a mental side but a somatic one, too. Freud crucially goes on carefully to discuss neurasthenia as becoming somatic too, even if it did not originate somatically: "I should like to make clear that I am far from denying the existence of mental conflicts and of neurotic complexes in neurasthenia. All that I am asserting is that the symptoms of these patients are not mentally determined or removable by analysis, but that they must be regarded as direct toxic consequences of disturbed sexual chemical processes—which are triggered by social or mental experiences."[25] This subtle formulation, making room for the role of somatic forces in neuroses, was a far cry from capitulating to the reigning somatic explanations.

CAUTION: OPTIMISM AT WORK

Foucault provides a classic if questionable metaphysical account of the social treatment of lunacy from the medieval times through the Enlightenment.[26] By the eighteenth century, once mass incarceration of the mad was under way and the need to claim "the insane as part of the legitimate domain of medicine" ignited administrative turf wars, which resulted in the subspecialty of psychiatry.[27] The "moral treatment" movement, led by Philippe Pinel in France and Samuel Tuke in England, viewed madness as a result of "shocks of life, not lesions of the brain," but this stance soon was relegated to a few tiny redoubts.[28]

Esquirol in France argued that disease was organic but regarded it as "having social triggers" and therefore being treatable.[29] Johann Christian Reil in Germany offered "moral treatment" too, largely his "powerful personality commanding the patient's imagination," combined with gimmicks such as submerging patients in a tub of eels, whipping them with nettles, and dripping sealing wax on bare skin.[30] Early treatments were a remorseless procession of purges, vomiting, bleeding, and cathartics.[31] No proof ever was needed for the utility of intrusive violent treatments for those designated mad.

By the 1840s insanity was deemed "purely a disease of the brain."[32] "Every change of mind," as Nicholas Robinson earlier argued, "indicates a change in the Bodily organs."[33] One must reduce the yellow and black bile buildup imagined to cause mental disorder.[34] The therapeutic idea of an empathic exploration of inner consciousness was too insubstantial to entertain. William Griesenger, the most eminent among German authorities, decreed "every mental illness is rooted in brain diseases," despite the fact that "he recognized that he could not prove this thesis."[35] The lesions were not traceable but why let one drawback spoil a good theory? The lesions must be found. Until then there was little one could do by way of cure. This therapeutic pessimism stoked a fierce hereditarian dogma, but what historians call "therapeutic optimism" wasn't any better for patients, because both versions were couched in a stern somatic doctrine.

What shapes scientific exploration are expectations of the model employed, not just evidence, which in any case is not easily separated from what one expects to find. In the nineteenth century B. A. Moreal, among others, reverted to a hearty degenerationist view: "Degenerations are deviations from the normal human type, which are transmissible by heredity and which degenerate progressively towards extinction."[36] Paul Mobius (1854–1907) and Max Nordau (1849–1923) popularized the degenerationist catechism. Mobius, no quack, taught that "women were slaves to their bodies," that "instinct makes the female animal-like," and, what's more, that "high intelligence in women was so unusual as to be a sign of degeneration."[37] Where, one wonders, are Freud's foes' prudent comparisons of Freud with these celebrated predecessors and contemporaries.

The patron saint of the medical model in psychiatry is Emil Kraepelin, an unapologetic archeugenicist, as were most physicians. Kraepelin held that dementia praecox (schizophrenia) was caused by internal factors and was incurable, even though one schizophrenic in six or seven, by his own count, recovered (which one might think would give one pause for thought).[38] In the nineteenth century the formal diagnosis for general paresis (syphilis—the pansexual AIDS of its day) saw it as a "disease produced by intemperance and immorality." The data seemed to attest that the disease ran in families and therefore "the tendency toward immorality was also thought to be inherited."[39] This rash extrapolation was not overturned until a spirochete for syphilis was found in early 1900s.

If mental illnesses ran a typical course, then it was reckoned by physicians that they must be organic. In the mid-nineteenth century psychiatrists, comfortable creatures of their environment, class, and state, duly labeled conscientious objectors as sick men, as "ethically inferior."[40] And that was all there was to it, like barroom yahoos braying. The social control function of psychiatry clearly outweighed the mission to heal, as psychiatrists policed the frayed borders of sanity in a world whose collective sanity was questionable. Krafft-Ebing obligingly devised a scientific nosology including a disease for "political and reformatory insanity," which medically damned any silly citizens who "have an inclination to differ from mass opinion."[41] People in the professions, raised to hug the party line or conventional wisdom, were scandalized and mystified by deviations from it.

Gilman suggests that a "powerful association between Jews and disease in fin-de-siècle racial biology" spurred Freud to reject sweeping biological claims of the day. Racial models of the Jew "are found not only in the crackpot pamphlet literature of the time; they are present in virtually all discussions of pathology published from 1880 to 1930."[42] Gilman, unfortunately, resorts to a dangerously double-edged argument, undercutting Freud's own acumen by reducing his resistance to orthodoxy to personal terms. Freud was a Jew, was thereby impugned, and so he rebelled. Presumably Freud would have caviled even if the degenerationist diagnosis was confirmed. One ought to note that some Jewish physicians bought into these beliefs.

Freud, Gilman more persuasively adds, later advocated lay (non–medical degree) analysis in large part because nonmedical practitioners would be "less gullible, less uncritical of the assumptions of the biological scientists." On every count the latter were held above suspicion, even when mutilating and maligning patients. Foes such as Gellner and Eysenck, who pride themselves on exacting standards, could not have helped but approve of these physicians' behavior based on the methodological standards of that time. Indeed, all we ever have are the methodological standards of our time—unless motivated to search more deeply, as Freud indeed did. By 1900, as Freud was emerging from his disputed isolation, "the optimism for curability had ended and cures were no longer expected."[43]

"The history of brain and behaviour research in the [twentieth] century," Young summarizes, "can be seen as the progressive abandonment of faith in a one-to-one correlation between the categories of analysis and the functional organization of the brain on the one hand, and the analogous variables in behaviour on the other."[44] A particularly embarrassing offshoot was phrenology, which held that mental traits were determined by localized parts of the brain. Beginning with Joseph Gall, phrenologists have had two characteristic reactions toward evidence. If it can be construed to support phrenology, it is proclaimed as confirmatory, If not, it is explained away.[45] Phrenology fizzled away but those defensive reactions did not.

Although Hale says neurologists and psychiatrists vaguely allotted a "role to the psychological factor and to environment," his study is a vivid description of the "somatic style" prevalent from 1870 to 1910 and beyond. "It is difficult to exaggerate the neurological sense of expectation, their faith that within the foreseeable future every puzzle would be solved" through a localization of function, and treatment of them, in the brain.[46] What accompanied this staunch belief was a "therapeutic optimism" that "disadvantageous heredity could be overcome. . . . by proper somatic hygiene." Therefore, physicians "felt free to create entirely speculative pathogens."[47] It was a most ominous form of optimism that drove this juggernaut enterprise. The relation of the neurological to the psychological went utterly unexplored, except insofar as causal arrows pointed in the one direction. Given this professional creed, anything went, and it did.

Freud's conciliatory statement that psychical distress might be found to be based on physical maladies allayed somewhat the suspicions of the medical community. It is hard to assay whether Freud actually believed it since he had abandoned the somatic accounts in the mid-1890s for being "too vague and too inclusive"—the charges ironically leveled against him later.[48] It was the abject failure of cerebral localization—plain to the minority who were unblinkingly honest scientists—that sparked the crisis that opened a cultural space for Freud's peculiar research paradigm.

When Freud arrived at Clark University in the United States in 1909, most doctors assumed "nervous and mental disorders resulted from inherited defects and from lesions" despite the considerable quibble that "no evidence could be produced to show that insanity had a somatic origin."[49] An inability to produce cures "was only of slight concern to their sponsors."[50] The "discipline of the ritual," as Scull calls it, became the basis for treatment: "The problem it was conceded must lie in the administration of the wrong remedies, of the right remedies in the wrong way, not in the nature of the undertaking itself."[51] Here is a potent attitude pervading a community of practitioners, morphing into the status of a principled stance. What it legitimized were such therapeutic devices as vomiting therapy, sulfur and turpentine injections, liberal use of laxatives, and peremptory removal of ovaries, gonads, and teeth. Latterly, chloral hydrate, morphine, and bromides came along as palliatives, usually for the hideous effects of the preceding batch of mistreatments.

ERROR AND TERROR

Medical science in the nineteenth century bordered on terrorism, and for the best of reasons, at least according to the self-understanding of authorities. In the 1840s a sudden fad for craniectomies on retarded patients resulted in 15 to 25 percent death rates in surgical units, with no hint of "progress." In 1889 a Kansas state hospital staff castrated forty-four boys and mutilated fourteen girls before a public outcry put a stop to it.[52] Institutes for the mentally retarded in Pennsylvania and Arkansas sterilized fifty-eight boys for masturbation with what they claimed were marvelous gains in tractability in all cases.[53] In the 1890s noted professor of obstetrics Alfred Hegar in Freiberg freely performed ovariectomies on hysterical women.[54] Freud's Dora would not have much enjoyed making his acquaintance, and well might have if family contacts had run in a different direction.

The cultural notion that masturbation causes physical ills harks back to the 1758 publication of Samuel Tissot's *Onania* (if not the Bible), listing in delectable detail the multitude of physical misfortunes that must ensue, excluding only hairy palms. Clearly, to these figures of rectitude, absolutely any measure that might discourage the sin of self-abuse was doing the weak-willed patient a favor. In 1883 ward physician Frank Hamilton ligated the vas deferens of patients to deter masturbation. Harry Clay Sharp later performed the first vasectomy not as a birth control measure but in order to "treat" masturbation among wretched prisoners in Indiana.

In 1899 the *Journal of the American Medical Association* featured an article advocating vasectomies on criminals as an alternative to prison.[55] In 1907 Indiana passed a compulsory sterilization law, enabling the author of the aforementioned article to sterilize of hundreds of young men.[56] As a "preventive measure," the chief surgeon of an Ohio hospital removed the clitoris of a self-abusive seven-year-old.[57] Cornflakes, apart from being devised for dining ease, were devised as a dietary remedy for Onan's sin. Hypnotism was tried. Circumcision was offered at all ages as a preventative, as were cold baths and intemperate enemas. Good middle-class people, it seems, preferred to mangle their children rather than permit them to masturbate. By 1912, incidentally, Freud had restricted his own concern to its psychological hazards, although he could "not rule out" the chance of organic damage.[58]

Meanwhile, up at the Burghölzli hospital in Switzerland, far from the reach of torch-bearing peasants, August Forel, to whom Breuer griped about Freud's alleged high-handedness, tried his hand at castrating violent patients. Doctor Frankenstein looks like a flower child compared to such grim, driven professionals. Mary Shelley sensed more than we appreciate about the physicians of her era, with dangerous conceits and medically approved prejudices.

The horrors performed with scientific zeal unfurl in a long bloody list. Freud, as foes admit, reproved himself for his minor gaffes with Dora but these physicians—whose credentials Crews and his cohort must find impeccable—persuaded themselves that their maimed patients were not only better for it but grateful too.[59] One can cite medical breakthroughs and a roll call of humane medical practitioners, but these aforementioned events are part and parcel of medicine too.

The era was saturated with eugenic beliefs. Beliefs are one thing, for no scientist is free of them, but knowing for sure what you are going to find is another. Krupp in 1900 dangled a thirty-thousand-mark award to the "scientist who most convincingly demonstrated the significance of biological and racial lineage to domestic political development."[60] Behind this money flow was a view that the paltry individual must meet a rigged society's demands. The tacit proviso is that special people providentially always have enough resources to attract the treatment they need. In Germany the brains of euthanized children were studied at the Max Plank Institute, a prestigious place dedicated to the proposition that "mental illness is genetically based."[61] Yet we are not dealing with science any longer when we witness researchers transfixed by doctrines as to what is a proper question and a proper answer.

In the United States Henry Cotton, superintendent of Trent State Hospital, racked up more victims than the *Texas Chainsaw Massacre* murderer could in a dozen sequels.[62] Here was a small-scale case of Arendt's "banality of evil" in action. Cotton embraced the creed of organic causation, a bet which proved to be both self-absolving and self-promoting. In hasty search of "obscure sites of focal sepsis," which is a medical fancy rooted in degeneracy theory, his great surgical snark hunt proceeded. Cotton yanked every tooth from his victims, adding tonsillectomies for good measure. The institutional presence of paresis (syphilis) victims—up to one in five patients—did offer a bare patina of credibility to these rough-and-ready interventions.

The mortality rate for colon resections in Cotton's busy facility was 30 percent.[63] Dora or Anna O. might well have fallen into these tender hands. Indeed, a woman like Dora, who was suffering depression and anxiety, was operated upon for "gatroenterostomy for her stomach ulcer followed by right-side colectomy. [Yet] she remained depressed, she then received, successively, a thyroidectomy, a complete colectomy, a double oophorectomy and salpingetomy (removal of both ovaries and fallopian tubes), encleation of her cervix, three series of vaccine treatments and two series of serum treatments . . . "

What was left of the lady was discharged and designated to the surgeons' satisfaction as "recovered."[64] Cotton operated, fatally, upon the hapless daughter of a fellow eugenicist who nonetheless endorsed the well-meaning butchery.[65] That's true believing. Cotton mitigatingly regarded the 1920s Chicago "thrill murderers" Leopold and Loeb as evincing "chronic sepsis" rather than homicidal lunacy derived from the corrosive chronic class privilege and sub-Nietzschean ideology he happened to share with them. Cotton claimed an 85 percent cure rate. Although by the 1920s Cotton was looked at askance for practicing an outmoded therapy, no one ever moved to stop him, Scull notes. Everyone knew mental illness had to be a symptom of underlying sepsis; Cotton was only onto the wrong sources of it. Even as theoretical tides turned against the focal sepsis assumption, actual practices took much, much longer to change. A generation had to die out.

One harbinger of change was Kanner's 1935 volume *Child Psychiatry*, which refers to Cotton's work as "as the starting point in a system according to which all mental difficulties are said to be rooted in some focal physical disturbances." Kanner notes that "such an attitude, if generally accepted, tends to do away with the desire to study the personalities of abnormally reacting individuals, make psychiatry superfluous, and leave behavior disorders entirely to the surgeon's scalpel and the dentist's forceps."[66] Kanner lampoons "the endocrinology fad," which "led certain enthusiasts to proclaim that ductless glands and their products as the one and only unrivaled sources of all functions of man."[67] What Kanner advocated instead is the formulation of "psychobiology as a pluralistic science"—as incorporating nonsomatic factors into diagnosis and treatment.[68] His plea would seem scarcely comprehensible even today to many professionals.

Freud conceded that the "hope of the future lies in an organic chemistry or the access to it through endocrinology/This is still far distant but we should study analytically every case of psychosis because the knowledge will do good to deviant therapy."[69] All Freud means here is that the analyst must cover every possibility, even undetectable or astronomically unlikely ones, because he never "allowed himself to forget that the mind is part of the body."[70] Patients will believe that they suffer mysterious but physical maladies because they are not stigmatized, as is "craziness," to which a stigma has been attached. Patients go along because they believe it is treatable. The doctor's authority is shored up.[71] Yet in the early twentieth century, even in physics and chemistry, the phenomenon of uncertainty disrupted all formerly cut-and-dried formulations. The savviest scientists in those fields coped and accounted for the factors causing it. What Freud was doing was incorporating "uncertainty" so as to understand and treat sources of human anguish. Psychoanalysis expanded the ameliorative influence of therapy. But it could not happen overnight or unopposed.

SHOCKING TROOPS

During World War I callous governments resorted to shock treatment for mental casualties. Side effects—compared to patients whom Freud's foes say were endangered by stray suggestions—were irreparable brain damage, headaches, dizziness, apathy, paralysis, disorientation, hallucinations, fear, loss of bowel control, amnesia, and miscellaneous tics and tremors. Thomas Szasz rather weirdly writes about this disgraceful period as if shock treatments were Freud's fault, when the entire "patriotic" medical fraternity on either side of no-man's-land favored them.[72] Julius Wagner von Jauregg, a towering medical figure, heartily advocated shocking soldiers suspected of cowardice. But Freud repudiated the approach as useless and, even if unintentionally, inhumane. Freud termed the treatments "expedient" at best, although he was "personally convinced that it was not intensified to a cruel pitch by Professor Wagner-Jauregg," an old schoolmate.[73]

Freud nevertheless argued that his therapy was more useful, pointing to Ernst Simmel's considerable successes.[74] (As in other experiences with electroshock, it wore off, though that was not Freud's point.) With satisfaction he noted that with the end of the war the incidence of such "war neuroses" plummeted—"a final and impressive proof of the psychical causation of the neuroses."[75] Because of his fierce empiricist background Wagner-Jauregg tried to "find a physical basis for mental maladies," adamantly oblivious to all else. Wagner-Jauregg became President of the Austrian League for Racial Regeneration and Heredity, which demanded "eugenic sterilization" for those allegedly of inferior stock.[76] His record during the Nazi takeover of Austria was one of distinct friendliness with the new regime.

The successes of psychoanalysis later in helping Allied soldiers in World War II helped to pry open the door to Freudian techniques afterward, but not of course without more fierce bouts of resistance. In 1946, Shephard notes the British Army, whose preferred prewar diagnosis of psychiatric casualties was "lack of moral fibre," took firm steps to reduce the "democratic influence" that psychiatric psychotherapy had introduced through its scurrilous treatment techniques, such as talking respectfully to afflicted soldiers of whatever rank on a one-to-one basis.[77]

Zwettler-Otte shows how common it was in Freud's lifetime for frustrated doctors to resort to the principle *ut aliquid fieri videatur* ("to create the impression of doing something") for ills they had no handle on. The urgency of creating an impression of doing something included electroshock.[78] Zwettler-Otte also notes the "deal repeatedly proposed to Freud: If he was prepared to play down the importance of the sexual drive in favor of other factors, hostility to his teachings would diminish."[79] Physicians would still sooner medicate their patients with placebos than explicitly touch on their sexual lives.[80] The brain was a safer organ to investigate than genitalia, and was far less complex than sexuality.

Yet the brain does not function as a single unit or organ. Contrary to the hardwired position bandied about in pop science books, the research discloses that all influences of personality, whether genetic or experiential, shape us by affecting the connection between neurons, altering the pathways according to the experiences that the infant undergoes. "We don't know how genes interact with each other and the environment (Mother, etc.) to produce a personality" (or schizophrenia) but we "do know that they do so interact."[81] As Horgan notes, fear "is a biological phenomenon," and emotions alter biology with dramatic consequences, such as PTSD.[82] The fact that the brain "does not mirror the world the way a camera does" (of which philosophers were well aware) should give pause to somatic explainers of mental disturbance.

Freud's foes are so worried about being gulled by a "subjective" account that they relegate all such explanations to the occult and instead believe naively in pure materiality, unaffected by perception and emotion. Every paradigm sets down guidelines which are useful for the purpose at hand, but which exclude vast areas of experience. And so, to paraphrase Wittgenstein, the foes' rule is that, of that which we cannot express in familiar terms, we cannot speak. What cannot fit in their framework does not exist or might as well not exist. The moral crime of Freud's foes is not only their failure to realize this historical reality of scientific life but their ploy to align Freud with medical sadism instead of seeing his work as a brave departure from cruel, if unwitting, orthodoxy.[83]

IN THE MEAN TIMES

The nineteenth century persisted beyond calendar dates in modern medicine. "Thryoidectomies, ovariectomies, male castration and removal of all or parts of all the glands of mental patients numbered in the tens of thousands around the world during the 1920s."[84] Sleep cures were reputed to remedy manic depressives and schizophrenics, with cure claims upward of 70 to 80 percent. Insulin shock therapy supposedly ended drug addiction and dissipated schizophrenia. The results either were made up or else indicated delusional states among attending physicians. By 1941 43 percent of U.S. mental hospitals utilized electroshock (and Metrazol) treatments. The newspapers, then as now, hyped technology-based "breakthroughs" in treatment, and saw nothing but benefits.

Coming into vogue in the 1930s were leucotomies and lobotomies, based on the "flimsiest of theories and on completely inadequate evidence."[85] Valenstein finds it "difficult to separate myth from fact" about Egas Moniz. Prefrontal leucotomy was endorsed not on the evidence but because there was nothing else on the horizon promising somatic relief. So Moniz's accompanying theory of "fixed thoughts in frontal lobes"—pure hogwash—was just trimmings. Moniz speculated that leucotomies "forced the brain to develop new neural pathways and more beneficial emotional responses."[86] A faith healer can offer more plausible reasons for why his or her prayers should work. Any likely story would do. There was at the time ample evidence that electroshock caused terrible impairments, but Moniz forged ahead anyway and so did the profession.

Chronic schizophrenics showed no improvement, yet Moniz claimed many cures and that the treatment was perfectly safe. Overcrowding and budget constraints played a key role too in the welcome of electroconvulsive therapy (ECT). "Almost any proposed treatment was considered worth trying, as long as it did not require much money or large numbers of skilled personnel," Valenstein writes.[87] "Certainly almost anything was tried with impunity, as malpractice suits and ethics committees were rare." The theory was that "specific brain pathways between the frontal lobes and the thalamus regulate the intensity of the emotions invested in ideas."[88] It was patent nonsense, even then. Unchallenged, "neuroelectric therapy spread. The tales of horrid side effects are numerous. In 1961 Ernest Hemingway was electro-shocked 30 days before he killed himself because he feared loss of memory and his writing ability after the shocks."[89]

The almighty knife had another of its heydays. From 1936 to 1951 eighteen thousand lobotomies were performed in the United States, propelled in part by the need to deal somehow with the long-term mentally ill, over 40 percent of whom were institutionalized more than 5 years. A *Life* magazine article denounced conditions in places that "degenerated into little more than concentration camps on the Belsen pattern."[90] The reporter exposed "snake pit" scenes of soiled people scattered nude on concrete floors in wards. The treatments of choice were hydrotherapy, electroshock, malarial therapy, and amateurish custodial care. A series of exposés termed the institutions "crowded, perverse, callous, abusive." Something, anything, had to be done, and as inexpensively as possible. The American Psychiatric Association said institutions were overcrowded by an average of 50 percent.

Life magazine in 1947 also published a panegyric article on psychosurgery claiming that only the "hopeless" were operated upon and that 30 percent returned to normal, 30 percent improved, and a mere 2 or 3 percent died.[91] Thin air seems to be the source of such statistics. The surgeries actually entailed frequent relapses, incontinence, dull affect, lack of initiative, and many deaths. Psychoanalysts opposed lobotomies but this rum cohort—whom Freud's foes depict as all-powerful in psychiatry—were completely ignored. (By the 1950s the dominant psychological school, contrary to the claims of foes, was not psychoanalysis but Skinnerian behaviorism.) So surgical procedures inflicting permanent damage of brain tissue went unhindered.

At best, lobotomy substituted an organic "deficiency" for a preexisting psychosis, if indeed there ever was one. The psychosurgeons talismanically invoked violent patients as justifying the procedures, but violent patients were not remotely representative of the average ward. The surgeons, however, were not responsible for clearing wards, which was due to other factors. Favorable publicity, as Valenstein surmises, created demand for the procedure, just as it does for mood-altering pharmaceuticals today.[92] Perhaps all psychosurgery did was to make things more orderly for orderlies. We're confronted with scientific bigotry; that is, scientists offering paradigm-derived prejudices as infallible truth. This was an era of therapeutic tap-dancing, when medicine conjured interventions that were guesswork but sounded solid, which is exactly the portrayal that the foes give of psychoanalysis.

A CASE STUDY

Those Freud's foes who endlessly carp at alleged systematic psychoanalytic abuses might peruse an instructive 1950s report by renowned psychiatrist Lauretta Bender, "The Development of a Schizophrenic Child Treated with Electric Convulsions at Three Years of Age."[93] Bender received substantial government funds to perform "experiments with shock on new clinical populations" and, according to investigators, she was a forerunner for the CIA's extensive MK-ULTRA "mind control" program.[94] The psychiatric community was involved in the atrocious experiments, as is an element of it today. The schools of psychiatry and medicine which countenance this mayhem have no grounds for invoking ethics; none are in evidence, overridden by diagnostic enthusiasms.

A two-and-a-half-year-old boy was referred in 1950 to Bellevue because of "distressing panic that frequently reached a state of panic" since he was four-and-a-half months of age (!).[95] The child initially was diagnosed as "mute and autistic" and finally as exhibiting "infantile schizophrenia." His father was "suspicious, irritable, high strung, and was discharged from the [military] service for a 'nervous heart.'" Dad also was impotent and "a schizophrenic, paranoid type." Mom showed "depressive moods, neurotic disturbance, high-strung, overreactive." Neither parent sounds like an ideal nurturer. Their child was prescribed phenobarbital, perhaps because at the ripe old age of two and a half he sometimes "wanted to be held like a baby." Concerned authorities sprang into action. Drugs were not enough: "It was felt that the greatest progress in therapy could be made if shock treatment was given as early as possible."[96]

So in April 1950, two months shy of his third birthday, the clingy little boy received the first of twenty shocks, "each of which stirred a grand mal convulsion." The boy "resisted being taken to the shock room and being prepared for treatment," Bender reports, "but was not more frightened or anxious than over other interruptions to his autistic behavior." So it's okay. She claims that the child afterward was "less autistic and was infrequently rigid and withdrawn" although, for some strange reason, he continued "clinging" to mother in new situations, and, yes, there were temper tantrums.[97] The writer can't imagine why a child would behave like that. Happily, by age five the child and his mother were in psychotherapy and the boy also found an interested teacher. Sustained improvements were noted, although the significance of these new factors was breezed over. Bender's report, fortunately, has appended to it a "discussion" by a group of psychiatrists.

Bender's conjecture that because the "symptoms that the boy eventually developed resemble the reactions which he probably manifested as a fetus it follows that his process of maturation in utero must have been defective will be difficult for many to accept." Bender had no evidence at all but her strained inference was regarded as a legitimate move on the scientific game board. In the name of "therapeutic optimism," Bender resorted to the most pessimistic portrayal of the origins of the symptoms. As a skeptical colleague observed: "The theory of maturational lag, like other theories that place the main emphasis on intrinsic hereditary or constitutional factors, not only is almost impossible to prove, but it leads to a pessimistic attitude towards the investigation and treatment of extrinsic factors, which are, after all, the only ones we are likely to have much power to alter. The question that cannot yet be answered by proponents of the extrinsic factor is why certain children and not others, exposed to pathogenic family environment, develop psychoses."[98]

The discussants of Bender's study conceded that it was likely that intrinsic elements were involved. Perhaps "some inborn sensitivity may be the 'hidden factor' determining that he react with a psychosis and not by psychosomatic disturbance or some other disorder [but] much further study is needed before we can feel confident that we are not deceiving ourselves."[99] The discussant carefully takes heed of the "bias of workers toward a theory which places primary emphasis either on extrinsic or in extrinsic factors—even though most people pay lip service to the inclusion of the factors too" and that "the difficulty of carrying out studies of clinical cases that are equally meticulous in their appraisal of all the factors involved, because of the one-sided interest or the experience of the workers."[100]

The discussants mention that until recently "most cases of childhood psychosis or borderline ego disturbance of the type manifested by [the child] were routinely diagnosed as mental deficiency, and the majority probably found their way into institutions for the feeble-minded, a fate which very nearly overtook [another child]."[101] The discussants found Ashley Montague's formulations of the interaction of prenatal constitutional factors with postnatal ones useful: "(1) indeed, there is little that is final about constitution, for constitution is a process rather than an unchanging entity . . . " It is "not a biologically given structure predestined by its genotype to function in a predestined manner. The manner in which all genotypes function is determined by the interaction of the genotype with the environment in which it undergoes development . . . Heredity is the dynamic integral of the genotype and its environment—the resultant of dynamic interaction between the two."[102] All these comments are as true today as then.

In 1975, despite negative reports on ECT the National Institutes of Health (NIH) awarded $10 million for research on somatic therapies, including ECT. The NIH *wanted* it to work. In 1990 the American Psychiatric Association (APA) reclassified shock as "safe" for depressed patients although no studies prove it. The APA also ruled that ECT could be used "regardless of age."[103] Yet ECT patients were more frequently hospitalized than non-ECT patients (41 to 15 percent).[104] Rarely did the allegedly good effects last more than 4 years. ECT also inflicts "acute brain syndrome," and has reduced patients to fetal positions. Several states ban ECT while thirty states limit it. More salient for those assaulting Freud is that ECT has been found to be used to "cover up sexual abuse of women and girls"—precisely the population Freud's foes say concern them most.[105] Concern about potential abuse seems to wane where physicians the foes approve of are involved.

COMEBACK OR BACKLASH?

Leaf through psychiatry journals and you will find much of the space is hogged by glossy drug advertisements. The illegible microprint listing side effects of each Food and Drug Administration (FDA)–approved wonder drug is often as long as the ad space itself. You would never guess that the FDA does not even conduct its own tests, relying on drug firms instead. This form of regulation is rather like a traffic cop pulling you over for suspected speeding and relying on you to tell him how fast you were going.

Politics determines what winds up in the small print. Tardive dyskinesia, for example, is a permanent physical disorder which manifests in a third of neuroleptic users within five years and is diplomatically downplayed.[106] One might think that consumer consciousness would heighten, given that by the 1990s the United States was consuming five times as much legal drugs as the rest of the world. But people (and physicians) are led by saturation campaigns to imagine that antidepressants like Prozac—which tripled in prescriptions from 1990 to 1997—and numerous other drugs are safe and effective. The methodological seesaw is hard at work here, with those findings that match the expectations of proponents of the dominant paradigm meeting lower verification standards than those challenging it or operating outside that paradigm.

Contrary to Freud's foes, biopsychiatry always has been dominant, although it underwent a brief spell in the 1950s and 1960s of having to reckon with psychoanalytic interlopers. Yet, at their peak in U.S. psychiatry, psychoanalysts made up less than 10 percent of the ranks.[107] In 1942, of 114 hospitals with psychiatric residents, psychoanalysts were in 38.[108] The American Psychoanalytic Association grew from 65 members in 1930 to 500 members and 700 students in 1950 and 600 members and 925 students (plus 61 laymen among its analysts) by 1955.[109]

NIMH grants expanded psychiatric ranks sixfold, from 4700 in 1948 to 28,000 by 1976.[110] A conceptual chasm always divided psychodynamic psychiatrists from the "organic" psychiatrists. Hale estimates that by 1957—a peak year—there were "no more than 1400 practicing analysts in the world in 1957 perhaps 14,000 people in analysis and no more than 100 thousand who completed treatment."[111] By 1962 fifty-two of the eighty-nine heads of psychiatry department were members of psychoanalytic associations. But they were mostly mediators among factions during a fleeting time when psychotherapeutic approaches had to be reckoned with.

The "revolution in psychiatry" was really a well-calibrated counterattack by the dominant core of American psychiatry. The first psychoactive drugs, it is rarely recalled, were discovered accidentally and only afterward were theories fashioned to explain them. Thorazine was created in 1952. Chlorpromazine arrived in 1954 after beginning its existence as an antihistamine. The hospitals already were emptying. Deinstitutionalization resulted in a drop of inmates from half a million in the 1950s to about eighty thousand today, with one result being tens of thousands of mentally ill people relegated to prisons instead.[112] The tranquilizer Miltown appeared in 1955, and Valium and Librium in the 1960s. The neuroleptics—Thorazine, Mellaril, Stelazine, Prolixin—poured out so that, as Breggin puts it, "patients don't lose their symptoms, they lose interest in them."[113]

Noting how "staggeringly fortuitous" was the discovery of penicillin, and the medical use of steroids, Le Fann concludes, "The actual state of medical knowledge about severe mental illness can be summarized as follows: we know that handful of drugs discovered by accident about fifty years ago are effective in relieving symptoms of schizophrenia and depression—but the way they work, the nature of the abnormal changes in the brain they correct and especially the causes of psychiatric illnesses remain a mystery."[114] But what the drug "revolution" enabled was a questioning of insulin, Metrazol, and, less so, electric shock procedures, since ready substitutes had come to hand. By 1970 lobotomies dropped to 6 percent of their quantity in the 1950s.

In psychiatry, according to one surveyor, "the neo-Kraepelinians" tend to be most interested in biological, especially genetic, explanations of mental illnesses. The neo-Kraepelinians "emphasize biological bases of mental disorders" and, with occasional exceptions, "are neutral, ambivalent, or at times hostile toward psychodynamic, interpersonal and social psychiatric approaches."[115] They in fact are throwbacks to the era of somatic dominance, and they hauled along all the old blind spots, largely because all they know is the smoothed-over textbook myths of an unbroken march of psychiatric progress. However, "to the extent that they are agnostic about the etiology of individual disorders," they differ from Emil Kraepelin himself—but not by much. These authorities played the decisive role in recasting *DSM-III*, which the author views as the emergence of a "new" paradigm. Psychoanalysts were somehow left out.

CONCLUSION

In *The Future of an Illusion* Freud considered the implications of philosophy for the positivist science: "Philosophy is not opposed to science, it behaves like a science and works in part by the same methods; it departs from it, however, by clinging to the illusion of being able to present a picture of the universe which [seems] coherent, though one which is bound to collapse with every fresh advance in our knowledge. It goes astray in its method by overestimating the epistemological value of our logical operations and by not accepting other sources of knowledge such as intuition."[116]

Here one can substitute what Freud's foes mean by science with the word philosophy, for that stunted sense of science has become a philosophy itself, one which overestimates logic, lionizes numbers, and disregards all other forms of acquiring knowledge. Science in this exclusivist form of philosophy is obstructive. The positivist foes could not be less scientific than when adopting these supposedly rigorous stances. Perhaps, as Norman O. Brown says, positivist science, like religion, "derives its strength from its readiness to fit in with our instinctual wishful impulses,"[117] which is the scientists' wish for omniscience by cutting everything down to our own size.

Freud took some comfort in the fact that Darwin's theory "met with embittered rejection and was violently disputed for decades; but it took no longer than a generation for it to be recognized as a great step towards truth [and indeed] the new truth awoke emotional resistances."[118] What Clifford Geertz said of social sciences is true in psychiatry: old theories never die; they tend to go into second editions—and await another chance. And there is nothing inherently wrong with that. A theory should be exposed to many competitors. Even obsolete or limited theories may have something to contribute to flushing out insights or refining one's own theory.[119] But this principled methodological stance differs considerably from one where the motive is to establish dominance of a favored model.

Sulloway says Freud abandoned his initial dream of "devising a neurophysiological, and hence, purely mechanical theory of defence (Repression)" but "he never abandoned the assumption that psychoanalysis would someday come to terms with the neuropsychological side of mental activity."[120] Sulloway insistently misunderstands Freud. Upon abandoning the project, Freud realized that medicine had to come to terms with a two-way traffic between psyche and soma, mind and body, soul and flesh. This is not at all what the authorities cared to hear.

"It is one thing to test a fruitful line of investigation," as Karl Mannheim observes, "and another to regard it as the only path to the scientific treatment of an object."[121] Oliver Sacks warns us of where dogmatic attitudes lead in his account of a neurologically impaired man who "construes the world as a computer construes it, by means of key features and schematic relationships," and is consequently lost in an "absurd abstractness of attitude—absurd because unleavened by anything else—which rendered him incapable of perceiving identity, or particulars, rendered him incapable of judgment."[122] Sacks sees cognitive sciences "suffering from an agnosia" similar to Dr. P., who is a warning of what happens to a science which eschews "the judgmental, the particular, the personal, and becomes entirely abstract and computational."[123] Hence, Sacks asks us to beware of the "downfall of judgment," which will not, one hopes, be an epitaph for science.

NOTES

1. Leo Kanner, *In Defense of Mothers* (Springfield, IL: C. C. Thomas, 1941), p. 64.
2. Jules Masserman, *A Psychiatric Odyssey* (New York: Science House, 1971), p. 25.

3. Edward Dolnick, *Madness on the Couch: Blaming the Victim in the Heyday of Psychoanalysis* (New York: Simon & Schuster, 1998), p. 27.

4. Todd Dufresne, *Killing Freud: Twentieth Century Culture and the Death of Psychoanalysis* (London: Continuum Books, 2003), p. 9.

5. John Haller and Robin Haller, *Physicians and Sexuality in Victorian America* (Carbondale, IL: Southern Illinois University Press, 1995), p. 203.

6. Haller and Haller, *Physicians and Sexuality*, p. 195.

7. Edward Cowles, "The Problem of Psychiatry and the Functional Neuroses," *American Journal of Insanity* 62, no. 2 (October 1905): 190. Also in the same issue, see the essay on differences between the "Aryan" and the "Semitic" by Major Charles E. Woodroof, U.S. Army Surgeon, "The Complexion of the Jews."

8. Cowles, "The Problem of Psychiatry," p. 189.

9. J. W. Whering, "Melancholia: The Psychical Expression of Organic Fear," *American Journal of Insanity* 62, no. 3 (January 1906): 369.

10. Whering, "Melancholia," p. 465.

11. Max Witte, "Surgery for the Relief of Insane Conditions," *American Journal of Insanity* 62, no. 3 (January 1906): 465.

12. Cited in Edward Tenner, *Why Things Bite Back* (New York: Knopf, 1996), p. 174.

13. Henry Herbert Goddard, *The Kallikaks* (New York: Macmillan Press, 1931), p. 12. "For the low-grade idiot, the loathsome unfortunate that may be seen in our institutions, some have proposed the lethal chamber. But humanity is steadily tending away from the possibility of that method, and there is no probability that it will ever be practiced" (p. 101).

14. Goddard, *The Kallikaks*, p. 30.

15. Goddard, *The Kallikaks*, p. 103.

16. Goddard, *The Kallikaks*, p. 107.

17. Ian Robert Dowbiggin, *Keeping America Sane: Psychiatry and Eugenics in the United States and Canada, 1880–1990* (Ithaca, NY: Cornell University Press, 1997), p. xi.

18. Freud, "Analysis of a Phobia in a Five Year Old Boy," *SE*, 10:252–53.

19. Sander Gilman, *The Case of Sigmund Freud: Medicine and Identity at the Fin-de-Siecle* (Baltimore, MD: Johns Hopkins University Press, 1993), p. 15.

20. Crews, *Unauthorized Freud*, p. 6.

21. Edwin Black, *War against the Weak* (New York: Four Walls, Eight Windows Press, 2003), p. xv. Also see chapter 4 in Kurt Jacobsen, *Technical Fouls: Democratic Dilemmas and Technological Change* (Boulder, CO: Westview Press, 2000).

22. "It appears, indeed, that man has a deep disinclination to understand the disturbances of his behavior in terms of psychology. He undoubtedly shuns the responsibility which results from such understanding and is ready to blame spirits, the devil and even mystical fluids in his body for his abnormal behavior instead of recognizing that it is a result of his own feelings, strivings, and inner conflicts," Franz Alexander and Sheldon T. Selesnick, *The History of Psychiatry* (New York: Mentor Books, 1966), p. 33.

23. Sigmund Freud, *An Autobiographical Study* (New York: Norton, 1962), p. 13.

24. Freud, *An Autobiographical Study*, p. 19.
25. Freud, *An Autobiographical Study*, p. 43.
26. See Michael Foucault, *Madness and Civilization* (New York: Vintage, 1973).
27. Andrew T. Scull, *Museums of Madness: The Social Organisation of Insanity in 19th Century England* (London: Allen Lane, 1972), p. 128.
28. Robert Whitaker, *Madness in America* (New York: Perseus Books, 2002), p. 27.
29. Roy Porter, *The Greatest Benefit to Mankind: A Medical History of Humanity* (New York: W. W. Norton, 1997), p. 502.
30. Porter, *Greatest Benefit*, p. 507.
31. Scull, *Museums of Madness*, p. 128. Also see Whitaker, who finds that "inducing nausea in patients was a medical tradition" (Whitaker, *Madness in America*), p. 7.
32. Scull, *Museums of Madness*, pp. 165, 168.
33. Porter, *Greatest Benefit*, p. 271.
34. Alexander and Selesnick, *The History of Psychiatry*, p. 22.
35. Robert Thomson, *The Pelican History of Psychology* (London: Pelican, 1968), p. 200. "Unfortunately, such speculation was of little use in diagnosis and treatment and offered no genuine explanation. 'Brain mythology' and 'speculative anatomy' were terms which contemporary physiologists used to describe much of the psychiatric writing of this period" (p. 201). If only.
36. Quoted in Thomson, *Pelican History of Psychology*, p. 199.
37. Porter, *Greatest Benefit*, p. 510.
38. Thomson, *Pelican History of Psychology*, p. 202.
39. Elliott Valenstein, *Great and Desperate Cures* (New York: Basic Books, 1986), p. 28.
40. Thomas Roder, et al., *Psychiatrists: The Men behind Hitler* (Los Angeles: Freedom Publishers, 1995), p. 78, 151. Also see John Cornwell, *Hitler's Scientists* (London: Viking, 2003), pp. 71–90.
41. Roder, et al., *Psychiatrists—The Men Behind Hitler*, p. 23.
42. Gilman, *Freud, Race and Gender*, pp. 3, 5, and Gilman, *The Case of Sigmund Freud*, pp. 5–7.
43. Porter, *Greatest Benefit*, p. 513.
44. Robert M. Young, *Mind, Brain and Adaptation in the 19th Century: Cerebral Localization and Its Biological Context from Gall to Ferrier* (Oxford: Clarendon Press, 1970), p. 31.
45. Young, *Mind, Brain*, p. 43.
46. Nathan G. Hale, *Freud and the Americans: The Beginnings of Psychoanalysis in the United States, University Press 1876–1917* (Oxford: Oxford, 1971), p. 50.
47. Hale, *Freud and the Americans*, p. 52.
48. Hale, *Freud and the Americans*, p. 179.
49. Nathan G. Hale, *The Rise and Crisis of Psychoanalysis in The United States: Freud and the Americans, 1917–1983*, p. 4.
50. Scull, *Museums of Madness*, p. 173.
51. Scull, *Museums of Madness*, p. 173.

52. Edward J. Larson, *Sex, Race and Science* (Baltimore, MD: Johns Hopkins University Press, 1995), p. 27.

53. Bert Sigurd Hansen, "Something Rotten in the State of Denmark: Eugenics and the Rise of the Welfare State," in *Eugenics and The Welfare State*, ed. Gunnar Broberg and Nils Roll-Hansen (East Lansing: Michigan State University Press, 1996), p. 14.

54. Hansen, "Something Rotten," p. 15.

55. Elof Axel Carlson, *The Unfit: A History of a Bad Idea* (Cold Spring Harbor, NY: Cold Spring Harbor Laboratories Press, 2001), p. 208.

56. Carlson, *The Unfit*, p. 208.

57. Brian Easlea, *Fathering the Unthinkable* (London: Pluto Press, 1983), p. 176.

58. Freud, "Concluding Remarks," *SE*, 12:252–53.

59. Philip Rieff, *Freud: The Mind of a Moralist* (London: Victor Gollancz, 1960), p. 86.

60. Roder, *Psychiatrists*, p. 147.

61. Roder, *Psychiatrists*, p. 156.

62. Andrew Scull, *Madhouse* (New Haven, CT: Yale University Press, 2005), p. 23.

63. Scull, *Madhouse*, p. 52.

64. Scull, *Madhouse*, p. 55.

65. Scull, *Madhouse*, p. 84.

66. Leo Kanner, *Child Psychiatry* (Springfield, IL: Charles Thomas, 1935), p. 3; Valenstein, *Blaming the Brain: The Truth about Drugs and Mental Health* (New York: Free Press, 1998), p. 12.

67. Kanner, *Child Psychiatry*, p. 4.

68. Kanner, *Child Psychiatry*, p. 17.

69. Letter to Marie Bonaparte, quoted in Valenstein, *Blaming the Brain*, p. 11.

70. Robert Coles, *The Mind's Fate* (New York: Little, Brown, 1997), p. 170.

71. Valenstein, *Great and Desperate Cures*, p. 216.

72. Thomas Szasz, *Anti-Freud: Karl Krauss's Criticism of Psychoanalysis and Psychiatry* (Syracuse, NY: Syracuse University Press, 1976), p. 137.

73. Freud, "Appendix: Psychology and War Neurosis," *SE*, 17: 213–14.

74. Jones, *Sigmund Freud: Life and Work*, vol. 3, *The Last Phase 1919–1939* (London: Hogarth Press, 1957), p. 236. He objected that "medicine was serving purposes foreign to its essence."

75. Freud, "Memorandum on the Electrical Treatment of War Neuroses," *SE*, 17:215. "If it was used in the Vienna clinic, I am personally convinced that it was never intensified to a cruel pitch by the institute Professor Wagner Von Jauregg" (p. 213).

76. Marius Turda and Paul J. Weindling, eds., *Blood and Homeland: Eugenics and Nationalist Racism in Southeast Europe 1900–1940* (Prague: Central European University Press, 2006), p. 311.

77. Ben Shephard, *War of Nerves: Soldiers and Psychiatrists in the Twentieth Century* (Cambridge, MA: Harvard University Press, 2001), p. 326.

78. Sylvia Zwettler-Otte, *Freud and the Media: The Reception of Psychoanalysis in Viennese Medical Journals* (New York: Peter Lang, 2006), pp. 30–31.
79. Zwettler-Otte, *Freud and the Media*, p. 39.
80. Zwettler-Otte, *Freud and the Media*, p. 66.
81. Horgan, *The Undiscovered Mind: How the Human Brain Defies Replication, Medication, and Explanation* (New York: Free Press, 1999), p. 68.
82. Horgan, *The Undiscovered Mind*, p. 28.
83. See Jeffrey Masson, *A Dark Science* (New York: Farrar, Straus and Giroux, 1986).
84. Valenstein, *Great and Desperate Cures*, p. 34.
85. Valenstein, *Great and Desperate Cures*, p. 62.
86. En-Lai, *The Lobotomist*, p. 10.
87. Valenstein, *Great and Desperate Cures*, p. 177.
88. Valenstein, *Great and Desperate Cures*, p. 171.
89. A. E. Hotchner, *Papa Hemingway* (New York: Random House, 1966), p. 346.
90. Valenstein, *Great and Desperate Cures*, p. 175.
91. Hotchner, *Papa Hemingway*, p. 177.
92. Hotchner, *Papa Hemingway*, p. 215.
93. Lauretta Bender, "The Development of a Schizophrenic Child Treated with Electric Convulsions at Three Years of Age," in *Emotional Problems of Early Childhood*, ed. Gerald Caplan (New York: Basic Books, 1955). Bender was the widow of psychoanalyst Paul Schilder, who died in a car accident in 1940.
94. See Steve Baldwin and Melissa Oxlad, *Electroshock and Minors: A Fifty Year Review* (Westport, CT: Greenwood Press, 2000). Also see Alexander Cockburn "The CIA and LSD," *Counterpunch*, 18 October 1999.
95. Bender, "The Development of a Schizophrenic Child," p. 407.
96. Bender, "The Development of a Schizophrenic Child," p. 418.
97. Bender, "The Development of a Schizophrenic Child," p. 418.
98. "Discussion," in Bender, "The Development of a Schizophrenic Child," p. 419.
99. Bender, "The Development of a Schizophrenic Child," p. 419.
100. Bender, "The Development of a Schizophrenic Child," p. 420.
101. Nic Waal, "A Special Technique of Psychotherapy with an Autistic Child," in *Emotional Problems of Early Childhood*, ed. Gerald Caplan, p. 482.
102. Waal, "A Special Technique of Psychotherapy," p. 522.
103. Breggin, *Toxic Psychiatry: Why Therapy, Empathy and Love Must Replace the Drugs, Electroshock, and Biochemical Theories of the "New Psychiatry"* (New York: St. Martin's Press, 1994), p. 137.
104. Breggin, *Toxic Psychiatry*.
105. Breggin, *Toxic Psychiatry*, p. 139.
106. Breggin, *Toxic Psychiatry*, p. 211.
107. Breggin, *Toxic Psychiatry*, p. 10.
108. Hale, *Rise and Crisis of Psychoanalysis*, p. 163.
109. Hale, *Rise and Crisis of Psychoanalysis*, p. 210.

110. Hale, *Rise and Crisis of Psychoanalysis*, p. 246.

111. Hale, *Rise and Crisis of Psychoanalysis*, p. 289.

112. Sasha Abramsky and Jamie Fellner, "No Exit: The Nation's Mentally Ill Used to Be Locked in Asylums. Now They're Stowed in Prisons," *American Prospect*, 8 January 2004.

113. Breggin, *Toxic Psychiatry*, p. 55.

114. James Le Fann, *The Rise and Fall of Modern Medicine* (London: Abacus Books, 1999), p. 61.

115. Gerald Klerman, "The Significance of DSM-III in American Psychiatry," in *International Perspectives on DSM-III*, ed. Robert Spitzer, Janet Williams, and Andrew Skodol (Washington DC: American Psychiatric Press, 1983).

116. Freud, *The Future of an Illusion*, p. 160.

117. Freud, *The Future of an Illusion*, p. 175.

118. Freud, "Moses and Monotheism," SE, 23:66.

119. See Paul Feyerabend, *Against Method: Outline of an Anarchist Theory of Knowledge* (London: Verso, 1975).

120. Frank J. Sulloway, *Freud: Biologist of the Mind* (New York: Basic Books, 1979), p. 131.

121. Karl Mannheim, *Ideology and Utopia* (New York: Harcourt, Brace, 1936), p. 8.

122. Oliver Sacks, *The Man Who Mistook His Wife for a Hat* (London: Picador, 1985), p. 9.

123. Sacks, *The Man Who Mistook His Wife for a Hat*, p. 10.

Chapter Five

Biological Veneers and Corporate Elixirs

> The belief that some one item fixes a person's lot in life for him is one of the things which the old and new superstitions have in common.
>
> —Leo Kanner[1]

For his TV act a famous mimic long ago arranged a row of bottles of various shapes on a table, each bottle labeled with a celebrity's name. The mimic sipped one and he stuttered out Jimmy Stewart. Swigging another, he rapidly rasped James Cagney. Sipping still another, he growled Humphrey Bogart. Then, upping the ante, he proceeded to mix Bogart and Cagney and conjured up Peter Lorre. The seductive notion that fixed blends of ingredients could make up a single predictable personality lies behind the apprehension—mixed with awe—of scientific research, or what we glean of it in the press, for science of this epic sort contains all the promises and all the threats that old science fiction B-movies exploited. Into this susceptible public climate somatic explanatory conceits sashayed back into the foreground in upgraded guises. All forgiven, or forgotten.

"Fundamentally, we believe that mental illness has a very strong genetic content," a NIMH honcho stated in 1989. "We just haven't found the genes yet."[2] Fundamentally, indeed. The fundamentalist element is the medical model injunction that mental disturbances must be caused by something one literally could put one's finger on. This paradigmatic faith is enticing, especially when there are persuasive simplicity, sincere proselytizers, and huge institutions to back it. The sales pitch to the public—especially the "educated classes" who are educated just well enough to buy system myths—was expertly conducted. Behind it all are enormous pressures in America, Porter notes, to "expand the diagnosis of treatable diseases" for the sake of profit margins.[3] "Low self-esteem is not a reimbursable condition," Murray observes.[4] "But if it is classified as minor depression, then reimbursement is possible. So there was a political and economic dimension to this process. The drug companies want to expand what is regarded as a disease in order to expand their market [because] psychiatric disorders with ill-defined boundaries are excellent playground in which to invent new diseases."

The first *Diagnostic and Statistical Manual (DSM-I),* published in 1952, listed 107 mental health disorders. Now, under the ingenuity of biopsychiatrists linked through many channels to drug firms, there are 365. "The very vocabulary of psychiatry is now defined at all levels by the pharmaceutical industry," says a professor of psychiatry at UCLA.[5] In 1999 the White House applauded biological psychiatrists in a ceremony that owed more to Big Pharma campaign contributions and hype than to the dicey scientific validity of their products.[6] Tipper Gore, scourge of racy music everywhere, confidently anointed mental illness—as if mental illness were one thing—a "physical disease." The conference concluded that the five to six million children then taking prescribed drugs were doing so because of "radical breakdowns in brain chemistry."[7]

"Do you know that in the entire [two-day] conference only on one occasion did one person up on that stage mention psychotherapy?" Psychiatrist Robert Epstein recalls. "The rest of it was all brain, drugs, brain, drugs."[8] In a 1937 essay on treatment technique Freud expressed his understanding for cries in various quarters to find ways to shorten therapy, but he also understood that "still at work in them as well is some trace of the impatient contempt with which the medical science of another day regarded the neuroses as being uncalled-for consequences of invisible lesions." Freud knew, and rued, the score: "If it has not become necessary to attend to them, they should at least be disposed of as quickly as possible." Freud particularly was annoyed at practitioners like Otto Rank, whose brand of analysis was "designed to adopt the tempo of analytical therapy to the haste of American life."[9]

Meanwhile, psychiatry, as Breggin argues, convinced much of the public that "psychosocial and spiritual suffering has no psychological or spiritual meaning whatsoever but stem instead from abnormalities in the physiology of the brain."[10] The American medical tendency to "diagnosis creep" appears irresistible and somewhat contagious. Physicians and patients are even trying to redefine obesity as a chronic disease, "like diabetes or hypertension, to be managed, rather than a problem to be solved."[11] Shyness too has been nominated in the twenty-first century as a lucrative disease to treat pharmacologically.

THE GREAT PANACEA HUNT

Freud's foes, with few exceptions, regard pharmacology as kosher science with the same alacrity that they denounce talk therapy as cant. Grunbaum, for example, seizes on a passage where Freud scrupulously says that even when psychoanalysis dissipates a neurosis it cannot be said to be "causal in the true sense of the word" unless it demonstrates that it can root out the earliest elements in the constitution of the patient "which first makes the patient as all vulnerable to pathogenic experiences."[12] Only this accomplishment, "perhaps by some chemical means," would be causal in the conventional medical sense.

Grunbaum gleefully hoists Freud by his own petard, which Freud, though not Grunbaum, already knew was flimsy. First, Freud here was only being perfunctory and humble, for any good scientist must allow that long shots—even a million or billion or infinity to one—cannot be dismissed totally. Thus, Freud was acting more positivistic than the positivists themselves while making no substantive concession to them. Second, the implication for Grunbaum is that only something like chemicals truly get at physiological predispositions that are nonetheless just *one* factor in generating a neurosis.

These "predisposing factors," however, may well turn out to be nothing but the human condition and all the "shocks that flesh is heir to." Third, if chemical means, in principle, might be found to treat the "earliest elements" in the patient, then presumably no mental illness will arise, no matter what force external conditions exert upon the subject, which Freud knew was a ridiculous but seductive proposition. Fourth, chemical means are assumed to counter deficits, except, as we see below in the "doctrine of the specific etiology," the specified deficits may not even exist and, if they do, may not be amenable to drugs.

Drugs are seductive for many reasons, including that of dispensing with a need to pin down the social or human sources of our problems. A best-selling author offers the twenty-first century's neoliberal motto, "It's nobody's fault," which people are relieved to hear, even if it isn't true.[13] Anything a drug can alleviate is nobody's fault. In 2004 over 57 billion dollars were spent by the pharmaceutical industry to market chemical panaceas to consumers, with 70 percent aimed at prescribing physicians, who must be a jaw-droppingly impressionable genus considering the impressive degrees they boast.[14] Is there a special element in their training that makes them such stunningly easy prey to advertising gimmicks and to indirect bribes (16 billion dollars of free samples from "detailers" pestering every doctor in the nation)?[15]

The cultural outcome of this perpetual advertising blitz is that mainstream America, the Breggins remark, is far "less skeptical about the scientific and medical establishment than the minority community, and is more willing to drug its children than is black America."[16] Until very recently, nowhere in the upper strata was heard a discouraging word about the outpour of miracle drugs. Only unchecked price rises drew U.S. public attention to pharmacologic oversell. In Britain too in the late 1960s half-a-dozen research units under the Medical Research Council of the Department of Health had been "dedicated to investigating social issues in psychiatry." Today there are none, which only adds to the imbalance of skills and approaches to psychiatry there.[17] Britain, though, is a haven of psychiatric pluralism compared to the United States.

It's not only the West; India too dishes out drugs based on a culture that sees "health in the short term can be [given] through the consumption of medicines."[18] The resurgence of biological psychiatry, propelled mainly by pharmaceuticals, is unstoppable. The new stream of nostrums provides abundant ammunition for medical model supporters. Forgotten in a snap of an ad man's fingers were the reckless brain mutilations and punitive electroshock forays of yesteryear conducted by all those immaculately attired, perfectly assured, and socially revered physicians. The current generation is just as confident of their capabilities as their predecessors, and just as fallible. They may be even more culpable than forerunners because they don't bother to peer into unabridged histories of medicine.

The flap over physicians abetting torture at Abu Ghraib, Guantanamo, and other post-9/11 Orwellian prisons shows that no one gets transformed into a moral paragon by dint of a swanky degree.[19] Physicians are as likely as anyone to collaborate with malevolent mega-institutions against the welfare of patients and the public. Freud, as noted earlier, upbraided authorities for mistreatment of shell-shocked soldiers, treatment delivered in the guise of therapy. Those doctors doubtless believed that they were acting out of the best motives and with consummate skill. They assumed that their blinkered patriotism should immunize them from reproach. But to accept their own subjective estimates, to accede to their (exculpatory) self-understanding, is to excuse the entire social order that shaped that subjectivity, too. No professionals are ever so helpless that they are unable to question the models, procedures, and "habits" handed down to them.

For the medical model to function the proverbial round pegs must be filed to fit available apertures. Human beings are beheld as puppetlike organisms whose neurological strings science soon will figure out how to pull with precision. The fact that a person with a loaded pistol pointed at him, or whose head is clouded with neuroleptic drugs, may do what he is told, is not news. Few people regard these exceptional situations as demonstrating anything revelatory about human behavior, but some ambitious authorities think otherwise. In this same vein, critics decry the explanatory privileging by some psychoanalysts of personal factors over all else. The early Freudians, usually deeply familiar with radical philosophies, understood that for psychoanalysis physical and social aspects were intimately interwoven.[20] Freud examined neuroses as social products, not natural diseases. One cannot sustain an argument that the forms that families take, and the rigors and pains they undergo, are immaculately separate from the societies in which they have to survive and get along.[21] But this separation is precisely what the medical model postulates, except in cases where specific families are seen as biological sites of imaginary pathogens.

The comeback of somatic explanations is attributable to the allure of simple theories and to the limits imposed by the tool kits at hand. The somatic dogma is resilient because it is attractive to an ineradicable subset of mentalities which search for formulaic solutions to problems. This refurbished doctrine blends a skin-deep understanding of science with a deliberate naiveté regarding external forces. The role of laziness—which, together with fear, fosters conformity—is great too. In 1954 an eminent psychiatrist casually suggested that "it was time to give up psychotherapy, as reserpine was good psychotherapy in pill form."[22] One doesn't get much lazier than that. Elite training is no proof against error. Psychiatrists in Nazi Germany were the most enthusiastic Hitler supporters among all professions, which were very supportive indeed.[23] There was nothing whatever wrong with their rigorous medical training except perhaps for much of the unquestioned content of it.

Psychoanalysis, in its classic one-to-one couch form, is shockingly expensive, always was. But detractors always avoid toting up how truly expensive a cheap drug therapy can be. Where is the inventory of the drawbacks? By both self-selection and training, "a psychiatrist is among the least likely people to help a child or a family with its problems."[24] Except, that is, by classifying the patient and drugging him or her up to the gills. Contrary to public images, a tiny percentage of psychiatrists have anything more than a smattering of training in talking to people about their problems, let alone any inclination to do so.

INDUSTRIALIZING PSYCHIATRY

In his study of aphasia, Oliver Sacks points out that Freud rejected Broca's notion of mapping functions to specific areas of the brain—the leitmotiv of this medical strain—as being too simplistic, finding instead that "all mental performance had an intricate structure."[25] Here is where the dramatic scientific rupture occurred, and not in the subsequent genesis of psychoanalysis.[26]

Freud in his abandoned "Project of a Scientific Psychology" tried to give his theories what Gellner calls "a firm physical or rather neurological basis."[27] For Gellner and like-minded foes, there is no other basis than a neurological one for medical theories, and neurological bases are always "firm." Both propositions are extremely questionable. When did coming to predesignated conclusions constitute a scientific approach? Isn't this what foes accuse Freud of doing?

But anyone who challenged the adequacy of the medical model was an apostate, a heretic, and a threat to a neat framework that served the personal and professional needs of a devout group. When Freud devised his "outline" for a scientific psychology he certainly would have tantalized this group. But Freud ultimately rejected the self-sufficiency of the medical model as too schematic, simplistic, sterile, and misleading. In science (as opposed to careerism) the evidence always contains the explosive potential of pushing the researcher beyond the textbook paradigm drummed into him.

Shorter oddly boasts that today the conversion of many diseases into treatable ones by wonder drugs—so-called—"was only possible because clinical psychiatry had enmeshed itself so massively in the corporate culture of the drug industry."[28] Examples include parent organizations such as Children and Adults with Attention Deficit/Hyperactivity Disorder (CHADD and National Alliance on Mental Illness (NAMI), which stump for biopsychiatric interventions and align themselves snugly as propaganda arms for Big Pharma.[29] The dispensing of drugs for every imaginable malady—"Sorry," as a New Yorker cartoon shrink advises a distraught parent, "there is no cure for adolescence"—leads to what the Breggins justly term "high tech child abuse," which troubles few in our culture so long as people in white coats approve. In 2008 an eminent Harvard child psychiatrist, whose work is credited with enormously boosting sales of antipsychotic drugs for juveniles (a fortyfold increase in pediatric bipolar disorder), was found to have earned about $1.6 million over the previous seven years from pharmaceutical companies. The good doctor did not report most of it to university officials, who were the ill-equipped site for monitoring such conflicts of interest.[30] The example is far from unusual in psychiatric ranks.

Is there really any prima facie reason why disturbed children are safer in the hands of such psychiatrists rather than with psychotherapists? The anti-Freudian feminist, if ever in distress, is not going to be rescued by the polite dispensers of psychoactive drugs, those avatars of true science and scorners of the unconscious. Indeed, as other feminists point out, the only reason "a therapist may dispense drugs [is] because he is uncomfortable with emotions aroused in therapy, to 'quicken' therapy, alleviate their own anxiety—a way to assert authority, a distancing technique."[31] Patriarchy comes in a pill bottle too.

A new mental illness contrived just for women by solicitous firms is "premenstrual dysphoric disorder," affecting 7 percent of women.[32] Happily for Lilly profit margins, PMDD—every marketable disease must be reduced to a few economical letters—requires an antidepressant, which turns out to be a refurbished form of Prozac renamed Sarafem. Hence, the medicalization of suffering masks the real causes, inverting Freud's foes' accusation that psychoanalysis masks physical problems. The difference is that no analyst can afford to overlook physical sources, while biopsychiatrists see nothing else. Brand spanking new PMDD, though, is indistinguishable from normal menstrual difficulties. The FDA under Bush II obligingly recognized the condition and approved the treatment. The World Health Organization is yet to be notified that it is supposed to exist.

So "everyday problems are a psychiatric condition" as the industry splashes out billions annually "teaching us to be hypochondriacs," proud middle-class junkies dependent on them.[33] Awareness-raising campaigns are, as many critics note, illness-creating campaigns. An ad campaign on TV was withdrawn under FDA pressure because the manufacturer failed to cite side effects, but no fines were levied or punitive consequences imposed. The advertisements increase sales, or they wouldn't be run, and they increase the risk of side effects without bringing any benefit to consumers.

The American Psychiatric Association in the 1970s sought drug company money, though largely, it is mitigatingly true, to do what most psychiatrists wanted anyway, which was to prove that "psychological suffering is a biologically based medical problem."[34] Correlating neurotic tendencies with the signs of the zodiac makes about as much sense and would probably proceed as successfully, given the sums involved. Eli Lilly, which manufactures Prozac, and Upjohn, which manufactures Xanax and Halcion, have slipped millions to the APA since the early 1990s. By 2006 pharmaceutical funding comprised 30 percent of the APA's $62 million budget.[35] Congressional investigators are just beginning to take interest in the implications for credible research and reliable products. The returns on tacit investments of this sort have been colossal.

Blaming the brain comprises the new "evil spirit" theory, explaining why good, or at least quiet, people (which is the same thing, in the estimate of authorities) do bad things. A typical headline reads: "Brain Seizure May Spark Crimes, Scientist Asserts." A researcher at Harvard develops "a seizure theory to explain otherwise inexplicable crimes after working with hundreds of murderers in a male prison."[36] Shy people and loners, including a monk, are hypothesized to be prey not to violent seizures, but to seizures causing violence, which is quite a different and more complicated thing. The article goes on serenely to explain why another researcher's finding lends support to the theory.

A neurologist found when "patients with brain disorders such as intractable epilepsy are given electrical stimulation to parts of their brain in preparation for treatment an unintended side effect is that people sometimes experience unbidden emotions"—laugh, burp, or feel sad for no reason other than electrical stimulation. You too might feel sad, laugh, burp, or break wind if you were cattle-prodded. These and many other specious findings are results of conceptual divides between doctor and patient, exactly the divides that Freud crossed to develop psychoanalysis. Is there no reason to suspect that the eruption of shy people into murder, robbery, or arson is traceable to emotional plights? This display of adamant cluelessness about the human condition reminds one of R. D. Laing's passage in *The Divided Self* on "reversing the gaze" so as to see Emil Kraepelin from the point of view of the patient as he is prodded and poked and treated as an inanimate object.[37]

Scientists again attribute virtually all crime, including mob violence, to brain disorders, especially from the 1960s onward.[38] As always such explanations cloak the power structure and blame the individual alone by the device of incriminating genes or errant toxins. We do not detect in the biopsychiatric gospels anything approaching a truly self-critical stance regarding the research enterprise. Instead they routinely side with a dominant public authority or private firm, which coincidentally usually pays the way. You rarely can cajole people, as the venerable axiom goes, to understand something that their paychecks depend on their not understanding. To boot, no one is more insecure than someone who is 100 percent sure of his or her ground. No one would differ except for the sake of mischief or because they are demented. Every form of puritanism is rooted in stark fear. Fanatics fear not just difference, but contamination by it. Hence, the extreme measures—from expulsion to extermination—these puritans always pretend to be reluctant to take.

Valenstein estimates that from 1945 to about 1965 biological explanation, as a dominant influence, receded into the background of psychiatry but definitely did not disappear, although disciples like to pretend it nearly did. Like all hard-pressed authorities, they are happy to play the victim in a narrative of their righteous resurrection. Ample funding always went on apace, but was shared to an annoying degree with some practitioners who took the other side of matters seriously too.[39] If all disorders must have a somatic origin, then those psychoanalysts must be blurring the lines, which is a threat. The optimal response is to redraw the old lines, expel anyone on the other side of them, and rewrite history to justify it, as winners always do.

The search for palliatives is a universal endeavor. It is no myth that the original secret ingredient of Coca-Cola was cocaine, replaced by caffeine. Until the late nineteenth century most patent medicines were laced liberally with opiate derivatives. How do you think we got through the Industrial Revolution? In 1898 Bayer advertised heroin as safe nonaddictive cough syrup, as opposed to codeine.[40] Nonetheless, the blunt verdict today too is that, despite all the advertisements, that "we really don't know what causes mental disorders or why drugs are sometimes helpful." For the prescribers, the impression must be spread that these pills, capsules, and liquids are magic potions sufficient to cure what ails you or your intractable nuisance of a neighbor. A tremendous amount of research money hangs on researchers reporting that they are on the right track.

SPECIOUS SPECIFICITY

The myth of specificity of drugs is the indispensable prop for the pharmaceutical revolution. People imagine that drugs were devised to solve particular behavioral problems and did so by filling a deficit or relieving a chemical overload, like insulin for diabetes or vitamins for vitamin deficiencies. That is not what these drugs do. Chlorpromazine, administered initially in France to mental patients in 1952 and first used as an antihistamine, has no direct effect on delusions. Any mental health facility staff member can testify that "neuroleptics are actively used in every institution in which social control and behavioral suppression are a top priority, and in which drugs can replace human services."[41] The pharmaceutical companies deploy the largest number of lobbyists in the United States of America. As a result, it is now second nature to presume that scientific research must ape "entrepreneurial market activity," as investigators cannot help but notice, so that "hardly any mainstream critics can see other ways to operate. Pharma has thus helped to foster a cultural mindset where any alternative to pharma-defined science has become literally unthinkable."[42]

The impulsion to ascribe everything to physical causes results in twists that hardly anyone notices. As quoted by Joan Didion in her bestseller about dealing with the death of a beloved husband, the Institute of Medicine in the 1980s admitted that "research to date has shown that, like many other stressors, grief frequently leads to changes in the endocrine, immune, autonomic nervous, and cardiovascular systems, all of these influenced by brain function and neurotransmitters."[43] That last phrase is thrown in to undercut any hint that emotions alone change physiology; it isn't grief really, but brain function and neurotransmitters that bring misery. Loss of a loved one is irrelevant, except as a trigger for chemical and neurological activity. By this logic, if you treat the latter successfully you will lift the grief.

The public is led to believe that neuroleptics cure, rather than muffle, disorders, that schizophrenia is genetic/biochemical, and that talking cures are frivolities for celebrities. Lobotomy and electroshock too have roared back in this propitious climate and what one booster calls the "second biological psychiatry" has regained dominance to the extent that psychiatric geneticists propose—and, in the press, proposals tend to become proclamations—that "some illness-causing genes expand in size when passed from generation to generation, as the mechanism behind the increasing severity of schizophrenia or manic-depressive illness."[44] This is raw unpasteurized eugenics, soft-peddled.

Phenothiazine is a byproduct of the synthetic dye industry, which might raise the question of how on earth it traveled from that use to human consumption? Wellbutrin originally was a weight-loss drug. No one knows why most drugs act in the way they do, except as impairing agents, not "cures." But if control, not understanding, is your ultimate objective, then it is easy to fudge the results or finesse the explanation so as to conjure the image of a cure: "See, the subject is sitting so still. That proves it works." Eli Lilly launched a campaign to "sensitize people to depressive symptoms" in the 1980s.[45] There is no evidence depression is related to serotonin levels. What exists is a whopping number of uncontrolled studies, faulty designs and executions, and "subjective" contaminating elements. Testing today is scandalously amenable to drug company bottom lines, not dispassionate analysis. A 2001 study found less than one in five medical journals had a conflict of interest policy and that a third of papers published were funded by firms involved in the products the authors assessed.[46]

Contrary to a scientific urban myth there are no grounds to believe there is a direct connection between a "neurotransmitter or receptor—and any psychological state."[47] The action of these ballyhooed drugs on the central nervous system is based on inferences—no less so, incidentally, than "inferential access" characterizes psychoanalysis.[48] We do know for certain that extrapyramidal motor disorders, such as Parkinson-like symptoms, were found at the start in Thorazine trials and then ignored. In one trial 61 percent suffered from extrapyramidal effects while 50 percent improved from the placebo.[49] How these drugs work remains "just speculative, hidden behind a veil of pseudoneurology."[50] Tardive dyskinesia and tardive dystonia—both with distressing ticlike symptoms—were considered small prices for patients to pay.

Things get worse with cynical campaigns to push drugs on youngsters even though "little or nothing is known about the effects of psychiatric drugs on the developing brain or the long term impact on social relations, academic achievement or personality in young children who take such drugs," as a *New York Times* reporter alertly notes. "And most of the medications have not been specifically tested or had their dosages calibrated for young children."[51] In any case, the line between normality and clinical illness in a three-year-old is no better defined now than when Bender applied those electrodes, yet everyone is pressured to act as if it is.

Iatrogenic effects are harmful ones caused by physicians or by the remedies they prescribe. In iatrogenic cases the drugs produce the very biochemical change that are claimed to be the cause of the disorder.[52] Recall the wisecrack that Karl Krauss made about analysis being the disease for which it purports to be the cure. That is what occurs often in pharmacological treatments and at a vast scale. Yet the most compelling scientific discovery is that different kinds of experience can modify brain chemistry—as in poverty-ridden environments versus rich environments.

Valenstein notes the findings that in the brain the "branching of neuronal dendrites is proportional to educational attainment."[53] Stress-related hormones undermine the immune system and impair memory. So it is clear which way causal arrows flow—both ways. "Organic changes in the organism must occur not only in [disturbed people]," Cleckley observed back in the 1950s, "but in other people in response to every item of experience."[54] Distinctions between organic and psychogenic cannot help but conceal more than they reveal.

"It would not be profitable to confine our concept of what is organic to the cellular level with so much already known which indicates that molecular and submolecular changes (colloidal, electrochemical, etc.) are regularly resulting from our acts of learning, or, if one prefers, from all of our conditioning," Cleckley writes. If anything, cutting-edge neurology research backs up this observation. Still, environment is just not supposed to matter. Cutting-edge work is, by definition, a thin wedge, while popular notions of neurology are broad. The situation replicates that of eugenics in the 1930s when the best scientists knew that eugenicists were peddling nonsense but were unable or unwilling to correct them publicly.

The *Bayh-Dole Act* enables universities to patent state-subsidized medicines to drug companies; previously they were in the public domain. A third or more of drugs "come from the tax-supported NIH or Universities and they are the most innovative ones."[55] The *Hatch-Waxman Act* in 1984 extended brand patents from eight to fourteen years. Combined profits for the ten drug companies in the Fortune 500 were more than the profits for all other 490 businesses put together—at least until the manufactured oil spike of the mid-2000s.[56] In 2002 the top ten U.S. drug companies had sales of 217 billion dollars, with 14 percent of spending going to research and development and 31 percent to "marketing and administration."[57] In August 1997 the Food and Drug Administration allowed drug companies to advertise directly to consumers with exquisite commercials promising bliss followed by a motor-mouthed whispered list of side effects or a superimposed sheet of small print of the same size as the Declaration of Independence.

After finagling federal largesse and license, these firms predictably are undergoing "a tidal wave of government investigations and civil and criminal lawsuits." Their first reaction is not to clean up their acts but to neutralize anyone and anything—gutting whistleblower protection and inserting tort "reform"—that impel them to clean up. The charges include "illegally overcharging Medicaid and Medicare, paying kickbacks to doctors, engaging in anticompetitive practices, colluding with generic companies to keep generic drugs off the market, illegally promoting drugs for unapproved uses, engaging in misleading advertising, and, of course, covering up the evidence. Some of the settlements have been huge," writes Marcia Angell.[58]

Prescription drugs are a $200 billion-plus business in the United States. In the low-inflation year 2000 prices rose 12 percent, several times the rise in cost of living, which means they drove up overall costs.[59] The vaunted drugs are derived mostly from taxpayer-funded research. Most new drugs, though, are forced variations on extant drugs so as to extend patent rights.[60] Half the largest drug companies are European. (Pfizer, Merck, Johnson and Johnson, Bristol-Meyers, Squibb, and Wyeth are American while GlaxoSmithKline and AstraZeneca are British, Novartis and Roche are Swiss, and Aventis is French.) In fact, it's the publicly sponsored research that lures foreign drug firms to locate in the United States, an investigator finds.[61]

A 1995 MIT study reports "that, of the 214 new drugs the industry identified as most medically significant in the preceding 25 years, 11 had their roots in studies paid by the government."[62] The pattern is that industry is feeding off basic research paid via NIH tax dollars. A 1997 study by the National Science Foundation looked at the most significant research papers cited on medicine patents and found that half were paid for with public funds, primarily from government and academia. Only 17 percent were bankrolled by industry. This means a huge slush fund remains for the hatching of marketing ploys.

The *New England Journal of Medicine* violated its own ethics by publishing articles by researchers with drug company ties.[63] The *Los Angeles Times* found in an analysis of thirty-six articles over 1997 to 1999 that eight articles were authored by people connected to drug companies that sold the very product they assessed. One is tempted to bring back the pillory and stocks for this misbehavior but a bit of hand-slapping is all that occurred. Medicine worldwide is not dominated, as yet, by slick opportunists. Thirteen leading medical journals recently assembled to chastise drug companies for distorting research for the sake of profits: "They tie up academic research with private contracts so they are unable to report freely [and] informed patient consent is a fabrication because they are not told who is in control of the trials."[64]

The FDA is not the watchdog the public imagines it to be but, as Eisenberg finds, "really exists to administer "proprietary rights in regulatory data, awarded to encourage certain kinds of innovation in drugs development, rather than to protect consumers from unsafe or ineffective drugs."[65] Of thirteen drugs withdrawn from the market between 1997 and 2004, seven were approved despite the objections of FDA safety reviewers.[66] The outcomes of drug experiments and tests "are negotiable, variable and subject to all manner of social variables," Angell finds. "Trials can be rigged in a dozen ways and it happens all the time."[67] Two-thirds of drug tests are industry funded and they are "four times as likely to be favorable as an independent inquiry."[68] Some 100,000 deaths a year stem from adverse drug reactions while one-and-a-half million people are harmed by drug reactions that require hospitalization—and 61,000 people have drug-induced Parkinsonism.[69] Is Freud worse?

It is shocking to read about a Government Accountability Office (GAO) report recommending that the FDA ought to be able to require drug makers, or its own commissioned groups, to conduct studies on the safety of existing drugs.[70] The reasons such powers do not exist stem from the origins and the dual purposes of these regulatory agencies—partly to protect the public from being poisoned and partly to perform as "*Good Housekeeping* seal of approval" marketing tools.[71] "The FDA's problems are systemic and cultural, not isolated or easily fixed," Senator Charles Grassley of Iowa sees. Fewer than a third of the follow-up studies promised to or by the FDA ever occur.

The regulatory climate is only marginally better in Britain, because the "New" Labour Party aped the neoliberal U.S. approach, which means letting industry alone, except for subsidies. "You could even say there is a positive disincentive to explore the data as fully as it could be explored," says Kent Woods, chief executive of the Medicines and Healthcare Products Regulatory Authority.[72] It turns out it was not legally possible for the regulatory staff to learn more than any company cared to tell them. Woods found GlaxoSmithKline had hidden negative data on its top-selling selective serotonin reuptake inhibitor (SSRI) drug Seroxat. The Authority banned the drug in 2005. In nine trials over 1994–2002 the first pair of trials showed no effect on depressed children and instead made some more suicidal.[73] It was the trials, not the drug, that were redesigned.

The Breggins cite a Yale study finding 50 percent of children age eight to sixteen developed behavioral abnormalities from taking Prozac.[74] They argue that these "anti-spunk" drugs mainly subdue mischievous or lively or unpliant kids, and they have a point. Downplayed in the pharmaceutical literature is "neuroleptic malignant syndrome" as a cumulative consequence of ingesting these drugs in the long term.[75] I have heard psychiatrists assert that these drugs exert a different effect on sane people than on disturbed, or brain disordered, people. How do they know? Have they sampled the elixirs?

Hyperactivity (attention-deficit/hyperactivity disorder [ADHD]) is the most common reason for prescribing drugs to kids. Yet there is no lesion associated with hyperactivity nor is there any evidence that it is a unitary affliction with a single cause, like a germ. The diagnosis rate ran up from 150,000 in the 1980s to 2,000,000 in the late 1990s—so whence the epidemic?[76] Inducements may have something to do with it. Poor people qualified for social security payment supplements if they had an ADHD kid. People so diagnosed were allowed untimed tests for the SATs—a boon that some canny affluent parents have signed up their children for in hope of making Harvard. But Ritalin, the iconic remedy, does not correct any known chemical imbalance. For all the ballyhoo otherwise, the brain is so dauntingly interrelated that it is impossible to localize the exact impact, and there is the utter failure to prove any brain abnormality in these cases even "after decades and tens of millions of research."[77] The "flattened emotional response" the kids often display is not an effect of a corrective drug experience, but of a chemical straitjacket laced tightly over a blurry psyche.

The search for what are regarded as scientific foundations is driven by a notion that Freud had the wits to abandon. The credo that every mental disorder has a somatic cause begs the question whether it is the mental state that causes somatic expressions or vice versa. For too many investigators the "vice versa" is not entertained as an alternate hypothesis, as one would in a genuine scientific investigation. Operating on the margin of a medical profession that credits only what is demonstrable on a dissecting table, a test tube, or a slide, psychiatry sought status on dubious terms that it instead should have been questioning.

The biopsychiatric paradigm and its devotees are awarded more leeway—the "seesaw" of standards—for error and inference than they ever grant a rival. That is the case with dominant paradigms. The effect of drugs on the central nervous system is inferred but it has no empirical support other than the eagerness of authorities to make the inference in the first place. The field of psychiatry is rife with the poor practices it accuses psychoanalysts of perpetrating, only they most certainly do it and they get away with it. That everything must have a physical cause is a belief, not a finding, which one can support to a degree as a guide, but not as an infallible one, and certainly not as a reason to ban inquires into other causative agents. Instead we get rote reaffirmations of the worst that the profession has to offer. Among Freud's foes, Crews at least has expressed skepticism toward pharmacological propaganda.[78]

SHOCK JOCKS

If you strike someone with a hammer under a doctor's prescription, because hitting a patient in a specific spot alters his or her behavior for the better, it would rate as a therapeutic act, if not a legal one. Indeed the Stanley Milgram experiments at Yale on obedience demonstrated that many people will do awful things if they believe they are doing it for sanctioned scientific purposes. (Mary Shelley need not take note.) Freud and kindred spirits opposed this inherent carte blanche tendency in psychiatric reasoning: anything goes if it cures or even looks like it does.

Electroshock, after a spell of disfavor, is back. Recent investigators remark that "the willingness of psychiatrists to promote electroshock for minors, in the absence of data to support this treatment, is paradoxical in the contemporary context and climate of 'evidenced-based' medicine."[79] Paradoxical is a kind word for what is happening. In the 1980s a policy climate of deinstitutionalization in mental health facilities—miserliness masquerading as benevolence—made electroshock as a quick cure seem attractive again. That is, powerful external agents, not the intrinsic merits of the technique itself, revived its use. The procedure accorded with the "biomedical model of mental life."[80] Following up on Bender's earlier sterling work, Ciardy and Rupf found that "half the kids were still hospitalized, and all 32 who had allegedly had temporary good effects from ECT relapsed in all cases."[81] Paradoxical, indeed.

Or it would be paradoxical if not for the obvious institutionalized seesaw of standards favoring a biomedical approach. In the United States in the 1990s an average of 3500 kids got ECT each year, and as the treatment of choice, not as a last resort.[82] Researchers find no evidence that it ever saved suicidal kids. Of 217 cases only 5 included a suicide threat. Horgan reports that "shock, which given to up to a hundred thousand Americans a year in the 1990s, apparently works about half the time," but that "87% regress within a year and usually within just 4 weeks."[83] The Breggins, who have documented painstakingly the NIMH "ideology of backing biomedical social control," find in the 1990s that of those one hundred thousand getting ECT every year, "the majority are women, and the elderly."[84]

Depression, more common among women, is always the exception for squeamish people who otherwise feel reluctant to apply shock treatment, but even then ECT helps 50 to 60 percent in the short term while 87 percent require another round of shocks within a year and usually within four months—facts which are carefully avoided, excluded, obscured, and overlooked.[85] Fewer than eight of every one thousand ECT patients stay well. Are psychotherapeutic results really supposed to be worse than this? Freud noted in 1920 that the ability to apply electric shocks insidiously appealed to the sadistic and punitive sides in authorities, who did not always resist such impulses.

Electroshock runs the gamut from well-meaning desperation to raw atrocities. The pre-apartheid South African Army tried to "cure" gays by electroconvulsion therapy, hormone treatment, and chemical castration.[86] Clockwork Orange–style, pictures of naked men were paired strategically with shock and then, presumably, naked women were shown without shocks. The full four-course treatment included narco analysis with "truth" serums and forced participation in gang rapes of Angolan women. The South African Army carried out fifty sex-change operations a year—from what to what else is not entirely clear. Shrinks electroshocked patients who had been administered LSD or Chlorpromazine.[87]

In a 1997 *New York Times* article headlined "A Journey Toward Independence: From Electric Shock to Glimmer of Hope for a Better Life," a reporter describes the electroshocking of a teen who "scratched at bugs under his skin."[88] Here caring people who were "determined to help the boy live on his own" approved it, so it must be okay: "Yes. The behavioral research institute used electric shock to get young people to alter dangerous behavior." What clearer definition of punitive use of shock is there? In an extreme case, one gets to try anything. In a center specializing in "aversive therapy" the boy was shocked for any of a litany of seventy-two actions, leading up to the scratching. We don't have the follow-up study with the usual relapse to report.

The media strives to portray technological and radical surgical procedures in the most radiant light. The *Chicago Tribune* recalled Egas Moniz's Nobel Prize in 1949 for "pioneering lobotomy," which he received because, as the reporter put it, "there was no other effective treatment for schizophrenia"! This typical journalistic portrayal blithely implies that the treatment was effective and assumes that no other approach mattered. The report more or less accurately concludes, "Today, some forms of psychosurgery are performed," but are quite rare.[89] It all depends on how many psychosurgeries you consider "rare." In the 2000s there are about three hundred psychosurgical operations every year to treat mental illnesses (down from a thousand a year in the 1950s).[90]

THE BLAME GENE

Daft genetic claims are everywhere. A recent specimen is the "loneliness gene" espied by researchers who conclude that 48 percent of the variation in human loneliness is due to genetics. "There probably is more than one loneliness gene, although no such gene has yet been identified," said a University of Chicago psychologist who was a coauthor of the study. The researchers found that loneliness genes in combination with life circumstances "likely determine how much loneliness a person feels."[91] Now there's an audacious statement.

An individual's loneliness genes determine to what extent such circumstances as losing a spouse though divorce or death, going to college, moving frequently, and becoming an immigrant cause loneliness. There simply is no way to parody the self-induced blindness in evidence here. Genes are the great one-stop-shop explanatory hope for somaticists. The eponymous chief of the J. Craig Venter Science Foundation believes finding the genetic component of human characteristics is "inevitable" and the danger is that we will find, after all, "we are not all created equal"—clearly relishing the prospect.[92] Such a society won't threaten him. Richard Dawkins resorts to computer malfunction analogies—not so different than the degenerative days of the Jukes—as a way of rubbing out responsibility for the defective soul, or for that matter, anyone. My genes made me do it. People, including scientists, believe these things—way out in front of any evidence this way or that—because they need to believe them.

Nothing about genetics is as simple as the media make out. As Keller explains, "Just how many other players—including regulatory sequences found elsewhere on the genome, the products of many other structural and regulatory genes, the complex signaling network of the living cell—are organized into a well-functioning and reliable whole is the question that dominates the attention of molecular biologists today."[93] Contrary to dystopian visions, "One might say that structural genomics has given us the insight we needed to confront our own hubris, insight that could illuminate the limits of the vision with which we began."[94]

The crucial turn toward genetic explanations, this stretch toward a genetic rather than environmental judgment, has political consequences. The notion that there is a gene "for" any single behavior is just bad science.[95] IQ heritability is put, at best, at a third, which leaves ample room for "inteferences."[96] There is no gene for loneliness or homosexuality or rudeness. One is sorely tempted, though, to hypothesize a gene for believing in single-gene explanations.

One of the capital crime charges leveled at psychoanalysis is that it trades in the blame game, that is, it points fingers when all adults are supposed to know nobody is to blame. This is a commercial society's self-serving ideology of exculpation, a paean to irresponsibility and especially scientific irresponsibility. The blame problem stems not from psychoanalysis itself but from puritanical American finger-pointing urges, relieving the finger-pointers of any need to examine themselves and their own role in their plights.

The fact that "blame" in the case of psychoanalysis is a means, not an end, escapes the average human being, or foe of Freud. If you can't zero in on the source, you can't come to grips with the changes needed to heal the wounds you carry. The fact is that analysts, and therapists of most descriptions, will help you deal with your impressions of what you experienced and not assume that they necessarily reflect solid reality. The reality is irrelevant to the fact that you experienced feelings and emotions in a harmful way. You own up to those feelings to understand how you can break out of the deleterious patterns you are in.

To brush aside a person's painful upbringing, whether due to abuse or exaggerated harm, is to be wildly unscientific. Consider the suffering inside families (often aggravated by economic or other insecurities) and compare it to the claim that physiology determines everything.[97] All the family tragedies in motion in the world are not responsible for deranged or damaged kids. That people cannot drive other people crazy is one of the comforting messages that biopsychiatry brings, and one of the greatest lies.

The notion of destigmatization for legal drug users, especially "unruly" children, is another great lie, an institutional deceit. The stigma merely takes another form. The belief that unruly children have a brain disease is a policy at the National Institute of Mental Health[98] in a land where 20 percent (up to third in cities) of children are raised in poverty, which itself is socially imposed abuse; parents struggle as the workweek has lengthened since the 1970s; and two in three families have both parents working because they have to. These are the benevolent results of policies hatched by family values–bleating yahoos who have ushered wealth and income to the very top over the last thirty years.[99] Who ignores these factors more—psychoanalysts or biopsychiatrists—would be an interesting debate.

Mental disorders among children and adolescents are on the rise.[100] These include childhood autism, autistic spectrum disorder, Tourette syndrome, and hyperkinetic disorder, which tripled in diagnoses at age five between 1992 and 1999. Here is a mad-hatter medical methodology, abetted by the complaisant media, at work. James Randerson cites data showing that, applying the same criteria for autism to every child in a British district over two periods (1992–1995 and 1996–1998), the prevalence of autism was unchanged.

This finding, however, occurred during a surge in autism diagnoses. One marvels as the reporter says this discrepancy suggests that although "the actual rate of autism in the community is staying the same" the "doctors are just getting better at recognizing it." Hence the "surge," even though there are no grounds for it. A member of the Institute of Psychiatry at King's College London chimed in that, "They have no way of distinguishing between [autism] having got more common and their clinicians having got better at recognizing it." No third option—such as misdiagnosing or overdiagnosing—is allowed.

As Mannheim writes, we choose our problems, and evaluate them, according to the interests we bring to the fray.[101] The average citizen mistakenly may believe that someone somewhere is objective and willing to confront results that fly in the face of expectations. But the truth is that doctors are not immunized against succumbing to unacknowledged biases. If anything, it is their biases that are immunized. We know that medical authorities like to put people in a context "that needs no further explanation": the disorder made him do it This robust tendency resembles an institutional Tourette syndrome where the institution provides profanities in the form of drug treatment no matter what the situation is and how inappropriate the response to it.

Thornton ominously says that the American Psychoanalytic Association conducted a survey of its membership the results of which were so disappointing that it refused to release them.[102] Perhaps. Everyone has their troubles. But Freud's foes might glance at the American Medical Association's problems since the onset of the pharmaceutical revolution. Over the last thirty years doctors have seen their autonomy erode, their prestige fall, and their competence challenged. Fewer are self-employed due to the prohibitive costs of starting an office, high malpractice premiums, and paperwork avalanches. Almost half say they would not enter medicine as a career again.

The reporter says the physicians get "little sympathy from government leaders and private organizations that are trying to slow the rise in medical cost, which are largely determined by physicians' decisions"—which is not the case, but it suits the view of media owners. The HMOs' aggressive practices triumphed, with the side effect that 72 percent of doctors say the public respects them less than a decade earlier.[103] Managed care, for reasons of insurance and economy, tends to be drug pushing to the exclusion of psychotherapy. That drugs also happen to cause brain disabilities is omitted from most reporting. None of this helps build trust in doctors who now are so subservient to the HMO bottom line.

The celebrative reporting of psychiatric research in textbooks promotes an otherwise weak biopsychiatric case.[104] In a vivid demonstration of the standards seesaw at work, Joseph examines a set of textbooks on portrayals of schizophrenia adoption studies—regarded wrongly as clinching the case for genetic explanations—and finds them permeated by what the publishers expected would be found in line with the dominant psycho-pharmacological paradigm and not what the studies, critically considered, actually had to say. Joseph finds that all scientific doubts about validity went unaddressed in textbooks. Indeed, the degree of shoddiness and bias on display in their pages makes anything the greatest Freudian charlatan imaginable is accused of pale by comparison.

These were not blind studies; adoptees mostly came from substandard homes or orphanages where unacknowledged harm was inflicted. The studies never reached statistical significance or rejected the null hypothesis.[105] A reanalysis disconfirmed the data yet the textbook said otherwise. In sum, Joseph finds a "failure to critically assess the original researcher's methods and conclusions, overreliance on secondary sources, a failure to discuss published critiques of the schizophrenia adoption studies; inaccuracy in reporting original findings, and a failure to discuss how the potentially invalidating environmental factor confounds the boasted conclusions." Ultimately, Joseph concludes that "without a theoretical or social content psychology erodes into technique."[106] Just so.[107]

The great exception to somatic determinism is supposedly posttraumatic stress disorder (PTSD), which was included in *DSM-IV* in 1980 as "a historical product."[108] PTSD starts out "as a psychological phenomenon," but one which causes the endocrinal system to overproduce hormones and chemicals that wear down the body. After Vietnam, 22.9 percent of high-combat veterans had digestive problems, 21.4 percent had urinary or genital problems, and 15.4 percent had arthritis—all much higher percentages than in those with low-combat experience.[109] This portrayal of the etiological path of PTSD differs from original theories in which literal shock waves caused the condition, reflecting the indelible neurological bias. For the sufferers in World War I who encountered them, "most any doctor believed that heredity and constitution have a determining effect 'in cases of war neuroses.'"[110] Yet when PTSD fought its way into the *DSM-IV*, it nonetheless was impelled to resort to an essentially biological framework of mental disorder.[111]

This raises the issue of the politics of professional bias in crafting the *DSM*, regarded as the bible of the psychiatric industry largely because the insurance industry insists on it.[112] *DSM-III* was seen as "a coup for neo-Kraepelinians."[113] For when the first *DSM* was composed in 1952, Adolf Meyer's psychodynamic approach influenced the field as much as psychoanalysis, and together their adherents made a space for themselves. *DSM-II* in 1968 preserved room for psychodynamic approaches. Most experts who prepared *DSM-IV* (2004), however, were exposed later for their dodgy relations with drug companies. Fifty-six percent of 170 *DSM* panel members had ties to pharmaceutical companies via research grants, as consultants (22 percent), and as speakers' bureau fodder (16 percent)—activities not thought worth mentioning. One hundred percent—yes, 100 percent—of the experts overseeing sections on mood disorders and schizophrenia had drug-firm ties. (Psychiatric drug sales amounted to $20.3 billion for mood disorders alone in 2004.) Officials ritualistically defended the experts as possessing, despite the heady emoluments, "impeccable integrity."[114] For the next revision, due in 2011, the APA promises full disclosure. Ah, but Freud is worse, isn't he?

One can count on Crews to leap to the defense of entrepreneurial *DSM* revisers, burbling that it could not possibly be that biopsychiatric biases and pharmacological allurements were in any way responsible for faults in the 1980 and 1994 editions. Perish this thought process. The "APA leadership's intentions in the late 1970s had nothing to do with pushing drugs and everything to do with lending greater scientific credibility to the psychiatric field."[115] So trust these guys. Crews has worked dauntlessly to identify scientific credibility with biological psychiatry. Even stranger in a Strangelovian way is Crews's peremptory dismissal of a critic of Big Pharma and the contemporary *DSM* (Christopher Lane) as "not a psychiatrist but a psychoanalytically inclined literary critic"—as was Crews himself, and which Crews remains, sans the "psychoanalytically inclined" part.

CONCLUSION

The record of psychiatry, even modern twenty-first-century psychiatry, is hardly as admirable as Freud's foes would wish it. Physicians do not seem to behave ethically because they are physicians but quite often in spite of it, because they somehow managed to hold on to a preceding set of values. But of course almost any psychologist, let alone psychoanalyst, could have told them that values formed late in life have little purchase. They are—exceptions always exist—prone enough to succumb to fashion, flattery, or bribery to make a used-car salesman look like the Dalai Lama.

Just as every profession has its paragons, so every profession has its dark side. Students of the history of science appreciate this inevitable mixture of motives in "real-world" research—this blend of paradigmatic dogmatism together with an eye for self-aggrandizing "breakthroughs"—with or without quotes. What is outrageous is the pretense by Freud's foes that psychoanalysis must be a pseudoscience when medicine is supposedly a pure enterprise populated by saints inside benevolent institutions, particularly in the United

States, where they are content to let you die or bankrupt you if your insurance is not in order.

NOTES

1. Leo Kanner, *In Defense of Mothers* (Springfield, IL: C. C. Thomas, 1950), p. 66.

2. Peter Breggin and Ginger Breggin, *The War against Children* (New York: St. Martin's Press, 1996), p. 60.

3. Mark S. Micale and Roy Porter, eds., *Discovering the History of Psychiatry* (New York: Oxford University Press, 1994), p. 711.

4. "Psychiatry and Schizophrenia: A Conversation with Robin Murray," in *What Scientists Think*, ed. Jeremy Stangroom (London: Routledge, 2005).

5. Judith Graham, "Top Mental Health Guide Questioned," *Chicago Tribune*, 20 April 2006.

6. Peter Breggin and Ginger Breggin, *Reclaiming Our Children* (New York: Perseus Books, 2000), pp. 2, 19. The president praised biopsychiatrists for working with violent children and for getting at the "biological brain disease"—treatable with psychiatric drugs even though one Littleton gunman was on Luvox and T. J. Solomon who killed six kids in Georgia was on Ritalin. So was Kip Kinkel in the Oregon shooting.

7. Breggin and Breggin, *Reclaiming Our Children*, p. 17.

8. Robert Epstein,"Discussion; Does Psychiatry Have a Split Personality?" from PBS, *Closer to Truth*, http://66.102.11.104/search?q=cache:DdIeiqtwybkJ:www.pbs.org/kcet/closertotruth/transcripts/309_psychiatry.pdf+%22peter+loewenberg%22&hl=en&ie=UTF-8/.

9. Freud, "Analysis Terminable and Interminable," *SE*, 23:216.

10. Breggin and Breggin, *Reclaiming Our Children*, p. 20.

11. Edward Tenner, *Why Things Bite Back* (New York: Knopf, 1996), p. 67.

12. Adolf Grunbaum, *The Foundations of Psychoanalysis: A Philosophical Critique* (Berkeley: University of California Press, 1984), p. 156.

13. Harold Koplewicz, *It's Nobody's Fault: New Hope and Help for Difficult Children* (New York: Random House, 1996).

14. Robert Weissman, "Letting Drugs Firms Market to Consumers Is Bad Medicine," *Chicago Sun-Times*, 22 May 2008, p. 31.

15. See Melody Petersen, *Our Daily Meds* (New York: Farrar, Straus and Giroux, 2008).

16. Breggin and Breggin, *War against Children*, p. 33.

17. Johan Leff, *Unbalanced Mind* (London: Weidenfeld & Nicolson, 2000), p. 4.

18. Michael Nunberg, "Why Psychiatrists in India Prescribe so Many Drugs," *Culture, Medicine and Psychiatry* 20, no. 2 (June 1996): 160. ECT is also "given to half the patients, 3 to 5 times a week" (p. 168).

19. On professional psychiatry and psychology associations and the question of torture see Frank Summers, "The American Psychological Association, and the In-

volvement of Psychologists at Guantanamo Bay," *Psychoanalysis, Culture and Society* 12 (April 2007): 83–92.

20. See Russell Jacoby, *The Repression of Psychoanalysis* (Chicago: University Of Chicago Press, 1986), and Bruno Bettelheim, *Freud and Man's Soul* (London: Penguin, 1980).

21. Wilhelm Reich, *Sex-Pol: Essays, 1929–1934* (New York: Random House, 1972), pp. 3–37.

22. Cited in David Healy, *Let Them Eat Prozac* (New York: Knopf, 2004), p. 14.

23. See Thomas Roder, et al., *Psychiatrists: The Men behind Hitler* (Los Angeles: Freedom Publishers, 1995).

24. Breggin and Breggin, *War against Children*, p. 82.

25. Oliver Sacks, *The Man Who Mistook His Wife for a Hat* (London: Picador, 1985), pp. 1–2.

26. See Sigmund Freud, *On Aphasia* (New York: International Universities Press, 1953).

27. Ernest Gellner, *The Psychoanalytic Movement* (London: Fontana, 1985), p. 6.

28. Edward Shorter, *A History of Psychiatry* (New York: John Wiley & Sons, 1997), p. 324.

29. Breggin and Breggin, *War against Children*, p. 89.

30. Gardiner Harris and Benjamin Carey, "Child Experts Fail to Reveal Full Drug Pay," *New York Times*, 8 June 2008. "Some 500,000 children and teenagers were given at least one prescription for an antipsychotic in 2007, including 20,500 under 6 years of age, according to Medco Health Solutions, a pharmacy benefit manager."

31. Jean Hamilton, Margaret F. Jensvold, Esther P. Rothenblum, and Ellen Cole, eds., *Psychopharmacology From a Feminist Perspective* (New York: Haworth Press, 1995), p. 80.

32. Ray Moynihan and Cassels, "A Disease for Every Pill," *Nation*, 17 October 2005, p. 22.

33. Moynihan and Alan Cassels, "A Disease for Every Pill," p. 22.

34. Breggin and Breggin, *War Against Children*, p. 29.

35. Benjamin Carey and Gardiner Harris, "Psychiatric Group Faces Scrutiny over Drug Company Ties," *New York Times*, 20 July 2008.

36. *Chicago Tribune,* 14 January 1996. "'I cannot prove my theory conclusively, said [Dr. Anneliese] Pontius, 'But I think if people start to apply this theory to pointless violent crimes, we may find more and more people who fit this pattern.'" No doubt we will. So what?

37. R. D. Laing, *The Divided Self* (London: Penguin, 1965), pp. 30–31.

38. Vernon Mark and Frank Erwin, *Violence and the Brain* (New York, Harper & Row, 1970).

39. Elliot S. Valenstein, *Blaming the Brain: The Truth about Drugs and Mental Health* (New York: Free Press, 1998), p. 206.

40. Valenstein, *Blaming the Brain*, p. 54. Also see G. A. Ross and A. Pen, *Pseudoscience in Biological Psychiatry* (New York: Wiley, 1995).

41. Peter Breggin, *Brain-Disabling Treatments* (New York: Springer, 1997), p. 21.

42. Philip Morowski, "'Johnny's in the Basement, Mixin' Up the Medicine,' Review of Angell, Avorn and Daemmrich on the Modern Pharmaceutical Predicament," *Social Studies of Science* 37, no. 2 (April 2007).

43. Joan Didion, *The Year of Magical Thinking* (New York: Knopf, 2005), p. 48.

44. Edward Shorter, *A History of Psychiatry: From the Era of the Asylum to the Age of Prozac* (New York: John Wiley & Sons, 1997), p. 246.

45. Healy, *Let Them Eat Prozac*, p. 9.

46. George Monbiot, "The Corporate Stooges Who Nobble Serious Science," *Guardian*, 24 February 2004.

47. Valenstein, *Blaming the Brain*, pp. 5, 54.

48. Grunbaum, *The Foundations of Psychoanalysis*, p. 27.

49. Valenstein, *Blaming the Brain*, p. 33.

50. Valenstein, *Blaming the Brain*, p. 34.

51. "The Battle over Child Behavior," *New York Times*, 4 April 2000.

52. See Ivan Illich, *Medical Nemesis* (New York: Pantheon, 1966).

53. Valenstein, *Blaming The Brain*, p. 127.

54. Hervey Cleckley, *The Mask of Sanity*, rev. ed. (New York: New American Library, 1982), p. 467.

55. See "Rx R&D: Myths: The Case against the Drug Industry's R& D 'Scare' Card," *Public Citizen*, July 2001, www.citizen.org.

56. Marcia Angell, "The Truth about the Drug Companies," *New York Review of Books*, 15 July 2004, p. 55.

57. Ben Goldacre, "Bad Science: Evil Ways of the Drug Companies," *Guardian*, 4 August 2007.

58. Goldacre, "Bad Science," p. 57.

59. Goldacre, "Bad Science," p. 52.

60. Angell notes the dubious classification of "new molecular entities" merely mean the drug composition is not in that exact molecular form already out in the market. "Priority review" refers to those which have potential for significant improvement. The two together seem to be scientific innovations: the number of U.S. drugs meriting these classes are sixteen in 1998, nineteen in 1999, nineteen in 2000, nine in 2001, and seven in 2002.

61. Angell, "The Truth about Drug Companies," p. 52.

62. "Drug Makers Reap Profits from Tax-backed Research," *New York Times*, 23 April 2000, pp. 1 and 20.

63. Terence Monmaney, "Med Journal's Ethics Questioned," *Chicago Sun-Times*, 21 October 1999, p. 36. "Among the articles questioned in the drug therapy series was a 1997 review of multiple sclerosis treatments. The lead author, Dr. Richard A. Rudnick of the Cleveland Clinic Foundation, received research money, speaking fees and travel expenses from three drug companies whose treatments were discussed in the article, he said in an interview. In another instance, the author of a 1998 review of breast cancer treatments, Dr. Gabriel N. Hortobagyi of the University of Texas, said he had received consulting fees, research money, and speaking fees from multiple companies that make drugs assessed in his article."

64. "Doctors or Drug Companies," *Guardian*, 10 September 2003.

65. Rebecca Eisenberg, "Patents, Product Exclusivity, and Information Dissemination," *Fordham Law Review* 72 (2003): 482.

66. Alicia Mundy, "Risk Management: The FDA's Deference to Drug Companies Is Bad for America's Health," *Harper's*, September 2004, pp. 83–84.

67. Marcia Angell, *The Truth about the Drug Companies* (New York: Random House, 2004), p. 95.

68. Darian Leader, "Prozac: Is This the End?" *Guardian*, 27 February 2008.

69. Sidney Wolfe "Worst Pills, Best Pills," *EXTRA* 14, no. 2 (March/April 2001): 11.

70. Andrew Bridges, "GAO Report Recommends New Powers for the FDA," *Chicago Sun-Times*, 24 April 2006.

71. See Grant McConnell, *Private Power and American Democracy* (New York: Knopf, 1966).

72. Sarah Boseley and David Leigh, "Watchdog Voices Dismay at Failure to Police Industry," *Guardian*, 7 March 2008.

73. Sarah Boseley, "Drug Can Trigger Suicide in Adults," *Guardian*, 22 August 2005.

74. Breggin and Breggin, *Reclaiming our Children*, p. 157.

75. Breggin and Breggin, *Reclaiming our Children*, p. 300.

76. Sydney Walker, *The Hyperactivity Hoax* (New York: St. Martin's Press, 1996), p. 17. Kurt Cobain had been on Ritalin for "being bright and overactive."

77. Breggin, *Brain-Disabling Treatments in Psychiatry*, p. 5.

78. Frederick Crews, "Talking Back to Prozac," *New York Review of Books,* 6 December 2007, p. 14. A review of Allan Horwitz and Jerome Wakefield (*The Loss of Sadness*), Christopher Lane (*Shyness: How Normal Behavior became a Sickness*), and Healy, *Let Them Eat Prozac*.

79. Steve Baldwin and Melissa Oxlad, *Electroshock and Minors: A Fifty Year Review* (Westport, CT: Greenwood Press, 2000), p. 4.

80. See Lauretta Bender and M. D. Keeler, "The Body Language of Schizophrenic Children following Electroshock," *American Journal of Orthopsychiatry* 22 (1952): 335–55, and Lauretta Bender, "One Hundred Cases of Childhood Schizophrenia Treated with Electric Shock," in *Transactions of the American Neurological Association* 72 (1947): pp. 165–69.

81. M. D. Ciardy and M. D. Rupf, "The Effect of Electroshock on Children having Schizophrenic Symptoms," *Psychiatric Quarterly* 28 (1954).

82. Ciardy and Rupf, "The Effect of Electroshock," p. 104.

83. Horgan, *The Undiscovered Mind: How the Human Brain Defies Replication, Medication, and Explanation* (New York: Free Press, 1999), p. 134.

84. Breggin, *Toxic Psychiatry: Why Therapy, Empathy and Love Must Replace the Drugs, Electroshock, and Biochemical Theories of the "New Psychiatry"* (New York: St. Martin's Press, 1994), pp. 130–34.

85. Horgan, *Undiscovered Mind*, p. 134.

86. Chris McGreal, "Gays Tell of Mutilation in Apartheid Army," *Guardian*, 29 July 2007.

87. Valenstein, *Blaming the Brain*, 208.

88. N. R. Kleinfield, "A Journey Toward Independence," *New York Times*, 23 June 1997, pp. A13–A14.

89. Mark Jacobs, "10 Things You Might Not Know about the Nobel Prize," Perspectives, *Chicago Tribune*, 14 October 2007, p. 4.

90. El-Hai, *The Lobotomist*, p. 310. "New operations target not just prefrontal lobotomy but also the cingulate gyrus, amygdala and their connecting networks; Neuroscientists amassed evidence that an individual's emotional response was not simply a product of communication between the thalamus and the prefrontal lobe but involved the entire limbic system, the central region of the brain that play a role in mood and attitude" (p. 291). More room to play.

91. Jim Ritter, "Genes May Be to Blame for Loneliness," *Chicago Sun-Times*, 11 November 2005, p. 36.

92. Alok Kha "Gene Discoveries Highlight Dangers Facing Society," *Guardian*, 2 January 2006.

93. Evelyn Fox Keller, *The Century of the Gene* (Cambridge, MA: Harvard University Press, 2000), p. 72.

94. Keller, *The Century of the Gene*, p. 8.

95. Kurt Jacobsen, "The Mystique of Genetic Correctness," *Logos: A Journal of Modern Society & Culture*, Winter/Spring 2007.

96. British Medical Association, *Human Genetics: Choice and Responsibility* (Oxford: Oxford University Press, 1998), citing a 1997 issue of *Nature* (388).

97. See Russell Jacoby, *Social Amnesia: A Critique of Contemporary Psychology from Adler to Laing* (Boston: Beacon Press, 1975).

98. Breggin, *Reclaiming Our Children*, p. 73. Also see www.breggin.com.

99. See David Cay Johnson, *Perfectly Legal* (New York: Portfolio, 2003).

100. James Randerson, "Study Shows Increase in Mental Disorders among Children," *Guardian*, 6 February 2007.

101. See Karl Mannheim, *Ideology and Utopia* (London: Routledge & Kegan Paul, 1936).

102. E. M. Thornton, *Freud and Cocaine: The Freudian Fallacy* (London: Blond & Briggs, 1983), p. 8.

103. Lawrence K. Altman, "Changes in Medicine Being Pain to Healing Profession," *New York Times*, 18 February 1990.

104. Jay Joseph, "Paradigms, Textbooks and Psychiatric Research: Inaccuracy and Bias in Textbooks Reporting Psychiatric Research: The Case of the Schizophrenia Adoption Studies," *Politics and the Life Sciences* 1, March 2000.

105. Joseph, "Paradigms, Textbooks and Psychiatric Research," p. 92.

106. Jacoby, *Social Amnesia*, p. xxii.

107. Joseph, "Paradigms, Textbooks and Psychiatric Research."

108. Allen Young, *Harmony of Illusions* (Princeton, NJ: Princeton University Press, 1997), p. 5.

109. John Dudley Miller, "Vietnam Vets Battle Illness," *ABC News*, n.d., http://www.11thcavnam.com/main/stress.htm.

110. Mark Micale and Paul Lerner, *Traumatic Pasts: History, Psychiatry and Trauma in the Modern Age, 1870–1930* (Cambridge: Cambridge University Press, 2001), p. 19.

111. Ben Shephard, *War of Nerves: Soldiers and Psychiatrists in the Twentieth Century* (Cambridge: MA: Cambridge University Press, 2001), p. 387.

112. The authors of a recent survey of the DSM ask whether professionals are too busy "inventing justifications for its use" rather than engaging in the understanding of mental illness. See Karen Eriksen and Victoria E. Kress, *Beyond the DSM Story* (New York: Sage Publications, 2004), p. x.

113. Young, *Harmony of Illusions*, p. 101.

114. Judith Graham, "Top Mental Health Guide Questioned," *Chicago Tribune*, 20 April 2006.

115. Frederick Crews, "Talking Back to Prozac," p. 14.

Chapter Six

Short Cuts to Tall Tales

> The more formal thinking becomes the more likely it is to provide short cuts from one area of ignorance to another.
>
> —Vladimir Nabokov[1]

Soma, the lotus-eater drug of Aldous Huxley's *Brave New World*, is an antique. Psychiatrist Robert Coles ruefully observed over a decade ago that even then he hardly knew anyone who was not either on medication themselves or was close to someone who was. I know of a psychiatrist who prescribed for his family the same feel-good drugs that patients swallow. One envisions the TV commercial with the shrink spooning out meds along with dessert at the dinner table. Indeed, one hardly can touch the topic of legal drugs at a dinner party without people sagely piping up that there really are some folks who need to be jacked up on very high doses—and somehow that makes it all okay.

Oliver James, an otherwise perceptive therapist, recommends dosing everyone with serotonin uplifters.[2] James is under the impression that SSRIs "increase realism"—that is, raise awareness of "real problems and make it less likely that people will buy into false solutions." To boot, the "psychic changes [SSRIs] bring about are almost exactly the ones required to make most people feel fulfilled." Feeling fulfilled, then, is almost as good as becoming fulfilled through actual accomplishments, or through managing to live a decent life in a crass universe. Any junkie can tell you that. The downside nonetheless is that feeling high esteem does not mean that anyone outside the striking range of your ego shares your opinion of yourself. It is a therapeutic act to induce mild delusional states in people, so long as they are ones of well-being, or can be passed off as such.

Aren't drugs fast and therapy slow? Is there not a happy medium for their applications? In the 1960s psychoanalyst Franz Alexander and Sheldon Selesnick urged a "kind of theory of complementarity" like that of physicists for psychiatry so as to interweave the psychological and the somatic. "Brain chemistry cannot be isolated from man, from what is at the core of his existence, his personality," they wrote. "Brain chemistry, indeed, can be altered by emotional stress, by anxiety, rage, fear and hopelessness."[3] Even then the best scientists were alert, contrary to the legion of vulgarizers, that this was true. The authors urged that "the integration of brain chemistry with psychology is the principal task which psychiatry is facing in our era." Instead, biopsychiatry shoved psychology unceremoniously aside.

Today's biopsychiatrists, Roazen cautions, "seem humane in their willingness to recommend various drugs, but any system of therapy can be used for keeping patients at a distance; the Diagnostic and Statistical Manual is too often misused for purposes of pigeon-holing, rather than helping, patients."[4] (Freud never doubted that the relationship with the analyst was the premier element in what was ultimately a "cure through love.") The "neurological approach has won the day," a Freud basher proclaims.[5] It certainly has in the realm of publicity. A *New York Times* hack can report the intriguingly abridged opinion of the director of the Schizophrenic Genetics Research program at the University of Chicago that the Nazis are to blame for "irresponsibly" linking schizophrenia to genetics.[6] Nazis, alas, made life tough for true scientists. The aggrieved director proposes to do this linking responsibly and, evidently, no matter what the case may actually be. Scientists know what they are going to find.

The easy compromise notion that "a combination of psychotherapy plus medication represents the most effective of all approaches" ought to be viewed with considerable suspicion anyway.[7] "The possibility of prescribing medication," Dr. Elio Fratorroli argues, "fosters the tendency to bring premature closure to an encounter" and that there is "an automatic assumption that in the face of the unknown the doctor should take control." Psychiatrists "get to know patients only well enough to match their diagnoses with the latest statistical outcome studies. When psychiatry is substituting statistics for Menschenkennen [an understanding of the person], it is hardly surprising that the Church of Scientology is flourishing."[8]

The overwhelming majority of patients are not violent, suicidal, or threatening, so why should one assume that drugging them is good for therapy? The short-range objective—a quiet or quiescent patient—is the familiar criterion stretching back to the first nervous asylum managers. Is what is good for administrators also good for therapy? There is no obvious reason to suppose that drugs automatically are a boon. Apart from a perpetual Big Pharma advertising blitz financed by overpricing consumers, this assumption stems from the fact that many HMOs pay 80 percent cost of drugs and, at best, only a quarter to half the cost of therapy.[9]

PSYCHED OUT

In August 2004 an NIMH study showed Prozac and cognitive behavior therapy together to be most effective for treating depression in adolescents. The NIMH research divided 439 adolescents into four groups: those given Prozac alone; those given Prozac plus cognitive behavior therapy (CBT—a short-term, quick-hit form of psychotherapy); those given placebo plus CBT; and those given placebo alone.[10] Over three months (not a span relevant to psychoanalytic treatment), 71 percent of the Prozac plus CBT patients allegedly improved. So did 60 percent of those taking Prozac alone, 43 percent with CBT alone, and 35 percent of those on placebos.[11] NIMH director Thomas Insel pronounced it a "landmark study" because "it's the largest publicly funded study and the only study this size that doesn't have pharmaceutical funding." But all is never what it seems in studies which exclude or downplay unwelcome data. As an independent journalist notices,[12]

> Insel would have been accurate if he'd said the NIMH study didn't get direct funding from the pharmaceutical industry. But lead investigator John March of Duke University Medical Center is on the Eli Lilly payroll, and five of his 10 co-authors also get drug-company grants. Few stories about the study even mentioned a higher incidence of harmful behavior among teens taking Prozac (11.9%) compared to those on placebo (5.4%) and CBT alone (4.5%). [And] few stories mentioned that teenagers to whom suicidal thoughts had occurred had been excluded from the study before it began.

Similar discoveries of selective reporting were found in the case of Paxil (GlaxoSmithKline) in 2001 with regard to suicide risk.[13] Meanwhile, the corporate version of the Prozac report, which is all the public hears, was wonderful news for CBT therapists and better news for Eli Lilly, which can market its product as indispensable to the conduct of psychotherapy, which allegedly isn't any better than Prozac alone.

Nonetheless, the public wants counseling, not drugs, by a 75 percent to 25 percent rate.[14] A 1995 *Consumer Reports* survey of four thousand people found that psychotherapy was the preferred route, fared better than drugs, and, contrary to the compromised NIMH report, much better than drugs plus talk (with 90 percent saying they improved using psychotherapy alone).[15] But, as Valenstein says with an implied sigh, today psychologists are "fighting to prescribe drugs" (which will boost drug company sales) and recently won that dubious right in New Mexico.[16] These would-be prescribers cannot help but be influenced by checkbook science and insurance company practices. (A survey of social workers, for instance, found 59 percent using *DSM* medical disorder diagnoses, and found that 86 percent used such categories for marital and family discords, that is, "massaging diagnoses" in order to get them to pay up.)[17]

"Checkbook science" is unpaid advertising.[18] The public relations firms, such as Excepta Medica, plant stories in medical journals by hiring physicians to do so and run speakers' bureaus by which to dish out honoraria and expenses to pliable MDs. The diet pill combination fen-phen, with seven million consumers, was yanked from the market in 1997 when it was linked to heart valve damage, but not before the manufacturer Wyeth-Ayerst issued studies to defend and publicize its product. The unreliability of industry studies of breast implants was known long before government action was taken. So too was the case with hormone replacement therapy. A *New York Times* headline on July 1, 2002, read "Hormone Replacement Study a Shock to the Medical System." An investigator complains, though, that

> Most media covered the story as if this was enormous news that came out of nowhere. The truth is quite different. For several years, article after article published in major medical journals had described the growing evidence that hormone replacement therapy increased the risk of breast cancer and did not help and possibly hurt women with heart disease. Although some of these studies were covered in major newspapers, without a PR machine behind them they received limited media attention.[19]

SPLITTING THE DIFFERENCE?

Luhrmann analyzes "two cultures" in psychiatry—the psychodynamic and psychopharmacological approaches—for which "halfies" might be the ideal solution; that is, blending potent therapeutic ingredients from both sides, as Alexander and Selesnick earlier urged.[20] Because there is no specific pathology, or any test, for any major mental illness, cultural values and professional inclinations shape the picture of whatever the psychiatrist beholds.[21] It is not that mental illness is a myth exactly, but just how problems are treated depends on diagnostic constructs that professionals bring to the fray. The plight now is that "a combination of socio-economic forces and ideology is driving psychotherapy out of psychiatry."[22] For example, "some insurance companies will not cover an inpatient unless the psychiatrist prescribes medications," in which cases the insurance company bookkeepers indirectly but powerfully are skewing clinical practices and, ultimately, professional training. "In fact, what people really have now," a psychiatrist observes, "is very limited benefits through an HMO, which might give them 10 sessions a year that might be 15-minute session."[23]

Given the upper hand biopsychiatry has regained, training in therapy has diminished over the last few decades from the status of a grudging component to a frill. "It has become standard practice in the US for you to get your drugs from a pharmacologist and to get therapy from a psychologist or counselor paid at a lower rate," David Healy finds. "This split is, I would have thought, disastrous. It means that the people who monitor the impact of therapy on you are not trained at all to know about the hazards of that therapy."[24]

A veteran psychiatrist recalls "the diagnostic and statistical manual lays out a set of criteria for every mental illness and, when we put them down, we thought, well, this'll help standardize things, clarify, create reliability, but what's in fact happened is that they've become reified over the course of the last 20 years, and people think these are absolutes handed down from God, and again, the Board Certification systems, when they test young psychiatrists, they're expected to have memorized all these silly criteria and, basically, increasingly, their interviews are limited to asking about the signs and symptoms in those criteria and they don't ask about the people. But, most of our young psychiatrists aren't trained that way and that is a, you know, a real loss."[25]

If anyone imagine that shrinks today typically are interested in subtle diagnoses, arrived at through sensitively conducted communication with distressed patients, a perusal of the eye-watering titles from one issue of the prestigious *American Journal of Psychiatry* (February 2006), devoted to bipolar disorder sufferers, may prove sobering.

> Treatment-Resistant Bipolar Depression: A STEP-BD Equipoise Randomized Effectiveness Trial of Antidepressant Augmentation with Lamotrigine, Inositol, or Resperidone
>
> Predictors of Recurrence in Bipolar Disorder: Primary Outcomes from the Systematic Treatment Enhancement Program for Bipolar Disorder
>
> Risk of Switch in Mood Polarity to Hypomania or Mania in Patients with Bipolar Depression during Acute and Continuation Trials of Venlafaxine, Sentraline, and Buproprion as Adjuncts to Mood Stabilizers.
>
> Randomized Placebo-controlled Trial of Olanzapine as Maintenance Therapy in Patients with Bipolar Disorder
>
> Risk and Resilience Markers in Bipolar Disorder: Brain Responses to Emotional Challenge in Bipolar Patients and the Healthy Siblings

Linear Relationship of Valproate Serum Concentration
to Response and Optimal Serum Levels for Acute Mania

Laboratory-Observed Behavioral Disinhibition
in the Young Offspring of Parents with Bipolar
Disorder: A High-Risk Pilot Study

Basal Ganglia Shape Alterations in Bipolar Disorder

Neurocognitive Function in Unmedicated
Manic and Medicated Euthymic Pediatric Bipolar Patients

Lower Switch Rate in Depressed Patients with
Bipolar II than Bipolar 1 Disorder Treated Adjunctively
with Second-Generation Antidepressants

Difference in Brain Chemistry in Children and
Adolescents with Attention Deficit Hyperactivity
Disorder with and without Comorbid Bipolar Disorder;
a PROTON Magnetic Resonance Spectroscopy Study

Comorbidity in Bipolar Disorder among the Elderly:
Results from an Epidemiological Community Study Sample

Evidence of White Matter Pathology in Bipolar Disorder
Adolescents Experiencing Their First Episode of Mania:
A Diffusion Tensor Imaging Study

Why Olanzapine Beats Risperidone, Risperidone beats Quetiapine,
and Quetiapine Beats Olanzapine: An Exploratory Analysis of Head-
To-Head Comparison Studies of Second Generation Antipsychotics

One wonders if anyone ever talks to anyone else, except their colleagues, and to too few and too narrow a sampling of those. To be fair, there is an introductory essay, "What is Bipolar Disorder." And, better still, an editorial entitled "What's Missing in Psychiatry" refreshingly chides APA members to remember to ask the patient "How do you feel?" Regarding talk therapy, the editors note that the "cost and pragmatics of conducting long-term psychotherapy studies makes most treatment trials unrepresentatively brief" and that such trials, geared to short-term drug actions, always are "disorder based, even though many patients wish to discuss problems of living that stem from personality characteristics that are intermingled with a specific disorder."[26] Fair enough.

"We do not propose that any of the methodology of efficacy and effectiveness be compromised," Gabbard (a psychoanalyst) and Freedman say. "However, when appropriate paragraphs or tables that use the patients' own words to report what happened are a desirable feature that contributes to the validity of the report, regardless of the treatment modality under study." The FDA recently announced it wants evidence from patients and families of change, not just neuro-psychological testing alone, before it approves drugs. This is encouraging. Some psychiatrists know the human race, not just anatomy charts, is out there.

Focus on a randomly chosen drug advertised in this same issue: Effexor, manufactured by Wyeth (remember fen-phen?), for alleviating panic disorder. Apart from increased suicidality in adolescents with "major depressive disorder," ingesting it comes at risk of anorexia, asthenia, constipation, dizziness, dry mouth, ejaculation problems, impotence, insomnia, nausea, nervousness, somnolence, and profuse sweating. You can "break the cycle with Effexor" while starting quite a few others. The small print warning "Commonly Observed Adverse Events in Controlled Clinical Trials" fills half the next page with an inventory of side effects. Scanning them, it's difficult to think of anything this drug cannot ruin in the course of making you feel better. You have to be a pretty cool customer to take panic medication these days.

Ivan Illich long ago described the "black magic" form of medicine designed to disempower the individual and remove from him any responsibility for his own condition and for his healing.[27] This deadly format was the opposite of the purpose of the therapy that Freud devised. But institutional power cannot help but sway the psychoanalytic profession toward more pseudosomatic stances that Freud did his best through the latter half of his life to defend psychoanalysis against. The prefix pseudo applies because portraying a phenomenon that is partly somatic as if it were nothing but somatic is to generate a deception.

David Healy, who believes therapy without drugs is a "romantic" notion, argues that psychiatrists are treating many more patients and not as safely as they used to. Given the dark history of many asylums this is quite a claim. Healy assembled statistics at a UK hospital over a one-hundred-year period. Patients in 1996 were discharged with prescriptions for neuroleptic and antidepressant drugs known to cause suicidal feelings. They had much higher suicide rates than those discharged in 1896. The implication for psychiatry is that "psychiatric patients of 1896 may have had better outcomes in the area of death rates than 19th century inmates despite, or even because of, the pharmacological revolution."[28]

What's at stake? Power, money, and status. More for them, less for you. "The power to define the standards of normality [or standards of scientific evidence] can be used either to change or stabilize society [or a profession]," a sharp critic writes.[29] Is it normal to prescribe antidepressants for most complaints, let alone take them? Are antidepressants the right remedy for lousy working conditions, inadequate pay, overwork, or any number of issues that are better settled through collective action?

Antedating psychoanalysis, the "defect model of emotional disorder" says society is OK, you aren't. Any treatment "that removes a patient's symptoms," many radical analysts see, "without simultaneously increasing the patients' awareness of his environment is potentially repressive."[30] The whole history of American psychiatry demonstrates how it is geared to isolate patients immaculately from their milieus and to pretend the latter have no influence on their disorders. Psychoanalysis is at least somewhat likelier to be open to socially sensitive correctives. In a comment on *DSM-III* in the 1980s a Latin American commentator registered his worry about abuse of the label "antisocial personality disorder" inasmuch as in poor countries such as his "a vast segment of the population may acquire or use some of the behaviors described in the diagnostic criteria as the only way to social survival." We should "not forget that in some countries failure to accept social norms has been elevated to the category of collective enterprise."[31] Medicalizing problems rubs out this critical dimension.

The medicalization of psychoanalysis since the 1930s accordingly produced a domesticated version, although exceptional analysts do sneak through. "Of course the rational ego must accept facts as facts, and avoid wishful thinking," Norman O. Brown concedes. "But recognition of the world as it is by no means precludes desire or activity to change it, in order to bring reality into conformity with the pleasure-principle."[32] "Know thyself" is the Socratic injunction that Freud aided and abetted. Freud was the quintessential creature of the enlightenment. Enlightenment does not happen by itself; an active hand must be taken, as Freud knew. The somatic injunction, however, is "Dose yourself," because, you know, it will help you fit in.

Psychoanalysis at its core is a rancorously rebellious therapy, despite the training regimen, developed since Freud's death, growing rather problematic because it so clearly induces conformity.[33] In something of an exaggeration, what Rieff calls "intelligent Normals" flooded the field and "they are, characteristically, without analytical talent."[34] Yet an old but telling joke among earlier generations was to say of a so-so colleague that he or she is "too healthy to be an analyst." The most talented analysts usually have overcome some wound or gap in themselves and thereby are sensitive to similar problems borne by others. This chapter emphasizes the importance of recovering an understanding of the humanism of Freud for the new high-tech age of quick cures and one-dimensional diagnoses.

MODEL PRISONERS

Progress in psychiatry, despite the Freudian "intrusion," always was based on the search for a biological defect or agent. Yet "it is not clear that even the most severe syndrome, schizophrenia, is in any good sense typified by detectable, quantified defects in brain structure or function."[35] Instead, neurology has made strides by approaching human beings from another direction. Neurologists do find that "within the central nervous system, repeated high intensity emotional signals lead eventually to neural change, which in turn leads to hyper-sensitivity and impaired potential for habitation and learning."[36] LeDoux finds that terrifying experiences change the brain.

Mark Solms asks how neurobiological processes in the brain "cause consciousness" and finds there is no answer since "we can never know an external process directly."[37] On the other hand, there is ample evidence that defense mechanisms can harm us more than the discomfort that they fend off (which may be imaginary). Freud only dumped the "the doctrine of the specific etiology" when he recognized the "self-injurious aspects of bodily and psychic defense"—as exemplified in the familiar "compulsion to repeat" in neuroses.[38] In the twenty-first century Collins and Pinch point to a reverse placebo effect by then widely known in medicine in which the "mind harms the body by thinking that a nonexistent disease is a real disease."[39]

Prominent neuroscientists, such as Gerald Edelman, hold Freud in high regard.[40] "Freud's most redeeming feature was his willingness to acknowledge the limits of science," which is anathema to zealots and their English-department PR men. John Horgan is, as he should be, "disturbed by the vast gulf between the field's modest achievement and the hyperbolic" worship it has attracted in naive quarters. None of the claims linking specific genes to specific, complex behavior traits "has been unambiguously identified."[41]

Medical model enthusiasts, however, do not disentangle the back-and-forth causal arrows between the mental and the physical. In depression, researchers reported that the hippocampus—essential for the formation of new memories—was 10 percent smaller in women suffering depression than in those who were not. The problem is that it may just as well be depression that shrinks the hippocampus, and not the smaller hippocampus that causes depression.[42] PET scans detect lower brain activity in depressed people but we don't know if this precedes or follows depression.[43] The tacit proposition is that nothing we feel has a significant impact on our physical functioning—an opinion that would be laughed out of court. Perhaps for that reason, one will not find this belief stated so starkly anywhere.

Contrary to Oliver James, raising serotonin levels in normal individuals has no effect. Doctors, lawyers, writers, and artists all have above average chances of depressive episodes, while managers are below average. Is this a genetic sorting of predisposed people in the job pool? Is a different gene (say, for empathy or bullying) responsible in each case, or is it the nature of the job that is responsible for episodes? Four out of five people recover from depression without treatment. What do genes or brain chemistry possibly have to do with it?[44] Social systems, however, can dictate what health is and what it is not. The medieval Catholic church, upset by the lack of productivity of despondent monks, labeled depression a sin. God isn't dead, just depressed over this behavior.

Why have there been two to three as many schizophrenics, proportionally, in Ireland as elsewhere in Western Europe?[45] Is it genes? Or the Guinness? Or the way statistics are recorded? Why are women five times more likely to exhibit PTSD symptoms after a traumatic event?[46] Genes? The resistance on exhibit here is based on believing, not Freudian "dogma" but only in the reality of physical injury. The assumption is that all the forces at work are internal, having nothing to do with an unchecked, unprotected, unregulated, unmerciful pace of life—a life that is not "natural" but geared to wring more work out of us and place all the added value and benefits of productivity in the pockets of the top 1 to 10 percent who then deploy it to buy influence, break unions, smear the world with propaganda, and monopolize the media. Earlier generations of psychoanalysts, unlike most shrinks today, were often acutely aware of power relations outside as well as inside the clinical setting.[47]

A selectively gullible culture, however, needs a scientific report to verify experiences everyone undergoes, such as emotional pain.[48] Behold the news item that science research "suggests that any emotional stress, such as the demise of a relationship or the loss of a loved one, might be far more closely linked to real pain than previously thought."[49] When a person is physically hurt, the anterior cingulate in the brain activates "like an alarm system," says a UCLA psychologist. "The response to this social exclusion was remarkably similar to what you see in response to physical pain."[50] A London professor says: "it's proving to the medical profession once and for all that emotional distress is a genuine thing, that people who are distressed and upset are not malingerers."[51]

So we—or our professional classes—are not so distant from the nineteenth-century medical prejudices as readers might like to imagine. What kind of world is it that needs "scientific" proof for such things, as if they otherwise were ghosts? The crux of this bias is expressed in the verdict that it "could not be simultaneously true that that one's psychological problems were caused by an abnormal relationship to the maternal breast and by a deficiency of serotonin."[52] Of course it can be true. One affects the other. The discovery, or imputation, of a serotonin drop eliminates further inquiry. Serotonin levels of any kind terminate intellect, at least that of certain investigators.

As for biology, "an overreliance on biological determinism can mask the fact that the evolution of biological potentialities also occurs as a function for environmental provision impinging at critical moments. Arrests, fixations or distortions of function, which occur at points on the developmental line cause the person, to be affected both qualitatively and quantitatively [as Freud maps out]. A proper respect for the epigenetic principle, wherein treatment interventions and environmental provision are critical at given points if maximal developmental potential is to be realized, enhances rather than diminishes the importance of biology . . . a sophisticated awareness of the interplay of these determinants in the processes of development and maturation is needed"—and that is just what psychoanalysis provided.[53] But psychoanalysis faced a decline. In 1945 one in seventeen psychiatric residents learned psychoanalysis while by 1968 just one in twenty did.[54] By 1980 there were twenty-eight thousand psychiatrists, fifty thousand psychologists and three hundred thousand social workers in the United States. Why go to an analyst?

ASSESSING FREUD

In an appraisal of the scientific credibility of Freud's theories Fisher and Greenberg apply a series of "conventional" tests to this vexing research realm.[55] They first translate Freud's ideas into positivistic scientific terms—a move many analysts unapologetically oppose—to see how well they fare in so inhospitable, and indeed antagonistic, a climate.[56] They also attend to "unexamined beliefs" in psychoanalysis not because of suspected deceit but because any model is liable to have unconscious errors and unacknowledged dictums. This scientific attitude is one Freud certainly endorsed.

At first Fisher and Greenberg indulge the foes' view that Freud "apparently became so fed up with 'alien' onslaughts that he could not open the door to any 'facts' besides those personally under his control."[57] However, they also say that the "imperfection [in making psychoanalysis measurable] does not lie in Freud's approach but in the scientific fragility of observations made in all clinical settings."[58] Do we require controlled experiments and observations, with a view to rules of evidence and replicability, given a method that is concerned with crafty beings unconcerned with rules who seek every ingenious way of evading them? How amenable to positivist methods is this rather inhospitable situation?

What laboratory scheme can encompass the odd behavior and multiple meanings marking an average analytic hour? Freud always was skeptical that therapists could predict anything; their job at best was to reconstruct the patient's pattern of defenses and work out a way of healing from there. The abiding problem, Freud always acknowledged, is overdetermination, fixing on one of many overlapping factors determining a somewhat unpredictable outcome. In any psychoanalytic situation, to predict is to control, and to control is to imply contempt for the subject, who senses it and rebels. What does a scientist do when the data gets angry at him or her? What page of which standard science manual does one turn to?

Although there is a "lack of 'real evidence' that the most effective therapists are the best adjusted ones," Fisher and Greenberg find evidence that "those less prey to unexamined anxiety and personal conflicts and hobgoblins do better as therapists."[59] The savviest therapists have blind spots, but by the same token, some will be more perceptive than others in their ability to ferret out violent or disordered or obsessive feelings. No psychoanalyst can afford to feel foolproof, for in the treatment room it is always possible, too, as psychoanalyst Jonathan Lear writes, for "the analysis and patient to collaborate in construction of a false self."[60]

The best analysts are wise enough to incorporate this element of doubt into their therapy. Freud's foes, apart from unfurling their own certitudes, expect full dispensations from any scrutiny of their own motives, conscious and otherwise (because there aren't supposed to be unconscious motives). Shall one merely assume that these critics, and the specific "scientific" means they champion, are free of all taint? Psychoanalysts, for all their intense introspective training, get run through the wringer. Some studies find that all psychotherapies offer a similar range of positive outcomes. This datum suggests that success may come down to matching the right patient with the therapist with the right personality, regardless of brand. Still, since "symptoms don't require an exploration of the whole person," Rycroft notes, "these are where brief psychotherapies may work."[61] All modern therapies but behaviorism are of course indebted to psychoanalytic explorations. As Freud justly remarked: "Psychoanalysis began as a method of treatment; but it did not want to commend it to your interest as a method of treatment but on account of the truths it contains, on account of the information it gives us about what concerns human beings most of all—their own nature—and on account of the connections it discloses between the most different of their activities. As a method of treatment it is one among many, though, to be sure, primus inter pares."[62]

One must mention the prosperous self-help industry servicing a society that thrives on exploitation.[63] Beholding unctuous finger-wagging sermonettes of a Dr. Phil or Dr. Laura and the unhinged "recovery" movement, even the worst cynical jokes about analysis seem true in spades about the vast weed patch of pop psychology. These slick gurus are dedicated to divine accumulation, not to therapeutic breakthroughs or to anything approaching truth. The reward structure of a society, or a subsection of it, is their guiding light and master. A pervasive feature of these hyperenthusiastic practitioners is to attribute their own psychologies, and the remedies, to everyone else, or to assume a one-therapy-fits-all solution for all woes.

Frustratingly, Fisher and Greenberg find "no simple association between therapist's work and patient outcome." The variables run wild. They do find, however, that "analyzed therapists *with experience* were able to maintain higher levels of empathy no matter what their personal attitudes toward the patients." In the short term, they note, an analyst can indeed muck up his or her patients because of his or her own dodging of dredged-up personal material—unpleasant material "which few of us would be glad to face in ourselves."[64] Of course, working through these ticklish countertransference situations so as to benefit the patient is what analysts are uniquely trained to do.

The very notion that one ought to be introspectively alert to one's foibles is foreign to most physicians. Typically, medical school students with any humane impulses find they have to suppress them to survive the sorting process.[65] You would be hard-pressed anyway to find many humble idealists among the lifelong, monomaniacal grade-grubber "hothouse children" who emerge from affluent suburbs to fill our gleaming professional schools. What does emerge from Fisher and Greenberg's studies, though, is the finding that psychoanalysts and their patients tend to be in great agreement—share the same view—about the mutuality of the warmth, empathy, and effectiveness of their relationships. Asking the patients how they feel about their therapist is, as noted earlier, a good idea, even if not a positivist one. In psychoanalysis it may well be true that there is no "uncontaminated clinical material" due to the very personal nature of the interaction. Applying conventional "tests" that insistently pretend that such a thing as uncontaminated clinical material is even possible, or which avoid the issue altogether, is usually a systematic distortion and a waste of time.

Yet the possibility of therapists' bias, no matter how much training one undergoes, distorting their account of the patient always must be on the table. "The truth could cure the patient," Erikson suggested, perhaps a tad too dramatically, "only insofar as the doctor had faced the corresponding truth in himself."[66] The patient correctly may see an analyst as inept, overbearing, or clueless. Patients do not respond in a vacuum, but to therapists' behavior (as they perceive it). Psychoanalysts are almost morbidly alert to this likelihood, freely admitting the point that it is "risky to assume a one-to-one correspondence between what goes on in the analysis and what is in the patient's mind." The analyst "makes a contribution to the projective identification of the patients" so it is best "to hold both poles in dialectical tension"—which is a tricky but necessary task.[67]

Insight is defined as making the "unconscious conscious" via free association, analysis of dreams, slips of the tongue, and so on. Fisher and Greenberg also endorse the move from intrapsychic to a more interpersonal process of therapy, explicitly integrating or utilizing therapists' personalities rather than minimizing their full role. They also contend that Freud's idea of insight has not been adequately tested, and not because it is untestable or silly, but because what crass researchers use is a "vague caricature of the approach outlined by Freud." Such mechanistic monitors are "naively out of touch with the nuances of the therapeutic process." The tests they used to discredit psychotherapy "were usually very brief exercises into chronic cases, hardly good tests."[68]

Fisher and Greenberg sum up by saying that psychoanalytic depictions of oral and anal personality trait clusters are reasonable; the etiology of homosexuality due to hostile and rejecting fathers is quite a strong one; the Freudian account of depression appears to be on the money; paranoid delusions do indeed tend to be defensive projections of homosexual impulses; the rivalry inherent in the Oedipal complex is partially confirmed; and the notion of dreams as a vent for anxieties is true.[69] Neurotic symptoms too usually are disguised expressions of forbidden wishes. Other medical researchers, as Solms points out, since have found neurological support for Freud's theory of repression, dreams as wish fulfillment, the id, and unconscious motivation.[70]

Still there is "no evidence that Psychoanalysis produces longer lasting change than other approaches that are less time consuming and costly." Fisher and Greenberg argue that the boy identifies with the father because of a nurturing positive attitude by father, not out of fear of him, although this difference (or addition) may well be traced to the different cultural roles played by fathers over time.[71] Anyway, many early child therapists appreciated this positive aspect of identification too, stretching back to major figures such as Fritz Redl, David Wineman, Edith Buxbaum, and her much-maligned cousin Bruno Bettelheim. What is a cure worth anyway in a world—or family—that one may be unable to change in any significant way? Freud, in reply, reasoned: "Much will be gained if we succeed in transforming your hysterical misery into common unhappiness. With a mental life that has been restored to health, you will be better armed against that unhappiness."[72]

Indeed, evidence suggests that depressed or anxious people respond far better to one-on-one therapy, and that the relapse rate is lower than with drugs (where it is 60 percent for vaunted antidepressants). Fisher and Greenberg also find, like Freud, that words alone and verbalization don't cause personality changes but, for that purpose, "the relationship context in which they are embedded . . . seem crucial."[73] They carefully and acidly note that some critics of Freud get "so deeply invested in the position that his views are mystical and untestable that they found it convenient to avoid the dissonance of confirming the real evidence."[74]

The foes, or the agents they champion, don't live up to their own professed standards, as the rampant high jinks in the pharmacological arena demonstrate. Even when impressive sober scientific reports do follow procedure earnestly, they are not and probably cannot always be as informative as they purport to be. "A story that is too well-told conceals the uncertainty and ambiguity of the real world," Michels writes. "I suggest that case reports that are offered as 'pure' scientific data are illustrations of implicit, concealed, or disavowed purposes."[75] Indeed, even when far away from the infernal analytical couch, double-blind procedures turn out to be remarkably ineffective in drug testing, which, for example, tend not to count "dropouts." Drugs rarely ever exceed placebo effect.[76] The efficacy of placebos in relation to antidepressants is closer to 7 percent than the 40 percent usually claimed. Two of three patients on lithium stop taking it because of its admittedly nasty side effects. Some 40 percent of Chlorpromazine users develop tardive dyskinesia, not to mention extrapyramidal effects and Parkinsonism symptoms (which, happily for Big Pharma, require anti-Parkinsonian drugs).

In Britain, as drug prices soared by 50 percent over 3 years, a vice-president at GlaxoSmithKline actually blurted out that "the vast majority of drugs—more than 90 per cent—only work in 30 or 50 per cent of the people."[77] The indiscreet company man attributed the difference, just as faultily, to genes because he happened to be in charge of GSK "pharmacogenomics"—which aims to match dubious estimates of drug actions with dubious estimates of gene activity so as to "improve" drug efficacy. Welcome one and all to the latest pharmaceutical industry ploy to salvage their own routinely overblown claims. Viewing Schering's adamant false claims for its oral contraceptives, the British Consumer Association's principle policy adviser was forced to sum up: "The drug companies are incapable of communicating honestly with health care professionals, let alone the public."[78] They, and biopsychiatric hangers-on, glory in pointing fingers at psychoanalysis instead. Depression and anxieties, though, respond better to therapy than drugs.[79]

Freud was a liberator, and not just of one privileged part of humanity. Freud worked with the specific sufferers he had before him. As human beings changed in their outward patterns (but not essential needs, desires, and ambivalences), as societies and mores shifted, so too would the psychoanalytic method and its preoccupations be expected to alter. History, for that matter, changes the expression as well as incidence of a neurosis, even if it does not change the underlying mechanism for it. (Hysteria, which we don't hear much about anymore, did not evaporate, it only had its designation changed.)[80] Creative ferment and dispute is always a sign of a lively and fertile research paradigm.[81] No innovator can keep control, or necessarily wants to keep control, of the implications, of their paradigmatic advances.

Science is a profoundly human enterprise, checked by whatever internalized ethical and external authoritative monitoring that can be arrayed in any given research field at a given time. True believers infest every profession. They become the people who, as Kuhn writes, "mop up" after a scientific revolution or major advance.[82] Every innovator and pioneer is followed remorselessly by what Max Weber calls routinizers. They cleave to whatever the orthodoxy is. They resolutely go by the book. There is no lack of fervent souls who ache to work where numbers (for which they just happen to have a knack) always seem to add up and where the experiments that they conduct not only are potentially replicable in exact detail but are assumed to reflect faithfully a reality out there, outside the lab. Indeed, these besotted people imagine—without the least clue they are imagining—that what they do is the whole truth and nothing but—and, of course, nothing else counts. That's certainly a point of view, but it is nothing but an ideology when it hardens into a crusty dogma of "objective knowledge."

"The epistemology of subjective knowledge," the Rudolphs note, stands counter to that of objective knowledge, knowledge based on a fiction of unsullied observation by impervious impartial observers. "Rigorous partiality recognizes and validates the situated, inflected nature of truth," the Rudolphs point out.[83] Rather than denying or repressing the sociology of knowledge, rigorous partiality self-consciously acknowledges that context shapes why and how knowledge is acquired and what it is taken to mean. This stance is consistent with Gadamer's hermeneutic stance that the "scientific ideal of objectivity is compromised by personal experience, cultural tradition, and prior understandings. Partiality also signifies that which is not whole, complete or being carried to completion. 'Rigorous partiality' makes the epistemological claim that knowing the whole truth is a capacity not given to mortals. The best they can strive for is partial truths. In this sense subjective truth is rigorously partial and contingent, not impartial and objective."[84] Here is the realm that psychoanalysis surveys and navigates.

Psychoanalysis cannot cure us in the same graphic sense as an appendix operation or the setting of a broken limb, so measuring it solely by positivist standards is a mug's game, or else is calculatedly disingenuous. "Unfortunately, both for the patient and the analyst, psychoneurotic symptoms are, in most cases the outward and visible sign of an inner distortion of the patient's total personality; and the exploration of the symptoms inevitable leads on to a consideration of the whole person, his development, temperament, and character structure," Anthony Storr posits.[85] "Even when cured," as Rycroft adds, "the [psychoanalytic] patient may want to explore further because being in "touch with basic instinctual drives the patient has ability to make better decisions" and may move from a "cure of symptoms" to the "big questions."[86] Try this conversational tack with your local pharmacist and see where it gets you. The harried physician—meeting his HMO quota—will shoo you out of the office as you clutch a quickly scrawled prescription.

NORMAL AND ABNORMAL SCIENCE

Are there any signs that society, or at least doctors, are sobering up from a long intoxication with the charms of pharmacology and biopsychiatry? Among promising indications of change is the AMA student association, where five thousand members signed a Pharma-free pledge to decline promotional items from drug firms.[87] Professionals are growing aware of the worrisome implications for their own credibility of studies of industry that find private-financed studies are "eight times more likely to produce results favorable to their funders, compared with studies which had no funding."[88] Streetlamp science descends further into streetwalker science. At a more technical level, a recent challenge to the pharmaceutical oligopoly has come from researchers at Imperial College in London, who seized on a standard drug company practice in order to "improve" the molecular structure of a drug so that it "is technically a new medicine" and therefore not under the twenty-year patent and so can be made available affordably.[89]

In the end the foes who accuse adherents of psychoanalysis of being suckers are themselves gulled by the most entrancing illusion of them all, that the mind-body relation is like playing a piano in a one-key, one-note fashion.[90] This scientific dream is so enticing because it appeals to the kind of intellect that wants anything that faintly resembles a two plus two situation to equal a nice neat four. These bookkeeper mentalities, useful in certain ways, diligently mistake a useful hypothesis, or fictions, for the whole truth or, at any rate, enough of it in order to suit inner psychic needs for certainty. They comprise a potent minority, often a majority, in every field, who seize on what they imagine is a safe indisputable model—rational choice, behaviorism, vulgarizations of neurology—to anchor their own anxieties and try to impose it on others. Interestingly, these misleading "scientific" views always dovetail with power relations, with the interests of those who have amassed the most wealth and influence in any given society, and these are the folks who hand out rewards and penalties.

Enthusiastic foes, playing the odds, therefore cut no slack to Freud while ignoring all the problems afflicting and infesting the facile (often misunderstood) positions they champion. The allure of single-cause explanations probably can never be banished for good. Neatness weaves its own resilient fairy-tale spell in the realm of explanation and, if not taken too seriously, can indeed be a useful aid. (Parsimony, as a requirement of a sound explanation, actually has a lot to answer for.) So is it not possible that Freud, well aware of this resilience of rivals, was protecting as best he could a rich method of inquiry well worth preserving as a major contribution to our culture—a theory of ambivalence, our deep-down ambivalence, about almost everything?

Freud really needs no defense, in the sense that anyone reading him can see and sense the power of his revelations about the way we feel and perceive and behave. Dismissing his whole body of work because some elements are overdrawn, or drawn into question, is in any case the height of idiocy about what grubby hands-on science actually does. No model of human activity can possibly survive the same verification demands made upon psychoanalysis. The Kuhnian definition of a strong paradigm is that it provides model problems for a community of practitioners, produces useful answers, and has an open-ended "fertile" program for further research into realms the founder(s) never dreamed of. Psychoanalysis surely fits that bill.

The somatic model is the ogre of the era, not Freud. These one-track models have generated more mayhem, inflicted more horror, salved more consciences that needed instead to have second thoughts, excused more mass crimes, wasted more time, and dealt out more harm than any psychoanalytic mafia could perform, even in the most paranoid or fanatical critic's fancies. Mechanistic thinking in society is normal; somatic thinking in psychiatry is normal. So what then constitutes normality? Are normal people supposed to be devoid of envy, jealousy, bitterness, or ambivalence? The primal Freudian crime, I submit, is his finding that the difference between normality and abnormality "is only a matter of degree."[91] Every normal person, as Freud said, is only approximately normal: his ego resembles that of the psychotic in one point or another, in a greater or lesser degree. Yes, even a scientist or a stockbroker nestled in a gated suburb is not exempt.

Perfectly normal people cheered racist drivel in *The Birth of a Nation* or *Jud Suss*, and acted upon it before and after the shows. Those audiences were normal in the widely accepted sense of fitting smoothly into their communities, unlike the mavericks, outsiders, and dissidents lurking in their midst. Normal people are probably the most dangerous people on earth. "Ordinary men" in Police Battalion 101 in Poland and western Russia, as Christopher Browning trenchantly shows, loyally played their lethal part in the Holocaust.[92] Were all the Hutus and Tutsis involved in mass slaughters in Rwanda and adjacent areas supposed to be abnormal people? Normal people, though, do know better than to stray dangerously away from the safe consensus, so far as they understand it.

This debased normality was not what Freud ever had in mind, despite the perfectly ignorant accusations that he only embraced "adjustment" as his therapeutic goal. Freud observed that "an 'ideally' normal person is a mixed type, and has narcissistic, obsessional, as well as hysterical layers to him" and, as Roazen ventures, "here Freud was undoubtedly writing about himself" too.[93] Perhaps we need a new definition of normality that includes a serrated critical edge, one suspicious of authority and alert to pious cant, one less likely to approve, say, torture simply because partisan nutcases insinuate themselves into the White House. "Our object will not be to rub off all the corners of the human character so as to produce 'normality' according to schedule," Freud advised. "Nor yet to demand that the person who has been 'thoroughly analysed' shall never again feel the stirrings of passions in himself or become involved in any internal conflict. The business of analysis is to secure the best possible psychological conditions for the functioning of the ego; when this has been done, analysis has accomplished its task."[94]

Freud understandably was cautious about psychoanalytic goals, though his own underlying radical thrust comes through in his writing. "Psychoanalytic education will be taking an uninvited responsibility on itself if it proposes to mould students into rebels," Freud stated. "It will have played its part if it sends them away as healthy and efficient as possible." Yet he immediately went on to say that "it also contains enough revolutionary factors to ensure that no one educated by it will in later life take the side of reaction and suppression."[95] Greater tolerance and, moreover, a greater sensitivity to injustice were reckoned to be the social results.

Rieff argues that Freud, foremost, defended the individual against society. Psychoanalysis involves a "skepticism about all ideologies"; it is "the doctrine of the private man defending himself against encroachment." This is a tad overstated. Freud held—perhaps even juggled—the legitimate needs of the individual and those of the social order in an exquisite dialectical tension in his metaspeculative works such as *Civilization and Its Discontents*. The newborn babe cannot be a self-sufficient monad; it must, and wants to, relate to others all the way to the grave.[96] Rieff is right, though, to laud Freud's subversive "ethic of honesty," extending from the wild couch out into the wider society, as a marvelous contribution to a better future. Honesty, however, is not a prized trait in either an authoritarian or a commercial society. Instead of reaping any appreciation, Freud regularly gets savaged as the sordid embodiment of envy, avarice, ambition, and zeal. These scurrilous portraits casually combine projection, pretension, exaggeration, and even, in some cases, doses of stupidity, though a form of stupidity the foes carefully reckon they can get away with.

The real problem with psychoanalysis, for foes, is that it is not a precise Newtonian clockwork, or cybernetic, model of how the human mind supposedly works. If it were, it might be hailed as impeccably scientific stuff.

Freudians long ago traced this prevalent kind of omniscient wish to a naive yet sinister urge for achieving control and predictability. The upshot of a psychoanalytic critique of positivist science is that we need to corral, or at least chide, the enthusiasts who seek so assiduously to corral reality in their fallible frameworks. So Feyerabend seems to have been wise to encourage many perspectives to bloom so as to play out their strengths and weaknesses on a fairly level playing field (which is a mighty rare condition anywhere).

The usual real-world route to success is for anxious researchers to isolate findings tidily from the wider context: one independent variable to a customer. What we really should keep an eye on is not the wild-eyed iconoclast but those high achievers dying to make their mark in whatever way encouraged by the system to which they eagerly adapt themselves. Here are the prismatic social "nests" where the Hannah Arendt's banality of evil breeds. Erich Fromm and his student David Riesman had intriguing things to say about "other-directed" personalities, who are back with us in abundance, if they ever actually went away.[97]

Phillips suggests that Freud, because he felt "science was the most exempt from wishfulness," fell into acceptance that the "relation to truth becomes a sado-masochistic one, truth being that which is better for us to submit to."[98] Phillips certainly scores a point here regarding Freud's essay "The Question of a Weltanschaaung." Nonetheless, the "basic structure of Freud's thought is committed to dialectics," Brown contends, "because it is committed to the vision of mental life as basically an arena of conflict; and his finest insights (for example, that when the patient denies something, he affirms it), are incurably 'dialectical.' Hence the attempt to make psychoanalysis out to be 'scientific' (in the positivist sense) is not only vain but destructive. Empirical verification, in the positivist test of science, can apply only to that which is fully in consciousness; but psychoanalysis is a mode of contacting the unconscious under conditions of general repression, when the unconscious remains in some sense repressed."[99] Gellner, as we saw in chapter 1, regards this argument as a cop-out, claiming there is no unconscious or else that it doesn't matter. Like Humpty Dumpty, for Gellner the word "science" is to mean what he means by it, no more and no less. It is not only psychoanalysts, however, who view Gellner's maneuver as a cop-out.

Alfred North Whitehead sees science as "one-sided," as one aspect of a total cultural situation: "a dull affair, soundless, scentless, colourless; merely the hurrying of material endlessly, meaninglessly."[100] Science then, Brown deduces, is an "awe-inspiring attack on the life of the universe; in more technical psychoanalytic terms, its anal-sadistic intent is plain." "Sublimation is the defense" of choice for nervous, driven inquirers who "transcend their own [ambivalently regarded] bodies" through deploying a handy abstract theoretical apparatus. "Our much-prized 'objectivity' towards our own bodies, other persons, and the universe, all our calculating 'rationality' is, from the psychoanalytic point of view, an ambivalent mixture of love and hate," Brown concludes. "Psychoanalysis calls permanently into question the 'subjective' attitude of the scientist, who may himself be schizoid."[101] So one can see why psychoanalysts aren't the first people that positivists want to invite to the scientific party, and also why the debate must continue.

CONCLUSION

The central proposition repeatedly weighed in the balance is if "mental activity is the result of unconscious mental forces which are instinctual, biological, and physical in origin then human psychology could be formulated in terms of the interacting of forces which were in principle quantifiable, without recourse to any vital mental integrating agency, and psychology would become a natural science like physics."[102] This is the crux of psychiatric debate on mental maladies, and psychotherapists and the biopsychiatrists clearly fall on different sides of the proposition.

If this determinist stance were correct, then Freud should never have abandoned his abortive "Scientific Project." Sulloway asserts, most implausibly, that he never did. Freud eventually was wrenched away from this enticing philosophical vision by the sheer accumulation of the clinical evidence. Responding to the charge that he "denied the significance of inborn (constitutional) factors because I have stressed that of infantile impressions," Freud rebuked critics with the sally that such "a reproach stems from the narrowness of the causal needs—*Kausalbedurfnis*—of mankind, which likes to posit a single cause if at all possible."[103] Certainty, or the search for it, is just another kind of intoxicant.

Therefore, contemporary "studies of the function of the brain—and therefore of man's place in nature," Young finds, "are less free from the constraints of philosophical assumptions than their positivist advocates have supposed."[104] Jules Henry adds that those who believe mental illnesses are nothing but biological thereby enjoy an exemption from needing to think it through. Anyway, as Henry sadly observes, "Every culture provides forms of rewarding intellectual waste and generates sabotage that dissipates the gifts of its most talented members in activities that leaves the basic social structure intact."[105]

The real conflict never was between Freud and science, but between psychoanalysis and "one form of knowledge" that managed to "identify it[self] as science" and for which "intersubjective validity is equivalent to objectivity" of science.[106] In debates over methodological paths to scientific progress, the poles are occupied by Kuhn's position, on one end, advocating that one ought to push a dogma as far as it can go until it begins to crack and only then deal with anomalies in a radical way. On the other end, opponents say "methodological pluralism" should reign because new knowledge, as Feyerabend argues, is "discovered by contrast, not by analysis."[107] The history of psychiatry, not to mention medicine, indicates that the optimal choice is methodological pluralism. Chapter 4 catalogued the mundane horrors that "methodological conservativism" has fostered. The only reason dogmatism ever seems a sound strategy is because the authority structures enable reason to be silenced, or lied about, or brushed aside. "The voice of the intellect is a soft one," Freud wrote, "but it does not rest until it has gained a hearing."[108] Still, reason can use all the bloody help it can get.

"Forgetting," Freud also observed, "is not without its reasons."[109] The motivation for forgetting what Freud wrote and did, who and what he contended with, and what his motives and strengths were is to plump up a pallid corporate-consecrated vision of how one ought to live one's life. The piquant irony is that Freud's foes fervently embrace a backward-looking positivist formula that long ago was shed elsewhere in so-called hard sciences. In any society only a few people really think "outside the box" because cultures (which are the boxes) discourage it. The distinguishing trait of Freud's foes is their utmost conventionality of vision, promoted in colorful words that conjure images of intellectual derring-do. They are the TV commercial heroes and heroines who battle a rabid cartoon dogma and then buy a hair gel or designer jeans to show they are the system's perfect housebroken citizens. Freud's raucous rebel spirit was a light-year leap beyond them. What Freud taught, as Roazen so nicely phrases it, is "to respect the past because of the control it can exert over the future."[110]

"And in the development of mankind as a whole, just as in individuals, love alone acts as the civilizing factor in the sense that it brings a change from egoism to altruism."[111] Resist it all you like.

NOTES

1. Quoted in Peter Brooks and Alex Woloch, *Whose Freud? The Place of Psychoanalysis in Contemporary Culture* (New Haven, CT: Yale University Press, 2000), p. 104.
2. Oliver James, *Britain on the Couch* (London: Arrow Books, 1998), p. 307.
3. Franz Alexander and Sheldon T. Selesnick, *The History of Psychiatry* (New York: Mentor Books, 1966), p. 34.
4. Paul Roazen, *How Freud Worked* (Northvale, NJ: Jason Aronson, 1995), p. 37.

5. Edward Dolnick, *Madness on the Couch: Blaming the Victim in the Heyday of Psychoanalysis* (New York: Simon & Schuster, 1998), p. 225.

6. Lisa Belkin, "What the Jumans Didn't Know about Michael," *New York Times Magazine*, 14 March 1999, p. 46. The "belief in a psychogenic causation for schizophrenia is "now discredited." The reporter calls it the "schizophrenogenic mother" theory. The father is never mentioned.

7. Edward Shorter, *A History of Psychiatry* (New York: John Wiley & Sons, 1997), p. 327.

8. Elio Frattaroli, "The Mind-Body Problem and the Choice of Intervention," *Psychiatric Times*, November 1991, p. 73ff.

9. Valenstein, *Blaming the Brain: The Truth about Drugs and Mental Health* (New York: Free Press, 1998), p. 215.

10. CBT claims to cure depression, agoraphobia, obsessive-compulsive disorders, and other anxieties in sixteen weeks of sessions. See the upbeat rendition presented in Richard Layard, *Happiness: Lessons from a New Science* (London: Penguin, 2005).

11. Fred Gardner, "Yet Another Prozac Scandal," *Counterpunch* 11/12, September 2004.

12. Gardner, "Yet Another Prozac Scandal."

13. Rick Giambetti, "Prozac, Suicide and Dr. Healy," *Counterpunch*, 20 March 2002. See the summary at www.pharmapolitics.com. The SSRIs such as Paxil and Prozac, says Dr. Healy, "cause more agitation in testing subjects than sugar pills, but they also tend to outperform sugar pills at getting depressed people better." The fact that companies have chose to market them as antidepressants rather than agents that cause agitation is a business decision rather than a scientific matter. It is certainly not one that was "ordained by God." You could say that the fact that some people who are depressed get better is a side effect.

14. Julian Leff, *The Unbalanced Mind* (New York: Columbia University Press, 2001), p. 107.

15. Horgan, *The Undiscovered Mind: How the Human Brain Defies Replication, Medication, and Explanation* (New York: Free Press, 1999), p. 121.

16. Valenstein, *Blaming the Brain*, p. 216.

17. Rachel Cooper, "What Is Wrong with the DSM?" *History of Psychiatry* 15, no. 5 (2004): 20.

18. See Diana Zuckerman, "Hype in Health Reporting: 'Checkbook Science' Buys Distortion of Medical News," *EXTRA*, September/October 2002.

19. Zuckerman, "Hype in Health Reporting."

20. Tanya Luhrman, *Of Two Minds: The Growing Disorder in Psychiatry* (New York: Knopf, 2000), p. 7.

21. Luhrman, *Of Two Minds*, p. 20.

22. Luhrman, *Of Two Minds*, p. 23.

23. Robert Epstein, "Discussion: Does Psychiatry Have a Split Personality?" including Peter Loewenberg, Nancy Anderson, Robert Epstein, and Robert Kuhn.

24. David Healy quoted in Rick Giombetti, "Prozac, Suicide and Dr. Healy," *Counterpunch* 20 March 2002.

25. Nancy Andersen in Robert Epstein, "Discussion: Does Psychiatry Have a Split Personality?"

26. Glen O. Gabbard and Robert Freedman, "Editorial: Psychotherapy in the Journal: What's Missing?" *American Journal of Psychiatry* 163, no. 2 (February 2006): 183.

27. Ivan Illich, *Medical Nemesis* (New York: Pantheon, 1966), p. 108.

28. Healy, "Prozac, Suicide and Dr. Healy."

29. Seymour Halleck, *The Politics of Therapy* (New York: Perennial Books, 1971), p. 111.

30. Halleck, *The Politics of Therapy*, p. 86.

31. Eenato Alarcon, "A Latin American Perspective on *DSM-III*," in Robert Spitzer et al., *International Perspectives on DSM-III*, p. 245.

32. Norman Brown, *Life Against Death* (Scranton, PA: Wesleyan University Press, 1985), p. 153.

33. See Joel Kovel, *The Age of Desire: Case Histories of a Radical Therapist* (New York: Pantheon, 1981).

34. Rieff, introduction to Sigmund Freud, *The History of the Psychoanalytic Movement* (New York: Collier Books, 1963), p. 33.

35. Fisher and Greenberg, *Freud Scientifically Reappraised*, p. 12.

36. Fisher and Greenberg, *Freud Scientifically Reappraised*, p. 12.

37. Mark Solms, "What Is Consciousness?" *Journal of the American Psychiatric Association* 45, no. 3 (1997): 688.

38. David Bakan, *On Disease, Pain, and Sacrifice* (Boston: Beacon, 1971), pp. 27, 29.

39. Collins and Pinch, *Dr. Golem*, p. 118.

40. Horgan, *The Undiscovered Mind*, p. 66.

41. Glen Gabbard, "Does Psychoanalysis Have a Future?" *Canadian Journal of Psychiatry* 2005. Other defenders include Drew Westin, Peter Fonagy, Rolf Sandell, and Anthony Bateman.

42. Robin Baker, *Fragile Science: The Reality behind the Headlines* (London: Pan Books, 2001), p. 69. How might this happen? "First, the chemistry of depression—say a long-term production of stress hormones—could actually kill off brain cells. . . . Or perhaps genetic depressives have a naturally slower rate of brain-cell replacement throughout their life, even before their first bout with depression."

43. Baker, *Fragile Science*, p. 71.

44. For hard core biopsychiatrists there also is no such thing as psychosomatic illness. Yet nearly 150 middle-aged Cambodian women in California went blind from witnessing horrors of the Year Zero slaughter, not from physiological deficiencies or brain lesions Arnold R. Isaacs, *Vietnam Shadows: The War, Its Ghosts, and Its Legacy* (Baltimore, MD: Johns Hopkins University Press, 1997), pp. 2–23.

45. John Ingham, *Psychological Anthropology Reconsidered* (Cambridge: Cambridge University Press, 1996), p. 159.

46. Christopher J. Hough and Robert Ursano, "A Guide to The Genetics of Psychiatric Disease," *Psychiatry* 69, no. 1 (Spring 2006), p. 5. "If the X Chromosome carried a susceptibility gene for PTSD, women would only be twice as likely to ac-

quire PTSD as man, assuming identical penetrance. There are clearly non-genetic factors involved in this difference."

47. Jacoby, *The Repression of Psychoanalysis*, p. 46.

48. The ironies implicit in the comeback of biopsychiatric dominance are lost on proponents. Parents still experience guilt when the child's ADHD diagnosis seems to be genetic, so reviving a dubious diagnostic tendency is commendable even though what is given with one hand (exculpation) is taken away with the other.

49. Ian Sample, "How Scientists Proved the Pain of Rejection Is all too Real," *Guardian*, October 10, 2003.

50. Sample, *Guardian*.

51. Sample, *Guardian*.

52. En-Lai, *The Lobotomist*, p. 146.

53. "Comment," Marc Amaya and W. V. Burlingame, "Training Child Psychiatrists and the Child Mental Health Professionals to Serve the Chronically Mentally Ill Youth," in *Chronic Mental Illness in Children and Adolescents*, ed. John G. Looney (Washington, DC: American Psychiatric Press, 1988), p. 165.

54. Hale, *Rise and Crisis*, p. 347.

55. Seymour Fisher and Roger P. Greenberg, *The Scientific Credibility of Freud's Theories and Therapy*, 2nd ed. (New York: Basic Books, 1995).

56. Bettelheim, *Freud and Man's Soul*, p. 3.

57. Fisher and Greenberg, *Freud Scientifically Reappraised,* p. ix.

58. Fisher and Greenberg, *Freud Scientifically Reappraised*, p. 4.

59. Fisher and Greenberg, *Freud Scientifically Reappraised*, p. 377.

60. Jonathan Lear, "Truth in Psychoanalysis," in *Whose Freud?* ed. Peter Brooks and Alex Woloch, p. 308.

61. Rycroft, "Introduction: Causes and Meaning," in *Psychoanalysis Observed*, p. 15.

62. Freud, "Explanations, Applications and Orientation," in *New Introductory Lectures*, pp. 152–53.

63. Steve Salerno, *SHAM: How the Gurus of the Self-Help Movement Make Us Helpless* (NT Crown, 2005), p. 8.

64. Salerno, *SHAM*, p. 381.

65. See the interview with Dr. David Buchanen on the medical school experience in Studs Terkel, *Hope Dies Last* (New York: New Press, 2003), pp. 198–99.

66. Erikson, *Gandhi's Truth*, p. 245.

67. Glen O. Gabbard, *Love and Hate in the Analytic Setting* (London: Jason Aronson, 1996), p. 46.

68. Fisher and Greenberg, *Freud Scientifically Reappraised*, p. 361.

69. Fisher and Greenberg, *Freud Scientifically Reappraised*, p. 394.

70. Mark Solms, "Freud Returns," *Scientific American*, May 2004. Also see David Westen, "The Scientific Status of Unconscious Processes: Is Freud Really Dead?" *Journal of the American Psychoanalytic Association* 47, no. 4 (1999).

71. Fisher and Greenberg, *Freud Scientifically Reappraised*, p. 14.

72. Freud and Breuer, *Studies in Hysteria* (New York: Avon Books, 1966), p. 351.

73. Fisher and Greenberg, *Freud Scientifically Reappraised*, p. 264.

74. Fisher and Greenberg, *Freud Scientifically Reappraised*, p. 396.

75. Robert Michels, "The Case History," *Journal of the American Psychoanalytic Association* 48, no. 2 (2000): 363.

76. See Fisher and Greenberg, *The Limits of Biological Treatment for Psychological Distress* (New York: Lawrence Erlbaum, 1989).

77. Steve Connor, "Glaxo Chief: Our Drugs Do Not Work on Most Patients," *Independent* (UK), 8 December 2003.

78. Sarah Boseley, "Pharmaceutical Adverts 'Inadequately Policed,'" *Guardian*, 23 September 2003, p. 10. Schering claimed their pills "unlike others, protect against weight gain and improve skin condition and premenstrual symptoms." Schering's lawyers threatened to sue the critics for defamation but eventually withdrew the drug.

79. Valenstein, *Blaming the Brain*, pp. 216–17.

80. Hysteria became "somatoform disorder: in which symptoms that originate from psychological processes often mimic physical disease." As Rosenfeld and Shapiro explain, a conversion reaction is an involuntary loss or "alteration in physical functioning, suggesting a physical disorder where the symptom enables avoidance of a noxious stimulus," the stimulus being some horrible life situation, such as incest, that the authors find the person is otherwise experiencing and needs "transient secondary gains" to get out of one compensated for. Alvin Rosenfeld and Elsa G. Shapiro, *The Somatizing Child: Diagnosis and Treatment of Conversion and Somatization Disorders* (New York: Springer-Verlag, 1987), pp. 1, 25.

81. See the essays in Lakatos and Musgrave, *Criticism and the Growth of Knowledge*.

82. See Thomas Kuhn, *The Structure of Scientific Revolutions* (Chicago: University of Chicago Press, 1962).

83. Lloyd Rudolph and Susanne Rudolph, "Engaging Subjective Knowledge: How Amar Sing's Diary Narratives of and by the Self Help Explain Identity Politics," *Perspectives on Politics* 1, no. 4 (December 2003): 682.

84. Lloyd Rudolph and Kurt Jacobsen, "Conclusion: Sovereignty Unbound," in *Experiencing the State*, ed. Rudolph and Jacobsen (New York: Oxford University Press, 2006), p. 363n4.

85. Anthony Storr, "The Concept of Cure," in Rycroft, *Psychoanalysis Observed*, pp. 52–53.

86. Rycroft, "Introduction: Causes and Meaning," in *Psychoanalysis Observed*, p. 15.

87. Jim Ritter, "Medical Students Just Saying No to Drug Company Gifts," *Chicago Sun-Times*, 30 March 2006.

88. Polly Curtis, "Researchers See Bias in Private-Funded Studies," *Guardian*, 9 January 2007, p. 8. The study comes out of the Children's Hospital in Boston with lead researcher David Ludwig.

89. Sarah Boseley, "Scientists Find Way to Slash Cost of Drugs," *Guardian*, 2 January 2007, p. 1. The team began with a drug for hepatitis C, which affects 170 million people worldwide. The key is that generics, as exact copies, cannot be sold back to the West. The "ethical" pharmaceuticals can.

90. See Maurice Merleau-Ponty, *The Structure of Behavior* (Boston: Beacon Press, 1963).

91. Freud, "Analysis Terminable and Interminable," *SE*, 23:337.

92. See Christopher Browning, *Ordinary Men: Police Battalion 101 and the Final Solution in Poland and Russia* (New York: HarperCollins, 1992).

93. Roazen, *Freud and His Followers* (London: Allen Lane, 1976), p. 102.

94. Freud, "Analysis, Terminable and Interminable," *SE*, 23:269.

95. Freud, *New Introductory Lectures* 2 (London: Penguin, 1973), p. 186.

96. Joseph Schwartz, *Cassandra's Daughter: A History of Psychoanalysis in Europe and America* (New York: Viking, 1999), pp. 225–27.

97. David Riesman, *The Lonely Crowd* (New Haven, CT: Yale University Press, 1950) and Erich Fromm's work on the "marketing personality."

98. Adam Phillips, "Psychoanalysis and Idolatry," in *On Kissing, Tickling and Being Bored: Psychoanalytic Essays on the Unexamined Life* (London: Faber & Faber, 1993), p. xvii.

99. Brown, *Life Against Death*, p. 320.

100. Brown, *Life Against Death*, p. 316.

101. Brown, *Life Against Death*, p. 294.

102. Rycroft, "Introduction: Causes and Meaning," in *Psychoanalysis Observed*, p. 13.

103. Quoted in Peter Gay, *Reading Freud* (New Haven, CT: Yale University Press, 1990), p. 83 (citing "The Dynamics of Transference").

104. Young, *Mind, Brain and Adaptation in the 19th Century*, p. 252.

105. Jules Henry, *Pathways to Madness* (New York: Random House, 1965), p. 388. "Biopsychiatry offers a rationale for disengagement" (p. 181).

106. Theodor Adorno, *The Positivist Dispute in German Sociology* (London: Heinemann, 1976), p. viii.

107. Paul Feyerabend, *Against Method* (London: Verso, 1975), p. 22.

108. Freud, "The Future of an Illusion," in *SE*, 21:53.

109. Freud, *Psychopathology of Everyday Life* (New York: Mentor, 1951), p. 14.

110. Roazen, *Freud and His Followers*, p. 35.

111. Freud, *Group Psychology and the Analysis of the Ego* (New York: Norton, 1965), p. 44.

Conclusion

> Protection against stimuli is an almost more important factor than reception of stimuli.
>
> —Freud, *Beyond the Pleasure Principle*[1]

Stephen Jay Gould, after detailing how extensively esteemed somatic enthusiasts like Paul Broca, Cyril Burt, and Francis Galton misshaped scientific data, concludes that they were "not conscious frauds."[2] Gould is probably right, and that is the insidious heart of the problem. Specialists, no matter how well versed in methodology, believe in their own models; they become emotionally attached, especially to models like positivism that appear to expel the icky horrors of subjectivity. Freud, however, a first-class neurologist, had no choice but to pay full attention to the dominant somatic explanation as he explored the dynamics of the psyche and its relation to human beings struggling in society. Some somatic researchers return the favor by considering seriously the psychological dimension, but the majority never have felt impelled to bother. Parsimony, as a wag said, has a lot to answer for.

Freud told students that the "man with the syringe," that is, modern pharmacology, was "right behind them" and so they had to hurry.[3] The reason for haste seems not so much that so-called hard scientists necessarily would devise superior explanations but that they very likely would trump psychoanalysis even when explanatory offerings were tenuous, incomplete, or plain errors.[4] The standards seesaw—tougher for challengers—always comes into play. The public, primed by a breathless booster media, tended, until at least very recently, to believe in science the way earlier generations believed in magic and witchcraft. Most any puff story could be propagated—at least long enough to make a profit—in the name of healing.

Contrary to the foes, resistance is not a bugbear solely for psychoanalysis. Every open-ended research field employs, and encounters, resistance in and outside its ranks. Psychoanalysis at the turn of the twentieth century, when biological models seemed exhausted and scientists were open to new approaches, was a bold enterprise exploring mysterious forces in places formerly ruled off-limits. Freud conceded the banal point that, in principle, somatic sources someday might be found to underlie the phenomena he painstakingly tracked down. Freud's obligatory concession did not mean that physiological accounts of mental woes therefore must be superior to, and displace, psychology. Cause and correlation, as Hume tells us, are different things. The comeback of the crushing dominance of somatic models, however, interwove with cultural cravings for explanations based on measurable events. Biopsychiatry purports to fulfill this criterion and consequently can get away with saying almost anything. Some practitioners, therefore, do.

One noxious result is that the gap between psychiatry and the pop self-help texts on megastore racks shrank to nothingness. These canny sound-bite books, with bullet points galore, coax the reader through arbitrarily selected steps to feel better. No objective test can tell you if you are depressed or schizoid or much of anything else emotionally. Yet this glib genre of pop psychiatry is part of a commercial trend to "somatize" any disorder or discomfort.[5] The smart money, you see, is investing in depression futures, a booming market. While ecstasy, according to ravers, may be an exception, psychoactive drugs actually distance you from your context, from your milieu, and from your relations with people (bosses, rivals, colleagues, family, etc.). The message inscribed on every prescription is that the problem is you, and you alone. Behold the sales pitch.

"When I became a psychiatrist, I learned to heal with words," one popular marketed author informs readers.[6] "For many years psychiatrists simplistically preached that words were enough." Of course this depiction seems extraordinarily unlikely considering that at the apex of Freudian influence of 9,000 American psychiatrists just 619 were psychoanalysts, who evidently ruled with an iron grip.[7] The author informs us that if the precious words she apparently was issued like boot-camp gear didn't work "then the words were wrong, they needed to be repeated and repeated or spoken by a different healer."[8] In short, these melodramatic "words" comprised a mantra, or a spell, to chant at bewildered sufferers, and were not a way of connecting with people and investigating their woes mutually so as to relieve suffering and its sources.

This psychiatric fairy tale serves the predetermined corporate moral that Prozac, unlike all those superstitious words, does the trick. Depression is depicted unequivocally as a physical illness, like tuberculosis, and is supposed to be caused by chemical imbalances. Even depressions due to trauma or grief stir chemical imbalances that the right doses correct.[9] These wonder drugs evidently make you forget that your beloved died, your job got shipped to Bangalore, your health maintenance organization (HMO) won't cover treatment of your strange new growth, or that you no longer can make the mortgage payments and still eat. That's asking a lot of an antidepressant.

Too much. A 2008 study, based on *Freedom of Information Act* requests eliciting unpublished data from reluctant firms, startlingly finds that Prozac is no more effective than a placebo in lifting depression, although this news was long known by insiders.[10] No one is picking on Prozac. The patterns of fluoxetine (Prozac), paroxetine (Seroxat), venlafaxine (Effexor), and nafazodone (Serzone) were consistent: "the overall effect of new-generation antidepressant medication is below recommended criteria for clinical significance." The National Institute for Health and Clinical Excellence, therefore, recommends that counseling should be attempted before (often useless or harmful) drugs.

Our author recommends pills and therapy, but with depression at skyrocketing levels, hitting one in five women, a prescription is going to be first resort.[11] The author promises working mothers under distress—most mothers work because they financially must—that if "you aren't convinced that that there's a biological abnormality here, [you] will believe it when you see the medication at work."[12] So if a drug suppresses an emotional state, this is evidence that the drug is curing an abnormality. This claptrap is offered in all seriousness as scientific thinking. There is a macabre humor in all the prim demands one hears for rigorous testing of the utility of psychotherapy, for the record abundantly indicates that the biopsychiatric end of the profession frequently applies tests sloppily or ignores them altogether when results conflict with interests.

In the late 1950s a Johns Hopkins University expert cheered a bracing new climate where "one is no longer compelled to accept the fantasy of physicochemical inadequacy or anatomical pathogenic tissue alteration as the only legitimate explanations for anything that goes wrong in the human organism."[13] This release from somatic dogma was a long time coming. "A systemic approach with psychobiological methods has given ample evidence of the eminent role which psychic motives play in the development and maintenance of somatic dysfunctions," Leo Kanner continued. "Studies have shown that emotional factors are potent also in diseases which have been previously regarded as exclusively organic."[14]

So words never have been a popular, let alone dominant, feature in psychiatry. Kanner gave Freud credit for demonstrating the power of therapy in cases of "conversion" of emotional states into physical manifestations, and lauded Adolf Meyer for prying loose psychiatry "from the nineteenth century of dehumanized cellular pathology."[15] As Jonathan Lear points out, contrary to Grunbaum, reasons too can be recognized as causes; that is, emotions such as anger alter conditions inside and outside the organism.[16] The medical model, which viewed this as anathema, was toppled from its perch and became one of several legitimate approaches to research and therapy.

This juncture amounts to a brief shining moment of pluralism in modern psychiatry. A counterrevolution always was in the works. The repressed always returns. The "stigmata of degeneration," the "neuropathic taint" roared back, though expressed in updated genetic-determinist terms. The worst tendencies within us, as psychoanalysis anticipates, will resurge at the first opportunity, if in slightly different and more pleasing guises.

Psychoanalysis is easy to make fun of: the arcane jargon, po-faced manners, Germanic accents, pointy beards, and the almighty couch. If you scan all the negative diagnoses applicable to us, you might deduce that only disturbed people are motivated to accomplish anything. The ideal picture of a well-adjusted person dwindles into, guess what, the unimposing figures of analysts themselves, an outcome which only warrants a guffaw. Some psychoanalysts demonstrate in small-scale ways that they too are prey to grandiosity and doctrinaire thinking. This book defends Freud's radical investigative method, not the foibles of its practitioners. "There is plenty to improve," as Freud would say. "I have nothing against that."[17]

Yet the latest batch of foes recycle antiquated critiques as if they were refreshingly new formulations and in doing so assemble a musty list of denunciations that amount to a catechism for biopsychiatry and carte blanche for the worst aspects of corporate medicine. The foes lack encyclopedic acuity, the courage to face their demons, the willingness to correct hunches and theories by experience, and the self-critical devotion to helping humanity that Freud evidenced throughout his life. As Fisher and Greenberg say of the fiercest critics, "By the very rigidity of their resistance, they have registered the impact of Freud's views."[18]

The version of science that foes promote is puerile in self-idealization and its propagation of promises of certainties. A sense of balance is missing. The rote response of professionals caught with their surgical masks down—from butchering "hysterical" women to endorsing crummy drugs today—is that they operate according to standard professional practice; they are not conscious frauds. The "safest way" for them is not the best way for the society as a whole, which is why all the monitoring and safeguards possible are needed to keep them and their corporate sponsors at least intermittently honest. "From a psychoanalytic point of view, belief changes being a question about the qualities of the object of belief to a question about the history of the subject," Phillips notes.[19] "What is the unconscious problem that your belief solves for you, or wish that it satisfies?"

Psychoanalysts are not more virtuous because of their profession; it may be, as a cynic might say, that they don't have anyone to whom to sell out anyway. Psychoanalysis at its best remains the enemy of deceit in personal matters and, for some, of humbug in public affairs too. Frederick Crews protests that he does not hate Freud but rather is "wholly lacking in respect" for him.[20] Guilty until proven innocent. One might endorse this sentiment if Crews and his compatriots were as diligently "wholly lacking in respect" for all potential scientific impostures. Then they might devise something approaching a fair assessment. Freud, for all his deficits, helped us along our idiosyncratic yet universal roads to becoming more alive, more attuned, less manipulable, and, as new-age mavens put it, more whole. The problem, ultimately, as Erikson remarked, is "creating a world worth being whole for."[21]

NOTES

1. Freud, "Beyond the Pleasure Principle," *SE*, 18:27.

2. Stephen J. Gould, *The Mismeasure of Man* (London: Penguin, 1981), p. 74.

3. Paul Roazen, *How Freud Worked* (Northvale, NJ: Jason Aronson, 1995), p. 185.

4. Freud told Richard Sterba that "the blind giant, the hormone man, will do a lot of damage if the dwarf psychologist does not take him out of the China shop," quoted in Paul Roazen, *Freud and His Followers* (London: Allen Lane, 1976), p. 151.

5. Robin Baker, *Fragile Science: The Reality behind the Headlines* (London: Pan Books, 2001), p. 62.

6. Valerie Davis Raskin, *When Words Are Not Enough* (London: Robinson, 1999), p. xv.

7. "The Explorer," *Time* Magazine, 23 April 1956.

8. Raskin, *When Words Are Not Enough*, p. vxii.

9. Raskin, *When Words Are Not Enough*, p. 9.

10. Sarah Boseley, "Prozac, Used by 40m People, does not Work, Say Scientists," *Guardian*, 26 February 2008. The study was conducted by Professor Irving Kirsch at Hull University and colleagues in the United States and Canada.

11. Raskin, *When Words Are Not Enough*, pp. 15, 21.

12. Raskin, *When Words Are Not Enough*, p. 8.

13. Leo Kanner, *Child Psychiatry*, 2nd ed. (Springfield, IL: Charles Thomas: 1949), p. 53.

14. Kanner, *Child Psychiatry*, 2nd ed., p. 58.

15. Kanner, *Child Psychiatry*, 2nd ed., p. 194.

16. Jonathan Lear, *Love and Its Place in Nature* (London: Faber and Faber, 1990), p. 49.

17. Joseph Wortis, *Fragments of an Analysis with Freud* (New York: Charter Books, 1954), p. 109.

18. Seymour Fisher and Roger Greenberg, *Freud Scientifically Reappraised* (New York: John Wiley, 1995), p. 6.

19. Adam Phillips, "Psychoanalysis and Idolatry," in *On Kissing, Tickling and Being Bored: Psychoanalytic Essays on the Unexamined Life* (London: Faber & Faber, 1993), p. 120.

20. Frederick Crews, *The Memory Wars: Freud's Legacy in Dispute* (New York: New York Review of Books, 1995), p. 293.

21. Erikson, Young Man Luther (New York: Norton, 1962), pp. 252–53.

Index

About the Author

Kurt Jacobsen is a research associate in the Political Science Department at the University of Chicago and the book review editor at *Logos: A Journal of Modern Society & Culture*. He is author or editor of seven books and has contributed articles and reviews to many professional journals, including *Psychoanalytic Review*, *Free Associations* (UK), and *Psychoanalytic Studies*. He has written for the *London Guardian*, the *Observer*, the *Independent*, the *Irish Times*, *Sunday Tribune* (Ireland), *Le Monde Diplomatique*, *New Statesman & Society*, *Economic and Political Weekly*, *Chicago Reader*, and many other periodicals. He also has cowritten and coproduced several documentaries.